RELIGION, CULTURE, AND PUBLIC LIFE

SERIES EDITOR: KATHERINE PRATT EWING

The resurgence of religion calls for careful analysis and constructive criticism of new forms of intolerance, as well as new approaches to tolerance, respect, mutual understanding, and accommodation. In order to promote serious scholarship and informed debate, the Institute for Religion, Culture, and Public Life and Columbia University Press are sponsoring a book series devoted to the investigation of the role of religion in society and culture today. This series includes works by scholars in religious studies, political science, history, cultural anthropology, economics, social psychology, and other allied fields whose work sustains multidisciplinary and comparative as well as transnational analyses of historical and contemporary issues. The series focuses on issues related to questions of difference, identity, and practice within local, national, and international contexts. Special attention is paid to the ways in which religious traditions encourage conflict, violence, and intolerance and also support human rights, ecumenical values, and mutual understanding. By mediating alternative methodologies and different religious, social, and cultural traditions, books published in this series will open channels of communication that facilitate critical analysis.

For the list of titles in this series, see page 281.

THE LIMITS OF TOLERANCE

For Michael Walzer, This ess,
in defense of tolerance,
in friendship and admiration

Denis Lacorne

Tahoe, CA   9/20/19

RELIGION, CULTURE, AND PUBLIC

THE LIMITS OF TOLERANCE

ENLIGHTENMENT VALUES AND RELIGIOUS FANATICISM

DENIS LACORNE

TRANSLATED BY

C. JON DELOGU
AND ROBIN EMLEIN

Columbia University Press   *New York*

Columbia University Press
Publishers Since 1893
New York   Chichester, West Sussex
cup.columbia.edu
Les frontières de la tolérance © 2016 Editions Gallimard, Paris
English translation copyright © 2019 Columbia University Press
All rights reserved

Library of Congress Cataloging-in-Publication Data
Names: Lacorne, Denis, author.
Title: The limits of tolerance : enlightenment values and religious fanaticism /
Denis Lacorne ; translated by C. Jon Delogu and Robin Emlein.
Other titles: Frontieres de la tolerance. English
Description: New York : Columbia University Press, 2019. | Series: Religion,
culture, and public life | Includes bibliographical references and index.
Identifiers: LCCN 2018038374 (print) | LCCN 2018059537 (ebook) |
ISBN 9780231547048 (e-book) | ISBN 9780231187145 (cloth : alk. paper)
Subjects: LCSH: Toleration—History. | Religious tolerance—History. |
Freedom of religion—History. | Freedom of speech—History.
Classification: LCC BJ1432 (ebook) | LCC BJ1432 .L3313 2019 (print) |
DDC 179/.9—dc23
LC record available at https://lccn.loc.gov/2018038374

Columbia University Press books are printed on permanent
and durable acid-free paper.
Printed in the United States of America

Cover image: *St. Bartholomew's Day Massacre*, c. 1572-84 (oil on panel),
Dubois, Francois (1529-1584) / Musee Cantonal des Beaux-Arts de Lausanne,
Switzerland / De Agostini Picture Library / G. Dagli Orti / Bridgeman Images

Cover design: Chang Jae Lee

Columbia University Press gratefully acknowledges the generous contribution to this book provided by the Florence Gould Foundation Endowment Fund for French Translation.

To the memory of Tony Judt and Al Stepan

CONTENTS

ACKNOWLEDGMENTS

The ideas behind this book emerged from a stay at Columbia University's newly created Institute for Religion, Culture, and Public Life in the spring of 2008 (supported by an Alliance grant) and a visiting fellowship at the Stanford Humanities Center in the winter of 2013. At Columbia I was fortunate to participate in a seminar, Challenges to Diverse Models of Secularism in the United States, France, and Turkey, co-organized with Al Stepan and Ahmet Kuru. While at Columbia, I had the chance to engage in numerous thought-provoking conversations with Al Stepan and Mark Lilla.

At Stanford I was able to develop my reflection on the management of religious symbols in the public square, centered on current debates about the permission or prohibition of Islamic veils. Stimulating discussions were provided by my Stanford colleagues, in particular Aron Rodrigue, Jack Rakove, and Keith Baker in the History Department; Michael McConnell, Richard Ford, and Avishai Margalit at the Stanford Law School; Cécile Alduy, Dan Edelstein, and Marie-Pierre Ulloa in the Division of Literatures, Cultures, and Languages; Charlotte Fonrobert in the Department of Religious Studies; and Bruce Cain, David Brady, and Mo Fiorina in the Political Science Department.

Generous support from the France-Stanford Center for Interdisciplinary Study allowed me to run an international conference, The New Politics of Church/State Relations, in December 2015. I am grateful to Laurent Cohen-Tanugi, an international lawyer who then taught at Stanford Law School, for his help in preparing and co-organizing this conference.

Back in France, many of the ideas tested in this bicoastal American environment were further developed in a three-year research seminar, Religion and Globalization, which I conducted at the CERI–Sciences Po with Joseph Maïla (then director of "CAPS," the policy planning staff of the French Ministry of Foreign Affairs) and Jean-Paul Willaime (then director of the Institut Européen en Science des Religions). Participants in this seminar generated lively discussions and provided an exceptional comparative and global perspective, and this book has greatly benefited from their contributions. A conference on "Religion and Foreign Policy" concluded the seminar on November 5–6, 2013. The proceedings of the conference were published under the title *La diplomatie au défi des religions* (Paris: Odile Jacob, 2014). I wish to thank the co-organizers of the conference (and coeditors of the book), Justin Vaïsse and Jean-Paul Willaime, for their enthusiastic support.

I am also particularly grateful to the successive directors of the CERI—Jean-François Bayart, Christophe Jaffrelot, Christian Lequesne, and Alain Dieckhoff—who supported my research and allowed me to expand its scope beyond the narrow field of American politics.

I could not have written this book without the constant, challenging, and stimulating discussions with my wife, Maria Ruegg, and with the invaluable help, critical comments, and friendly support of my two editors—Ran Halévi at Gallimard and Wendy Lochner at Columbia University Press.

This book is dedicated to the memory of Tony Judt and Al Stepan—two great friends and mentors who knew that good research cannot be restricted to a single scholarly discipline. They both understood that history, to be meaningful, must be long-term history and that political science and political philosophy gain much from a genuine comparative perspective.

NEW INTRODUCTION FOR THE AMERICAN EDITION

There are numerous historical examples of religious tolerance, from ancient Greece to the Roman Empire, medieval Spain to the Ottoman Empire and the Venetian Republic. But, generally speaking, these are not examples of tolerance in the modern sense of the term. They are rather examples of "toleration": systems in which diverse religions are "suffered" for the sake of keeping the peace. The Latin root for toleration, *tolerantia*, is derived from the verb *tolerare*: to accept, endure, put up with, support with courage a burden or a difficult condition of life.[1] Tolerance in this sense is commonly associated with a political act, something that is within the power of a ruler to impose or refuse to allow, such as the coexistence of established and minority religions.[2]

Today, however, tolerance is more often understood as the welcoming acceptance of a wide variety of beliefs and viewpoints where diverse communities respect one another and act collectively for the common good. This modern concept of tolerance began to emerge in the Age of Enlightenment and is closely associated with Enlightenment values, in particular, freedom of speech, free exercise of religion, separation of church and state, and the principle of equality. These values were not readily accepted. It was only through the pervasive and growing influence of philosophers such as John Locke and Voltaire; the efforts of political activists such as Thomas Paine, Thomas Jefferson, and Mirabeau; and the acquiescence of modern rulers that these conceptions eventually prevailed and were enshrined in written constitutions and bills of rights at the very end of the eighteenth century.

The elaboration of the modern concept of tolerance took place against a backdrop of religious wars and difficult attempts to put an end to these wars. Treaties, for example the Peace of Augsburg (1555), the French Edict of Nantes (1598), and the Peace of Westphalia (1648), brought periods of truce that were rarely definitive. Princes and their subjects were unable to conceive of tolerance as the peaceful coexistence of religious communities separated by strong doctrinal differences. Tolerance was a "burden" that would only last until the next clash of religions. It took only a local revolt or the intervention of some foreign power in favor of a dissident community for the hard-won civil peace to dissolve into open violence.

During the same period, however, a more positive conception of tolerance was gradually developed by thinkers such as Michel de l'Hôpital and Sebastian Castellio in the sixteenth century; John Locke and Pierre Bayle in the seventeenth century; and Montesquieu, Voltaire, and Kant in the eighteenth century. They all denounced the use of force to convert dissidents and insisted that only persuasion could change a person's faith, provided that her conversion was authentic and sincere. They also emphasized the advantages of religious pluralism to overcome the most dangerous religious passions. Voltaire insisted, "If there were only one religion in England there would be danger of despotism, if there were two they would cut each other's throats, but there are thirty, and they live in peace and happiness."[3] Other writers went further in linking the virtues of pluralism to direct economic benefits. Montesquieu, for instance, observed that a multiplicity of religions strengthened the state because the members of tolerated religions were more likely to be hardworking than those of the dominant religions, who would only be eager to collect the benefits of unproductive, honorific functions.[4] Kant's moral philosophy expanded the meaning of tolerance further in calling for the full respect of human beings as moral persons, detached from narrowly defined religious passions. What was needed, in an Age of Enlightenment, was "a prince . . . who considers it his duty, in religious matters, not to prescribe anything to his people but to allow them complete freedom."[5] Enlightened tolerance was thus conceived as an instrument of liberation not just from religious fanaticism but from outmoded religious dogmas and scriptural precepts. And its best safeguard was to be found in the "freedom of the pen," the only way to protect the rights of the people in a constitutional monarchy or a republican commonwealth.[6]

Certain thinkers at the end of the eighteenth century even believed that new republican political norms would render tolerance unnecessary. In a key speech before the French National Assembly, on August 22, 1789, Mirabeau rejected the concept of tolerance because he perceived it as exclusively dependent on the will of a sovereign: "I do not come here to preach tolerance— the most unlimited freedom of religion is, in my view, a right so sacred that the word 'tolerance' used to express it strikes me as itself tyrannical since the authority that tolerates can just as well not tolerate."[7] In the same vein, George Washington, in a famous letter to the Hebrew Congregation of Newport, Rhode Island, written on August 18, 1790, explained that Jews no longer had to be tolerated since they possessed full "liberty of conscience and immunities of citizenship."[8] Thomas Paine, one year later in the

Rights of Man (1791), thought it was time to move beyond "toleration," understood as a concession granted by a prince or priest to his subjects: "Toleration is not the *opposite* of Intolerance, but is the *counterfeit* of it. Both are despotisms. The one assumes to itself the right of withholding Liberty of Conscience, and the other of granting it. The one is the Pope armed with fire and faggot, and the other is the Pope selling or granting indulgences."[9]

Despite these critiques of the very notion of tolerance, the concept did not disappear. Indeed, the use of the term "tolerance"—in the positive sense—continued to grow. Critiques of the notion of tolerance were without exception based on the assumption that tolerance was a favor granted by an all-powerful sovereign, and that is the particular notion of tolerance that was rejected. Tolerance as such was not abolished; it remained a fundamental operating principle for a well-functioning republic (or constitutional monarchy), open to a plurality of competing religious communities.

In the twentieth century, the concept of tolerance was gradually expanded to apply to groups that have been marginalized on the basis of race, ethnicity, cultural identity, and gender. Indeed, by the end of the century, debates about tolerance most often referred to racial, ethnic, and gender issues and not to religion.[10] These debates raised important political questions about power relations, social hierarchies, and systems of domination. For critics such as Wendy Brown, tolerance—or, more accurately, the discourse of tolerance—is used as a smokescreen by Western liberals to reinforce the oppression of ethnic minorities and nontraditional gender groups. Borrowing loosely from Foucault, Brown views tolerance as a form of "governmentality" designed to affirm the superiority of Western values against less tolerant, "primitive," or "barbarian" societies.[11] In fact, if one substitutes "governmentality" for "absolute Monarch," Brown's critique of the notion of tolerance is very much like that of Mirabeau, Paine, and Washington.

Admittedly, Brown is very effective in exposing the hypocrisy of Western political and cultural elites who attack the intolerance of Islam and its related cultural traditions while at the same time attempting to regulate or even prohibit the wearing of headscarves on the grounds that this practice reflects a lack of choice or a submission to authoritarian religious leaders. "Choice," as she rightly points out, is indeed a relative concept, and Western women who claim their superiority in being free to dress as they wish are in fact equally constrained by social and cultural norms but in a different way, determined by the market forces of a consumer society.[12] The problem with Brown's analysis is that—again like Mirabeau and Paine—she views tolerance only in a negative light, as an act that, in an ideal world, would have no reason to exist. At the same time, by limiting the scope of her argument to the twentieth century, Brown ignores the complex and changing modes of tolerance that evolved over time and tends to exaggerate the Manichean dimension of a conflict opposing a supposedly tolerant and "civilized" West to a supposedly intolerant and "barbaric" non-West.[13] The fact that Western elites have used the concept of tolerance as a mask for intolerance is no reason to throw out the concept.

Tolerance properly understood requires the open acceptance of diverse religious communities that are not treated as "superior" or "inferior." They all possess equal rights and benefit from constitutional guarantees enforced by the courts and state authorities. In such a context, members of minority or dissident religions are respected, even though their beliefs or religious practices may not be necessarily approved.[14] For instance, I may object to the wearing of a niqab (a full-face veil) in the public space because it seems to imply the subordination of women. But should it be completely banned as it is today in France and in Denmark? There is no easy answer, particularly if wearing a hijab (a headscarf) or a niqab has been chosen by a free autonomous subject for religious reasons.[15] In fact, the debate about the Islamic veil exists only because Western secular elites are reluctant to admit that religious beliefs cannot really be separated from cultural practices. The question, again, is not whether wearing the veil expresses a religious obligation (it may not be the case) but whether it is *experienced*, rightly or wrongly, as a religious obligation by the faithful.[16] But this does not imply that all religious practices should be blindly accepted by state authorities. Parliamentary leaders may choose to limit or ban certain religious practices in the name of public order. But such a ban should be carefully designed and balanced against preexisting fundamental rights, such as the free exercise of religion. In the end, restrictive measures limiting the rights of a particular religious group should only be accepted if they do not impose an excessive burden on the members of the group.

The different regimes of tolerance examined in this book do not offer a single universal model of toleration. Each regime, in its own way, draws boundaries between the tolerable and the intolerable, the permitted and the prohibited, the religious and the political. Moreover, these borders fluctuate as a result of wars and political revolutions. Public order, political survival, dynastic succession, established religions, and population migration may all impose limitations to existing regimes.[17] These constraints vary over time as attitudes and customs change. Dissident religions that were hardly tolerated in France, England, and Italy in the sixteenth and seventeenth centuries are today perfectly accepted without any restrictions. However, recent religions, such as Mormonism or Jehovah's Witnesses, and older religions in new settings, such as Islam and Sikhism in Europe and North America, may cause alarm because they are poorly understood and seem to challenge local customs and habits. This, in turn, may facilitate the rise of intolerant, xenophobic movements and present a difficult challenge to the advocates of modern tolerance.

The history of tolerance, examined over a long historical period, is a complex story of breaks and continuities, advances and regressions.[18] That history cannot be a simplistic narrative opposing a "tolerant West" to an "intolerant non-West," nor can it be reduced to a linear progression from an ancient age of persecution to a modern age of tolerance and peaceful accommodation.[19] Indeed, the "tolerant" West has regularly experienced periods of extreme intolerance and episodes of extreme brutality: the Thirty Years' War, the St. Bartholomew's Day massacre, the execution of Michel Servet in Geneva, the execution of Chevalier de La Barre for blasphemy in the France of Louis XV, the revocation of the Edict of Nantes, and the persecution of Quakers, Baptists, and "witches" in North America. In fact, the same country could be tolerant, then intolerant, in a recurring cycle. Consider, for example, the curious treatment of French Huguenots: the first Edict of Tolerance—the Edict of Nantes— reconciled Catholics and Protestants in 1598; it was later revoked with the Edict of Fontainebleau in 1685, which was in turn superseded by a new Edict of Tolerance—the Edict of Versailles—in 1787. Given such recurrent cycles of tolerance and intolerance, the fear of intolerance, real or imagined, is always with us, and it is reinforced by a new postrevolutionary cycle of tolerance and intolerance opposing, both in France and the United States, secular forces to committed believers.

At the same time, there are numerous examples of tolerant regimes in non-Western societies, in Indonesia, for instance, with the coexistence of Buddhism, Hinduism, and Islam; in the Indian subcontinent, both before and after the intrusion of Islamic conquerors; and in Turkey, after the conquest of Constantinople.[20] To illustrate this phenomenon and challenge, in my own way, the much abused notion of a "clash of civilizations," I will examine the rise of a unique form of Islamic tolerance, better defined as "bureaucratic and imperial," which emerged in the Ottoman Empire and survived for nearly four hundred years at a time when Europe was experiencing violent and devastating religious wars.[21]

The concept of religious tolerance, if it is of any use today, makes sense only if it denotes a right that exists independently of any political or religious authority—a right that does not derive from the arbitrary will of a political ruler, a principle as fundamental as the "Universal Right of Conscience" defended by Thomas Paine. But this right is workable only if people (and their rulers) can detach themselves from their own religious (or secular) conceptions of the good and agree to cooperate in the public sphere. In this context, the concept of tolerance, as applied to religion, can be conceived of as a consensual system of harmonious coexistence between a multiplicity of comprehensive religious doctrines and a secular political order. The difficulty, of course, is to find a proper balance between the uniformity of the rule of law and a variety of religious beliefs and nonbeliefs.[22]

Why write a book about religious tolerance? By the 1980s, religion no longer was a fashionable topic. And why should it be? The globalization of the world and the rising secularism of modern societies seemed to suggest that religious tolerance had finally become a universal norm accepted by all without much resistance. The antidiscrimination policies implemented in the United States, France, Canada, and Great Britain paved the way for a new form of "multicultural tolerance" that emphasized diversity rather than religion.[23]

The religious question, partially eclipsed by new and vigorous debates on gay marriage, gender, and ethno-racial diversity, regained the center stage when extreme forms of intolerance challenged the very notion of free speech—one of the major achievements of the Enlightenment. A new spiritual despotism reintroduced the long-forgotten notion of "blasphemy." Ayatollah Khomeini's unexpected and brutal fatwa calling for the death of Salman Rushdie, the author of a controversial novel—*The Satanic Verses*—reactivated the old debate on the limits of tolerance.[24] A new form of religious fanaticism, fueled by Islamist passions, led to outbreaks of violence that reached a climax with the denunciations of cartoons mocking revered scriptures and religious figures such as Muhammad. Terrorist attacks targeting writers, journalists, and cartoonists in Denmark, France, Pakistan, and other countries raised new, difficult questions. Should we tolerate the intolerant? Should we appease the fanatics in forbidding certain forms of artistic expressions perceived as offensive by true believers? Is censorship or self-censorship a valid strategy to calm the anger of the faithful? Is the risk of a "clear and present danger" the ultimate limit to tolerance? I attempt to address these fundamental questions in the last two chapters of the book and in the epilogue to the American edition.

1

TOLERANCE ACCORDING TO JOHN LOCKE

J ohn Locke is probably the most systematic—if not the first—thinker of modern tolerance and for that reason deserves a special place in this book. Locke was fully aware of the many theological, philosophical, and political debates on tolerance that proliferated in the second half of the sixteenth century in the Dutch Republic, Switzerland, France, the German states, and England. His most notable precursors strongly believed that tolerance was integral to the pacification of societies torn apart by the wars of religion. For these thinkers, tolerance was inseparable from a larger set of principles and practices that the sovereign was encouraged to embrace, including civil peace, freedom of conscience, freedom of religion, and the separation of spiritual and temporal powers.

THE PRECURSORS

Pierre Du Chastel (1504–1552), the leading chaplain and counselor to King Francis I, denounced the execution of the "heretic" Étienne Dolet while extolling a certain measured skepticism that prefigured the right to freedom of thought. He argued that no mortal should be condemned for heresy, since God alone can know the absolute truth.[1] A few years later, Michel de L'Hospital (1507–1573), the chancellor and counselor to Queen Catherine de Medici, used a medical metaphor to illustrate the progress of tolerance and the need to respect the freedom of thought of the king's subjects. Since the violent remedies of "fire and iron" had not stopped the advance of Protestantism, a different medicine should be tried, one using "softer remedies" that would replace force with persuasion. The proposed solution was "pure politics"; in other words, it did not involve the religious beliefs of the sovereign.[2] In a famous speech, Michel de L'Hospital insisted on the necessity of bringing the two sides together in the interest of peace. "Let us abolish those devilish words: partisan, faction, sedition, Lutheran, Huguenot, Papist. Let us not change the name of Christian."[3] This conception of tolerance favored the political over the religious. It advocated the "disestablishment of the church" and the abandonment of the old absolutist principle of "one faith, one law, one king."[4]

Étienne Pasquier (1529–1615), a famous jurist and historian of the French monarchy, echoed these principles in his "Exhortation to Princes" and insisted on the importance of encouraging and protecting freedom of conscience. In an unsigned text that circulated widely in Europe, he harangued his readership in strong terms: "For God's sake, Sirs, *do not force our thoughts at sword point. We* are all (both Romans and Protestants) Christians, united as one by the holy sacrament of baptism. We worship and revere the same God, if not in the same way at least with the same zealous devotion. . . . Let us voluntarily obey all the human edicts of our prince."[5] Respect for the conscience of individuals and freedom of religion contribute to the national interest and the peace of the kingdom. The only limit to the form of civil tolerance advocated by Pasquier was the politicization of religion by ministers or overzealous preachers, who might trouble the public order if their sermons veered into calls for sedition. Such excesses deserved to be severely punished.[6]

Among the Protestants, one finds the best defense of modern tolerance in the works of the humanist teacher and theologian Sebastian Castellio (1515–1563). Residing in Basel after a short stay in Geneva, Castellio provoked an uproar by denouncing Calvin's intolerance in his *Traité des hérétiques* (1554). He held Calvin responsible for the trial and execution for heresy and blasphemy of the Spanish physician and theologian Michel Servet, who was burned alive at the stake before the gates of Geneva on October 27, 1553. In particular, Castellio accused Calvin of acting cruelly, in a manner consistent with the Old Testament but contrary to the teachings of the Gospels, and of confusing the temporal and the spiritual. The prince or magistrate had a duty to punish proven crimes such as theft, murder, or adultery. But he should never place himself in the position of God by ordering the execution of those whose religious opinions he considered erroneous. "Killing a man is not defending a doctrine, it is killing a man." And what is a doctrine? It is a dogma upheld by the doctors of the church, who have every right to punish nonconformist thinkers by excommunicating them or condemning them to exile. The use of the sword, however, should be reserved for civil authorities to punish common-law crimes committed against citizens: "If Servet had wanted to kill Calvin, the magistrate would have been right to defend Calvin [by executing Servet]. But since Servet fought with his writings and reasons, it was *with reasons and writings* that he should have been refuted."[7]

By systematically deconstructing the notion of heresy, Castellio highlighted the absurdity of persecuting men over dogmatic subtleties whose meaning varies from one denomination to another, from city to city, and from country to country. The only important thing was to live a Christian life and ignore useless controversies arising from the "enigmas and obscure questions" that come up so often in Holy Scripture. The truth, Castellio concluded, is a matter of individual conscience and sincerity. It consists in affirming "what one believes, even when one may be mistaken."[8] With these declarations, Castellio laid out the promise of a future utopia: a pluralist society, tolerant, open to all religious faiths, where all men would live "amicably, without any debates or strife, in loving harmony with one another."[9]

These authors and many others were all known to John Locke, who had amassed an impressive collection of works devoted to the major religious controversies of the sixteenth and seventeenth centuries.[10] An extended stay in France (1675–1679) had also exposed him directly to the effects of the Edict of Nantes and to the multiple challenges it faced during the reign of Louis XIV. Another stay, in the Republic of the United Netherlands (1683–1688), allowed Locke to become familiar with the important theological debates that divided the country's Protestants and to observe that religious controversies were not incompatible with civil peace and the prosperity of a tolerant population.[11] It was in Holland, at the end of 1685 or the beginning of 1686, that Locke wrote, in Latin, his famous *Letter Concerning Toleration*, during a time of troubles and uncertainty.

In France, Louis XIV had just signed the Edict of Fontainebleau (October 18, 1685), which revoked the Edict of Nantes and accelerated the persecution of Huguenots, who were forced to flee into exile or convert. The same year, in England, a Catholic, the Duke of York, became King James II at the very moment when thousands of Huguenots were going into exile in Germany, England, and the Dutch Republic. In the years before this, Protestant elites and the Anglican leadership had tried to block the Duke of York's possible accession to the throne. Their failure pushed certain leaders within the Whig party, including Locke, to go into exile in Holland to escape the repressive measures of the duke's brother, King Charles II, who was already suspected of wanting to create an absolutist Catholic monarchy. Threatened with extradition on charges of subversion, Locke was obliged to change addresses frequently in Holland and to use pseudonyms to hide his real identity.

A LETTER CONCERNING TOLERATION

Locke dedicated his *Letter* to a personal friend, the Dutch Remonstrant theologian Philipp van Limborch, and he wrote it at a time when he was cultivating relationships with Quakers, Arminians, and Latitudinarians, who all favored new forms of religious tolerance. The *Epistola de tolerantia* was published anonymously in 1689, simultaneously with William Popple's English translation. That year marked Locke's return to his native country directly following the Glorious Revolution and the forced abdication of the Catholic James II.[12] The military invasion of William of Orange and the accession to the throne of William and Mary (the son-in-law and daughter of James II) put an end to the Jacobite dream of restoring a Catholic dynasty. William justified his military intervention by claiming the need to restore religious freedom to England and, by extension, reestablish the supremacy of the Anglican religion.

The *Letter Concerning Toleration* is not a simple political commentary on the recent events that Locke had witnessed but rather an attempt to go beyond those events to offer a comprehensive reflection on the principle of tolerance.[13] The *Letter* begins with a spirited protest against "fiery zealots" who persecute "upon pretence of religion." Locke does not name them, but he suggests

that they are powerful men who aim to impose either an orthodoxy founded on the "antiquity of places and names" and "the
pomp of their outward worship" or an ascetic discipline invented
by the founders of the Reformation. The reader is therefore
encouraged to contemplate both the excesses of the Catholic
Inquisition and the rigors of the Republic of Geneva.[14] The per-
secutors, whoever they may be, are enemies of humankind
because they demean true Christian virtues, which, says Locke,
are founded on "Charity, Meekness, and Good-will."[15] The persecution of schismatics and heretics was extremely violent; no
means were too extreme, including "Confiscation of Estate,
Imprisonment, Torments." In the event of failure, the inquisi-
tors' "burning zeal for God" led to burning the infidel "literally
with Fire and Faggot."[16] The persecutor appears all the more
detestable because he often acts hypocritically: "cruel and
implacable towards those that differ from him in opinion, he
be indulgent to such iniquities and immoralities as are unbe-
coming the name of a Christian." The immoralities he names,
"Adultery, Fornication, Uncleanness, Lasciviousness, Idolatry,
and such like things," form a long list of sins that jeopardize
the salvation of those who wish to impose their own idea of
salvation.[17]

Locke's argument therefore advances the notion of a true faith
and true Christianity perverted by zealots pretending to act in
the name of a self-proclaimed orthodoxy. Locke ridicules this
orthodoxy, underscoring its absurdity by imagining himself in
the place of an impartial observer, a Turk, witnessing the discord between Christians in the Ottoman Empire:

> Let us suppose two Churches, the one of Arminians, the other
> of Calvinists, residing in the City of Constantinople. Will any
> one say that either of these Churches has Right to deprive the

Members of the other of their Estates and Liberty (as we see prac-
tised elsewhere) because of their differing from it in some Doctrines or Ceremonies, whilst the Turks, in the mean while, silently
stand by and laugh to see with what inhumane Cruelty Christians thus rage against Christians? But if one of these Churches
hath this Power of treating the other ill, I ask which of them it is
to whom that Power belongs, and by what Right? It will be
answered, undoubtedly, that it is the Orthodox Church which has
the Right of authority over the Erroneous or heretical. This is, in
great and specious words, to say just nothing at all. For every
Church is Orthodox to itself; to others, Erroneous or Heretical.
Whatsoever any Church believes, it believes to be true; and the
contrary thereunto it pronounces to be Error.[18]

Locke's example is an apt illustration of his quest for the true
religious pluralism underpinning his conception of tolerance.
Since an impartial observer in Constantinople would be incapable of identifying which is the true religion in the endless disputes
between churches, no religious institution has a legitimate right
to impose its truth on another or use its powers of coercion.

Contrary to appearances, Locke is not defending a relativist
point of view. Certainly, there is not, nor can there be, a pre-
established religious orthodoxy. But there exists some transcendental truth that can be grasped by the individual while in
solitary communion with his creator. The sole arbiter of ultimate truths is not of this world but is rather "the Supreme judge
of all men, to whom also alone belongs the judgment of the
erroneous."[19]

Locke's thinking leads to political considerations: the power
to control individuals and their possessions or to use "fire and
faggot" against recalcitrant subjects does not rightfully belong
to ecclesiastical authorities, whose orthodoxy and legitimacy are

by definition uncertain. At most, a church, which is no more than "a society of men" united to serve God, may excommunicate wayward members for their lack of faith or for the seriousness of their sins. However, this act of exclusion is symbolic and may not be accompanied by physical violence or the confiscation of the possessions of the excommunicated person. The use of force, reserved for the political authority, prince, or civil magistrate, has the sole objective of protecting the worldly belongings of the state's subjects, among them "life, liberty, health, and indolency of body [freedom from pain]; and the possession of outward things, such as money, lands, houses, furniture, and the like."[20] There is nothing arbitrary about the use of force; it must obey major political principles and in particular justice, the only guarantor of an impartial execution of the laws.[21]

The notion of a strict separation between temporal and spiritual powers had emerged in the sixteenth and seventeenth centuries, but Locke is one of the first to insist on an enduring separation of the two: "I esteem it above all things necessary to distinguish exactly the Business of Civil Government from that of Religion, and to settle the just Bonds that lie between the one and the other." These two spheres of power do not have the same means at their disposal to impose their authority. On the one hand, the head of state (the prince, magistrate, or legislator) has a monopoly on the use of force; his only goal is to secure the wealth of his subjects and to punish those who violate the laws of the state. On the other hand, even the most powerful ecclesiastical authorities possess only one method for drawing "the Heterodox into the way of Truth." It cannot use force or penalties "to convince the mind."[22]

Locke's reasoning is perfectly consistent with his radical individualism: no prince may forcibly convert a group of people, even if he is acting perfectly democratically on behalf of subjects who gave him their consent. Freedom of thought excludes all mediation, for "the Life and Power of true Religion consists in the inward and full persuasion of the mind."[23] In a first version of the *Letter* published eighteen years earlier as *An Essay Concerning Toleration*, Locke defended a similar position, insisting on the necessity of a direct relationship to God. The search for salvation is a manifestation of "the voluntary and secret choice of the mind"; the preference of a believer for a particular form of religious worship can only be determined by a "commerce . . . between God and myself."[24]

The importance Locke accorded to freedom of conscience and to a direct, transcendental connection with God had revolutionary political implications that were also expressed, in similar terms, by contemporary philosophers—some of whom went so far as to conclude that acting against one's conscience amounted to a mortal sin.[25] Freedom of conscience, as long as it is exercised sincerely in a genuine attempt to find what is "true," or seemingly true, must be granted to all, including heretics.[26] The individual is released from all political or religious subordination; she acts according to her intimate convictions. Tolerance, therefore, is not "a condescension, an indulgence toward that which cannot be prevented," as defined in the first edition of the *Dictionnaire de l'Académie* from 1694,[27] nor is it an accommodation or privilege granted to a small group of heretics (in France) or dissidents (in England). Rather, it is an active principle founded on the convictions of an individual conscience engaged in a reasoned quest for truth.[28]

Does the principle of tolerance, founded on freedom of conscience, apply to all, including Catholics, Jews, Muslims, pagans, and atheists? This raises the question of the limits of tolerance—limits that are inseparable from the notion of public order and from an implicit hierarchy between the political and religious spheres.

The regime of tolerance imagined by Locke is radical for its time because it extends to non-Christian monotheistic religions as well as to pagan beliefs such as those of Native Americans. The philosopher explains this vast expansion of tolerance in four different ways. First, he invokes the principle of a strict separation between church and state. As we have seen, the sole duty of the latter is to defend the community of citizens and their possessions. Churches, on the other hand, are voluntary associations with no civil authority, whose members share a singular preoccupation, that of finding the path to salvation in a solitary undertaking reflective of the "sincerity of the heart." No state or civil magistrate may "force [men] to be saved against their will." Therefore, "no private Person has any Right, in any manner, to prejudice another Person in his Civil Enjoyments, because he is of another Church or Religion." And the "other" mentioned here, says Locke, can be "Christian or Pagan." He cites the example of a Jew who refuses to consider the New Testament as the word of God, a pagan who rejects both the Old and New Testaments, and a "Turk" or "Mahometan" who considers the "Alcoran" the only true sacred text.[29] A person's religion is of no importance so long as its exercise does not disrupt public order or harm the interests of other citizens.

The second argument has to do with the virtues of commerce in a state that needs "honest, peaceable, and industrious" subjects to ensure the prosperity of all. The exchanges required by modern society necessarily imply encounters between people of different nationalities and religions. Hence the double objection that Locke addresses to advocates of intolerance:

Shall we suffer a Pagan to deal and trade with us, and shall we not suffer him to pray unto and worship God? If we allow the Jews to have private Houses and Dwellings amongst us, why should we not allow them to have Synagogues? Is their Doctrine more false, their Worship more abominable, or is the Civil Peace more endangered by their meeting in publick than in their private Houses?[30]

In the case of Jews, Locke is hereby demanding a clear extension of tolerance in countries such as England and the United Netherlands, which allowed Jews to worship privately (and discreetly) but prohibited the construction of synagogues.[31]

The third argument is based on international relations and what is essentially the principle of reciprocity. Forbidding pagan worship in one's own country will only incite neighboring countries to disallow Christian practices; the resulting breach in good relations between the two countries may in turn damage the possibility of profitable commercial exchanges. Locke once again admonishes those who favor religious uniformity and seek to "extirpate by Violence and Blood the Religion which is there reputed Idolatrous,"[32] arguing that claims of orthodoxy in one camp will only provoke the sectarianism of another, and the result will be useless violence against individuals deemed heretics: "And what if in another country, to a Mahoumetan or a Pagan Prince, the Christian Religion seem false and offensive to God; may not the Christians for the same reason, and after the same manner, be extirpated there?"[33] Locke establishes a new, peaceable conception of international relations; a virtuous circle of mutual tolerance will put an end to the escalation of intolerance triggered by princes or civil magistrates who ceaselessly meddle in religious affairs. According to this argument, rare in its time, tolerance should not be the exclusive practice of a few Western countries but a universal principle applicable in all nations regardless of religion—in Asia, the Ottoman Empire, the American colonies, etc.

A fourth and last argument is founded on the notion of religious diversity favored at the time by most "tolerationists." Locke adopts a line of reasoning exactly the opposite of that advanced by Hobbes in *Leviathan* and by other partisans of absolute monarchy, such as Bossuet in France. Hobbes considered religious uniformity throughout a republic as the best way to prevent religious wars. Orthodoxy imposed from the top down and the prohibition of all forms of heresy are, he claimed, the only way to maintain civil peace.[34] For Locke it is just the reverse: the repression of minority churches generates a "spirit of revolt" that eventually triggers religious wars. Such a spirit of revolt is a natural defense mechanism; it "proceed[s] not from any peculiar Temper of this or that Church or Religious Society, but from the common Disposition of all Mankind, who when they groan under any heavy Burthen endeavour naturally to shake off the Yoke that galls their Necks." This is why, Locke adds, "Just and Moderate Governments are every where quiet, every where safe. But Oppression raises Ferments and makes Men struggle to cast off an uneasy and tyrannical Yoke." It is not diversity of opinions that creates disorder but "the Refusal of Toleration to those that are of different Opinions . . . that has produced all the Bustles and Wars that have been in the Christian World upon account of Religion."[35]

Other writers made similar arguments, often emphasizing a factor that Locke neglected: the beneficial effects of a free market of religions. Pierre Bayle (1647–1706), a Huguenot refugee living in Holland, became famous for his writings criticizing the established religions, which were widely circulated in Europe but censored in France. His *Commentaire philosophique* (1686) championed the concept of a "multiplicity of religions." In his view, an "honest emulation" between religions would reinforce the authority of the sovereign by giving him the means to govern without excessive partiality. To illustrate this conception of religious pluralism, Bayle used a musical metaphor, polyphony, which he thought was appropriate to describe the functioning of a modern state, as opposed to plainsong, which he deemed anachronistic and better adapted to a feudal nation-state. If there were ten religions within a country, wrote Bayle, just as there are dozens of artisans in a city, the result would be harmonious, "a beautiful concert formed by different voices and melodies." The ten religions would mutually support one another while competing to show which was best in the eyes of God; at the same time, to the extent that the sovereign treated each religion fairly, the loyalty of each to his authority would be reinforced.[36]

With this idea of polyphony, Bayle countered Hobbes's classical argument by demonstrating that the fusion of political and religious authorities could only result in a cruel tyranny. He concluded with a stinging indictment: "All disorder comes not from tolerance, but from the want of tolerance."[37] For Bayle even more than for Locke, tolerance was essential to civil peace, which could only be maintained through the virtuous competition of all religions, under the guidance of a neutral sovereign.

NO TOLERANCE FOR THE ENEMIES OF TOLERANCE

While seemingly universal, Locke's principle of tolerance is not without limits. Theoretically, as he admitted in a text published earlier, in 1667, tolerance is an "absolute and universal right." But this absolute right can only apply to "purely speculative opinions," such as "belief of the trinity, purgatory, transubstantiation, antipodes, Christ's personal reign on earth, etc." By this measure, the "pompous ceremonies of papists" are as acceptable as the "plainer way of the Calvinists." It is a fact, according to Locke, that "wearing a cope or surplice in the church, can no more alarm or threaten the peace of the state, than wearing a cloak or coat in the market." Freedom of belief comes with a condition: it must express a purely individual choice and remain in the realm of transcendental ideas. Speculative beliefs are acceptable only insofar as they are detached from the world of political action. They must in no way create trouble for the prince or his fellow subjects.[38] Here the notion of public order is central to the philosopher's reasoning, and it will become a rallying cry for all those who favor toleration within reasonable limits.

In principle, Catholics who believe in transubstantiation are tolerated by Locke—their belief is a superstition like any other. But their speculative opinions are inextricably linked to political opinions that run counter to civil peace. Catholics "mix with their religious worship, and speculative opinions, other doctrines absolutely destructive to the society wherein they live."[39] And how do these dangerous doctrines threaten the legitimacy of the monarch? Locke's answer is blunt: English Catholics constitute a state within the state, a sort of fifth column that undermines the English monarchy from within, since the only prince they recognize is the pope. Their freedom of conscience is an illusion because "they owe a blind obedience to an infallible pope *who has the keys to their consciences tied to his girdle*, and can upon occasion dispense with all their oaths, promises and the obligations they have to their prince, especially being a heretic, and arm them to the disturbance of the government."[40] It is impossible under these conditions to grant the "benefit of toleration" to such subversive agents manipulated by an intolerant and unscrupulous clergy.[41]

Catholicism would be perfectly acceptable if the political opinions of its followers were clearly dissociated from their religious opinions, but Locke doubts that "Papists" are capable of separating the two. For one thing, they do not behave as autonomous subjects possessing true freedom of conscience because "they openly pledge allegiance to a foreign prince who is our enemy." In any case, it does not make sense to tolerate Catholics because, should they come to power, they would themselves refuse to tolerate Protestants.[42] The *Essay Concerning Toleration* published in 1667 clearly delimits the regime of tolerance imagined by Locke. Its boundaries are determined by a higher principle: the necessity of maintaining civil peace. Catholicism cannot be tolerated because it contains within itself the threat, implicit but nonetheless real, of using force to overthrow the Anglican monarchy. At the time of its publication, the *Essay* represented a significant progress for proponents of tolerance because, as we have seen, it proclaims a universal right to tolerance and vigorously criticizes the intolerance of the Anglican monarchy toward nonconforming Protestants.[43]

Eleven years later, Locke's worst fears were realized: the Catholic King James II succeeded his brother, Charles II, while another Catholic king, Louis XIV, revoked the Edict of Nantes, forcing thousands of Huguenots into exile. Given the circumstances, one can understand why the author of the *Epistola de tolerantia*, then in exile in Holland, felt compelled once again to exclude Catholics from his ideal regime of tolerance. Yet in the later work his thinking on the matter had nonetheless evolved, and he offered instead a general theory of tolerance. The enemies of tolerance are only alluded to, and the word "Catholic" is almost never used in the *Letter Concerning Toleration*. Still, a close reading of the *Letter* clearly suggests that a monarch who seeks to impose Catholicism on his subjects would be undermining the established political order and destroying any serious possibility of securing toleration. Should a people oppressed by a Catholic king revolt? Locke is careful on this point—his personal survival, after all, is at stake—but the implications are clear: a prince who embraces religious dogmas detrimental to the common good loses all legitimacy. The only religion that meddles in politics and assumes "the power of deposing Kings" for the sole reason that they do not believe in the "true" religion is manifestly (even if Locke does not call it by name) Roman Catholicism.[44] The members of this peculiar religion, Locke concludes, are enemies of tolerance because "they are ready upon any occasion to seize the Government, and possess themselves of the Estates and Fortunes of their Fellow-Subjects."[45]

At the same time, to emphasize that his opposition to Catholicism is politically and not religiously motivated, Locke affirms—and it is the one time in the text when he deliberately employs the word "Catholic"—that the civil magistrate must tolerate all beliefs that do not threaten civil peace. It does not matter, after all, if a Catholic believes that a piece of bread is really the body of Christ or if a Jew refuses to believe that the New Testament is the "Word of God" so long as those beliefs do no harm to others and do not challenge existing "Civil Rights."[46] Thomas Jefferson, an enthusiastic reader and admirer of Locke, makes roughly the same argument in his *Notes on the State of Virginia* (1785) when he claims: "It does me no injury for my neighbour to say there are twenty gods, or no God. It neither picks my pocket nor breaks my leg."[47]

The only danger to be feared is the confusion between religious power and political power that happens in an absolute monarchy. In such a case, one can expect the worst: a state religion established by force, producing "endless Hatreds, Rapines and Slaughters . . . unto Mankind."[48] This somber portrait, which calls to mind the France of Charles IX or Louis XIV, allows Locke to emphasize just how much the Catholic clergy had violated the message of gentleness and tolerance advocated by the apostles and their successors.[49] In doing so, the English philosopher sought to expose Catholics as being inconsistent with themselves and their own religious tradition.

The case of America's "innocent Pagans" was of particular interest to Locke, who was the primary author of *The Fundamental Constitutions of Carolina* (1669), which was commissioned by his sponsor, Lord Ashley. The realities of trade and the success of the British colonial experiment in North America required establishing a regime of tolerance that could attract an array of peoples to the new territories, notably "Pagans, Jews," and, above all, "natives of that place [who are] utterly strangers to Christianity." Every community comprising at least seven people was authorized to found a church or denomination with its own name. The "natives" would have the right to keep their lands—it was out of the question to expel them or otherwise mistreat them on account of their ignorance of the Christian faith.[50] Twenty years later, Locke developed the same idea even more emphatically in his *Letter Concerning Toleration*. He insists that the faith and possessions of the "infidels" of North America be respected and that they not be stripped of their lands simply because they do not embrace the faith of a Christian prince. No religion should be forcibly imposed on them. "If they are persuaded that they please God in observing the Rites of their own Country and that they shall obtain Happiness by that means, they are to be left unto God and themselves."[51]

These "innocent Pagans" must be tolerated in spite of their "idolatry." Their religion, writes Locke, spurs them to be "strict observers of the Rules of Equity and the Law of Nature" and encourages them to embrace the laws of the colonizers. They should therefore be trusted, and there is no reason for Christian settlers to abuse the "most inviolable rights" of the country's natives by dispossessing them of their lands or by refusing to respect the solemn treaties signed with them.[52]

Atheists, however, were excluded from Locke's regime of tolerance essentially for economic reasons. What value, he argued, could one assign to the "Promises, Covenants, and Oaths" of an atheist who might lie with impunity without the least fear of divine retribution and who, in doing so, would destroy "the Bonds of Humane Society"?[53] Here Locke is too categorical to be completely credible. Doesn't history offer many examples of Christians who break their word and act in bad faith without displaying the least fear of divine punishment? In New England, did not Christian settlers often use specious reasoning and flimsy pretexts to violate treaties signed with the Native Americans?

Pierre Bayle, on the other hand, has no problem tolerating atheism on certain conditions. He offers a two-part argument. First, he challenges the idea of there being a direct link between an individual's professed convictions and his actual behavior. A Christian may live his whole life in sin while outwardly displaying the most admirable piety. By the same token, an atheist, despite his rejection of the notion of divine order, may behave in a perfectly virtuous manner.[54] Second, it is possible to imagine a society of atheists who, contrary to the fears expressed by Locke, do not succumb to disorder or general confusion.[55] In a well-managed society with a penal code that severely punishes infractions, there is no reason to think that an atheist would behave less virtuously than a believer. Social pressure and an age-old conception of honor would prevent him from "doing harm to his neighbor." In contrast, no human justice will impede the zeal of a fanatic believer who is persuaded that by exterminating heresy and blasphemers he will advance the will of God and assure himself a glorious place in heaven.[56] For Bayle, atheists should only be admonished if their excessive zeal imperils social order.[57] The atheist is accepted so long as he is discreet and his convictions do not go beyond the realm of conjecture.

Voltaire, unconvinced by the arguments of Bayle, also refused to tolerate atheists and more or less reiterated Locke's reasoning on this point. Atheism, he writes in the *Dictionnaire philosophique*, "is not so mischievous as fanaticism, [but] it is almost ever destructive of virtue." Why is the gentle and tolerant society of atheists imagined by Bayle unacceptable? "Because it is thought that men under no restraint could never live together; that laws avail nothing against secret crimes; and that there must be an avenging God, punishing in this world or the other those delinquents who have escaped human justice."[58] More importantly, Voltaire asserts that in a modern society of commerce and contracts, "the sacredness of oaths is manifest and necessary, and they who hold that perjury will be punished, are certainly more to be trusted than those who think that a false oath will be attended with no ill consequence."[59] By refusing to include atheists in his regime of tolerance, Voltaire, according to René Pomeau, was drawing "a line that he would never cross."[60] One could hate religion, deny the holiness of the Bible, denounce the absurdities of theologians, combat the abuses and fanaticism of priests, or recall the atrocities of Christianity, Islam, and Judaism—but God deserved man's respect. The idea of a supreme being was necessary because it ensured the smooth functioning of a "policed" society, guaranteeing property rights, the validity of contracts, and the sanctity of oaths.

John Locke, as we have seen, was not the first philosopher to take up the matter of tolerance, but he was certainly the author on the question whose views were the most widely read and discussed during the Enlightenment. His great originality was the central place he gave to liberty of conscience and to the necessity of separating an individual's spiritual opinions from any ecclesiastical orthodoxy. Locke's regime of tolerance is revolutionary because it posits the complete autonomy of the individual, or, more precisely, the splitting of the individual into two parts: the believer, who alone has the power to judge his true faith, and the citizen, whose acts must conform to the rule of law. Freedom of conscience eliminates the need for an established church; all that matters is the sincerity of individual beliefs in an open environment of diversity and respectful competition between religions. The authentic exercise of freedom of thought distances the individual from his religious community, for he is alone before his creator. As for ecclesiastical authorities, they still exist, of course, but they lose a considerable share of their customary prerogatives. In the system imagined by Locke, there is no longer a single official church but rather a multitude of churches all subordinate to a civil power, with the state retaining its monopoly on the use of force to maintain public order. In the religious domain, everything is permitted, even paganism and other superstitions, on the condition that religious leaders avoid meddling in politics. Hence the necessity of establishing "fixed and immovable boundaries" between church authorities and the monarch—what will come to be known, at the pinnacle of the Enlightenment, as the separation of church and state.

2

VOLTAIRE AND
MODERN TOLERANCE

I n his late writings, Voltaire turned his attention to the subject of tolerance, inspired by numerous incidents of extreme
intolerance throughout history. For Voltaire, intolerance was
associated with fanaticism, "enthusiasm," and religious zeal,
inevitably leading to murder, torture, massacres, and civil wars.
Tolerance as such only appears as a fundamental theme in the
Lettres philosophiques (1734), written at the end of a three-year
stay in England. Voltaire's personal commitment to rehabilitat-
ing Jean Calas constitutes the high point of his thoughts on the
subject.

RELIGIOUS WARS

The real effects of fanaticism are described in vivid detail in *La
Henriade*, Voltaire's first published epic poem from 1728. The
poem focuses on the glory of Henri de Bourbon, king of Navarre
and future Henry IV. It offers a forceful indictment of the Saint
Bartholomew's Day massacre (1572) and its leading instigators:
Catherine de Medici, her son Charles IX, and the Duke of

Anjou, the king's brother and future Henri III. Voltaire describes the event in excruciating detail:

> What waves of blood the streets of Paris stain'd;
> What piercing shrieks were heard, what dying groans:
> Torn from her breast, and dash'd upon the stones,
> The mother, dying, mourned her infant dead![1]

He denounces the wild mob of Charles IX's followers:

> What Fate reserv'd for our devoted times,
> By frantic priests the pious monsters led,
> Call'd God to witness all the blood they shed:
> On altars of the slain his name invok'd;
> Where, mix'd with human blood, their horrid incense smok'd![2]

In a commentary at the end of the poem, Voltaire states that it is important not to forget such barbaric events because they can degenerate into religious wars. There is a duty to remember, which must be renewed with each successive generation, even if the memories cast a shadow over the reputation of the French people. It must never be forgotten that "at a court obsessed with politeness," a brilliant woman and her young son ordered the massacre of "more than a million" subjects.[3] Voltaire never forgot. Every year on the anniversary of the Saint Bartholomew's Day massacre he was overcome with bouts of fever that always astonished those close to him, less sensitive as they were to the crimes of history and their aftereffects.

In his *Essai sur les mœurs*, a general history of Christianity from the early Middle Ages to the reign of Louis XIII, Voltaire offers a list of barbaric deeds committed in the name of religion. He analyzes in succession iconoclasm in the Byzantine Empire, the brutal subjugation of Saxon idolaters by Charlemagne, the bloody battles of Ferdinand III of Castile against the Moors, the massacre of Jews and Muslims during the first Crusades and the conquest of Jerusalem, the carnage of the Albigensian Crusade, the arrest and torture of Jan Hus during the Council of Constance, the expulsion of the Jews from Spain in 1492 and their persecution in the Holy Roman Empire, the misdeeds of the Inquisition throughout Europe, the assassination of Henri IV by Ravaillac in the name of divine justice, and so on.[4] No act of cruelty escapes the philosopher's attention, not even those of John Calvin—formerly persecuted, then the persecutor—who, yielding to "the furor of his theological hatred," ordered the unfortunate Michel Servet, accused of Socinianism, to be burned alive.[5] For Voltaire, fanaticism is the result of theological opinions whose content, scope, and true influence on the history of customs (*mœurs*) must be elucidated.

Can social customs be changed? Voltaire hopes so, and his account, steeped in Enlightenment thought, seeks to demonstrate that the "only arm against this monster [of fanaticism] is reason. The sole means of preventing men from being absurd and cruel is to enlighten them. To make fanaticism detestable, one need only describe it. Only the enemies of mankind would say, 'You are shedding too much light on men, you are writing too much about their mistakes.'"[6] Voltaire's argument would be challenged a century later by Ernest Renan, who contended in *What Is a Nation?* that France needed to forget in order to create a strong, unified country after France's defeat at Sedan (1870). "The essence of a nation," Renan explains, "is that all individuals have many things in common; and also that they have forgotten many things. . . . Every French citizen has to have forgotten the massacre of Saint Bartholomew, or the massacres that took place in the Midi in the thirteenth century."[7]

Voltaire, however, has forgotten nothing. He is unwavering in his conviction that it is never too late to repair old injustices, as his personal involvement in the rehabilitation of Calas brilliantly demonstrates. Voltaire's fight for tolerance is therefore founded on a scrupulous examination of all forms of intolerance and a conviction that the truth will emerge for the enlightened reader from the somber chaos of events.

But Voltaire does not merely analyze historic facts; he denounces theologians whose reading of the Bible serves to justify intolerance. He insists there is no natural right to intolerance. No massacre can be attributed to "natural causes." Fanatics schooled in theology invoke an odd "right to intolerance" to justify the unacceptable: massacres perpetrated in the name of a highly dubious conception of good and truth. "The law of intolerance," Voltaire claims, "is therefore absurd and barbaric. It is the law of the jungle and, indeed, it is even worse because wild animals kill others only to eat, while we human beings are exterminating each other for the sake of a few paragraphs."[8]

IN PRAISE OF ENGLISH TOLERANCE

The outlines of Voltaire's philosophy of tolerance are already perceptible in the *Lettres philosophiques*. In that text the author commends Quakers, especially William Penn. He also sings England's praises, referring to that "country of sects" where every citizen is first and foremost a free man who "goes to heaven by whatever path he chooses."[9] While certain sects—Episcopalian and Presbyterian—dominate in England and Scotland, "all sects are welcome there and all live together comfortably enough," although not without occasional public quarrels, reminiscent of those opposing French Jansenists to their Jesuit rivals.[10]

To further extol the merits of English tolerance, Voltaire claims (against all evidence) that Arians, Socinians, and anti-trinitarians are fully tolerated by public authorities.[11] He even adds that Scottish Presbyterians, strict Calvinists, are perfectly within their right to address Anglicans and Catholics in insulting terms and call them "whores of Babylon."[12] But such insults do not prevent these religions from peacefully coexisting, thanks to the regime of tolerance imposed by William and Mary.

Reading Voltaire, one has the impression that English tolerance knows no limits, even if it operates within a framework shaped by the "church *par excellence*," the Anglican Church. It is dominant for reasons that are purely utilitarian and pragmatic; only Anglicans have access to the best civilian and military positions. And since this religion is the church "where one can make one's fortune," many nonconformists felt obliged to convert to Anglicanism.[13]

The *Treatise on Toleration* (*Traité sur la tolérance*, 1763) is the high point of Voltaire's thinking on the subject. But is it really the work of a philosopher? It is certainly not the sort of manifesto generally associated with the Lockean tradition. Instead, the *Treatise* presents itself as a case study. It is part of the great political struggle by the "hermit of Ferney" to obtain redress for the Huguenot Jean Calas, a Toulouse merchant wrongly accused of strangling one of his sons in order to prevent him, according to popular rumor, from renouncing "the so-called reformed religion" and converting to Catholicism. Condemned to death by the Toulouse parliament on March 9, 1762, Calas was tortured before being executed. He was first submitted to the *question ordinaire*, which meant having his arms and legs stretched, and then to the *question extraordinaire*, which consisted—in an early form of waterboarding—in being forced to ingurgitate twenty jugs of water, but the "parricide" still refused to confess. He was then tortured on a wheel, strangled, and burned alive. It is said that his courage and resolve impressed those who witnessed his last moments.

Convinced of Calas's innocence, Voltaire and his friends succeeded in gathering enough evidence and testimonies to persuade the king's counsel to intervene. Eventually the decision of the Toulouse parliament was overturned in June 1764. One year later, the Chambre des requêtes de l'hôtel (the court of the French parliament) exonerated Jean Calas and his family. The senior judges of the Chambre des requêtes

> ask[ed] His Majesty to compensate this family with gifts for the ruin they had suffered. . . . The king responded by granting 36,000 pounds to the mother and her children. . . . By this act of bounty, as by so many other actions, the king earned the title [the Beloved] that the nation's love had granted him. May this example serve to inspire toleration among people, without which fanaticism would devastate the whole world or at least make it permanently miserable.[14]

The rehabilitation of Calas was a testimony to the increasing influence of the Enlightenment. But it was also an occasion for Voltaire to draw up a hundred-page world history of the rise of tolerance, from the first European religious wars to the mid–eighteenth century. In adopting a global perspective and in "examin[ing] what happens in the rest of the world," the philosopher demonstrates that religious wars, outside of Europe, were rather rare.[15]

Voltaire asserts that tolerance has always reigned in countries as diverse as India, Persia, Turkey, China, Japan, and in the "other hemisphere," North America. For four thousand years, he claims, the Chinese and Japanese were the most tolerant of people until Jesuits introduced intolerant dogmas previously unknown in the Orient. The virtuous Quakers in Pennsylvania and the wise measures proposed by Locke for the Carolinas created exemplary regimes of tolerance in North America. The great sultan of the Ottoman Empire succeeded admirably in governing

> twenty peoples of different religions who live together peacefully. There are 200,000 Greeks living safely in Constantinople; and the Mufti himself nominates and presents the Greek Orthodox patriarch to the Emperor; they also allow a Latin rite patriarch in the same city. . . . This empire is full of Jacobites, Nestorians and Monothelites; there are also members of the Coptic rite there, members of the Church of Saint John, Jews, Gebers and Banians. Nevertheless, the annals of Turkey never mention any rebellion that was initiated by any of these religions.[16]

Europe appeared to lag behind the rest of the world. But a half-century after the signing of the Treaty of Westphalia (1648), which put an end to the Thirty Years' War, "philosophy" produced a break with the past that changed the face of Europe. By "philosophy," Voltaire means the progress of reason against fanaticism and superstition; the influence of "good books" written by new tolerationist authors; and the impact of "more agreeable manners" fostered by the expansion of trade and the construction of strong states with disciplined armies that prohibit "a return to those anarchic times when Calvinist peasants fought Catholic peasants, who were recruited hastily between the sowing season and harvest time."[17] Germany, England, and the Dutch Republic had set a good example. Now, Voltaire asserted, "religious differences cause no problems in these states. Jews, Catholics, Greek Orthodox Christians,

Lutherans, Calvinists, Anabaptists, Socinians, Moravians, and so many others live together peacefully in these countries and contribute equally to the welfare of the society."[18]

The Calas affair revealed how far behind France was compared to the rest of Europe, but the rehabilitation of the tortured man showed that the spirit of tolerance was advancing in the France of Louis XV. It allowed Voltaire to plead in favor of allowing the return of Huguenots who had been unjustly exiled by an illiberal monarchy. In fact, France need only follow the English example or that of a prosperous French province where tolerance was already practiced. In Alsace, explained Voltaire, "Lutherans are more numerous than Catholics. . . . The province has never been disturbed by the slightest religious quarrel since it began to be ruled by our kings. Why? Because no one was persecuted there. Do not try to interfere with people and you will win their loyalty."[19] The English model was imperfect, however, since Catholics were suspected of "supporting the Pretender" and were "denied access to public offices," although they still enjoyed "all the rights of a citizen."[20] In France, Protestants did not obtain those rights until 1787 with the promulgation of the Edict of Tolerance that finally recognized freedom of conscience and allowed Huguenots to legally marry and exercise full property rights.[21] But the public celebration of the reformed religion was not yet authorized. The Catholic Church remained the single official religion of the kingdom, and public positions in the military or civil service were reserved for Catholics.

THE BENEFITS OF *DOUX COMMERCE*

Tolerance was not just an abstract idea. It was facilitated by the rise of trade in an increasingly competitive commercial environment. Montesquieu had already posited in *The Spirit of Laws* (1748) that "Commerce is a cure for the most destructive prejudices; for it is almost a general rule, that wherever we find agreeable manners, there commerce flourishes; and that wherever there is commerce, there we meet with agreeable manners."[22] Voltaire gives a striking formulation of this in three different texts: in the "Sixth Letter on the Presbyterians," in the article "Tolerance" in his *Questions sur l'Encyclopédie*, and in the article "Tolerance" in the *Philosophical Dictionary*. Tolerance, he observes, is to be found in the "stock exchanges of Amsterdam, London, Surat, or Basra."[23] Although adversaries or strangers to one another, these merchants (Jewish, Catholic, Protestant, Muslim, Chinese, etc.) get along fine because they have bracketed their differences. Trade, by definition, is not a proselytizing activity but a utilitarian act of exchange. Each individual trusts the other and receives a promise of delivery for a certain quantity and for a certain price. The stock exchange, therefore, is that magical place where "the Jew, the Mohammedan, and the Christian negotiate with one another as if they were all of the same religion, and the only heretics are those who declare bankruptcy."[24] Commerce produces tolerance, but it also prospers in places where religious tolerance has already taken root. This is the case in the British colonies of North America, where, according to Voltaire, freedom of conscience is well established, and "thanks to this trade flourishes and the population increases."[25]

The second factor identified by Voltaire is the multiplicity of religions and the thriving competition between them. "Were there only one religion in England, despotism would be a threat; were there two, they would be at each other's throats; but there are thirty, and they live happily at peace with one another."[26] Defending freedom of conscience guarantees religious pluralism, and the latter necessarily entails the promise of tolerance. This lesson was not lost on the founders of the American republic, beginning with James Madison, who, like most of his contemporaries, was an avid reader of Voltaire. Madison presents a similar argument in *The Federalist Papers* (1788). He stresses the rights of minority religions, which often find themselves under threat from the dominant churches, such as the Anglican Church in Virginia or the Congregationalist churches in Massachusetts and Connecticut. For Madison, it is the "multiplicity of churches" that protects religious rights.[27] In much the same way, the multiplicity of factions and political interests guarantees the existence, however fragile, of civil rights. Voltaire and his followers are thus proposing a form of circular argument: freedom of thought, granted by a political power, leads to the multiplication of religions, which in turn reinforces religious liberty and protects it against the authoritarian tendencies of dominant churches. Competition properly exercised blocks monopoly; competition produces the "honest emulation" described by Pierre Bayle in his *Commentaire philosophique*, as indicated in chapter 1 of this book.

In addition to this circular argument, Voltaire elaborates a theory of parallel powers—the temporal and the spiritual—that he sees as originating in the Gospels of Matthew, Mark, and John: "'Render unto Caesar the things that are Caesar's.' 'Among you there is neither first nor last.' 'My kingdom is not of this world.'"[28] The drama of the ten centuries of history surveyed in the *Essai sur les mœurs* derives from the multiple entanglements between these two powers and the countless quarrels provoked by their proximity. "Since Charlemagne and down to our own day," Voltaire writes, "in the Catholic quarters of our Christian Europe, *the war between the authority of the prince and the priesthood* has fueled every revolution—it is the red thread running through the labyrinth of modern history."[29]

How can one interrupt the course of history and put an end to religious wars? Voltaire gives a particularly striking answer in his entry for "Priests" in the *Philosophical Dictionary*. He develops a theory of the separation of church and state in answer to a fundamental question: How should the prince or magistrate behave toward the clergy? Voltaire's response is based on an analogy: "Priests are in a state more or less what tutors are in the homes of its citizens: employed to teach, pray, and set an example. They can have no authority over the masters of the house unless it can be proved that he who pays the wages must obey him who receives them." A confusion of the two powers—tutors and masters, "priesthood and empire" (*sacerdotum* and *imperium*)—would constitute "the most monstrous of systems." No priest should ever attempt to dominate his prince or his emperor.[30]

Here Voltaire repeats the argument already defended by Locke in his *Letter Concerning Toleration*. An end to religious wars is only possible if "fixed and immovable" boundaries are established between civil and religious authorities. Hence the necessity of dissociating the power of the church from that of the commonwealth.[31] In a similar way, Voltaire explains that the priesthood must never control the empire—"prayer is not domination"; the only acceptable role for the priest in society is that of a doctor of souls.[32]

Voltaire defends the same position in the article "Religion" in the *Dictionnaire*, but with an important nuance: The separation of temporal and spiritual powers must not be envisioned as absolute. Accommodations are possible and even desirable from the point of view of the political power. A "state religion" is perfectly conceivable. But for it to be tolerated, it must be confined to subaltern administrative tasks, such as the keeping of religious registers where priests, ministers, and imams record the names of the baptized and circumcised. Other acceptable areas would be the religious oversight of days of rest and religious holidays in the official national calendar. None of these rites threatens public order. They are entirely acceptable, especially since they give religious leaders "respect without power."[33] On the other hand, Voltaire is severely critical of the opposite of state religion, namely "theological religion,"[34] which he considers unacceptable because it encourages proselytizing and thereby threatens to disrupt public order. It cannot be completely prohibited out of respect for freedom of conscience, but it must be excluded from the public sphere and contained by all means necessary because it is "the mother of fanaticism and civil discord" and "the enemy of mankind."[35]

In the final analysis, the most beautiful religion, the most pacific, the most reasonable, and the least threatening for the powers that be is the Quaker religion. For Voltaire, it presents all the advantages of a counter-religion or inverted Catholicism: a religion without priests, without dogmas, without rites, and without sacraments. Its fundamental principle is "to prohibit maltreatment of anyone because of his religion, and to consider as brothers all those who believe in God."[36] Quakerism is the perfect embodiment of the regime of tolerance inaugurated by the English, but it goes even further by establishing true equality between all members of the church and by forbidding access to the benefits of an established religion: "The Quakers cannot be members of Parliament, or hold public office; to do so they would have to swear an oath, which they refuse to do. They are reduced to earning money by commerce."[37] What does the future hold for them? Voltaire is both ironic and pessimistic. Success brings honors, and the quest for honors risks destroying the Quakers' reason for being. "Their children, made wealthy by the industry of their fathers, now want to live in comfort, have titles, wear buttons, and lace wristbands; they are ashamed of being called Quakers, and, to be fashionable, they have joined the Church of England."[38] English tolerance, therefore, despite the radical example of the Quakers, is not without its limits. The evolution of customs and habits, along with greed, ultimately benefits established churches.

3

TOLERANCE IN AMERICA

What did the French know about tolerance in North America at the end of the eighteenth century? Voltaire's writings on the Pennsylvania Quakers were familiar to readers of the time, as were texts by Benjamin Franklin, Thomas Paine, and William Robertson on the British colonies in North America and the early years of the War of Independence. But the most influential work, without a doubt, was the *Philosophical and Political History of the Settlements and Trade of the Europeans in the East and West Indies* by the Abbé Raynal. This encyclopedic work, prepared with numerous collaborators (the most famous of whom was Diderot), offers a compilation of travel writing, statistics on trade, maps, and political commentary on the imperial expansion of the great European powers to India, Africa, Southeast Asia, and the Americas. North America holds a special place in the last volumes of this encyclopedic publication.

The *Philosophical and Political History* was reedited and published many times in French as well as in English, German, Russian, and Spanish, and it became a bestseller in Europe.[1] Its success had largely to do with its critical stance toward absolute monarchies, dominant religions, colonization, and slavery. The

History predicts the decline of religion and the future triumph of a regime of reason inspired by the most radical thinkers of the Enlightenment. This explains why its publication was banned in France, first by the king's Counsel and then by the Parlement of Paris and the faculty of theology. Raynal was forced to live in exile for a time, becoming a martyr to the cause of the Enlightenment, and his personal story only contributed to his notoriety and boosted sales of the book.[2]

A REVOLUTION IN SOCIAL NORMS

One does not find in the Abbé's work, as one of his first critics, Frédéric Melchior Grimm, claimed, "the moderate tone of history." It is much more, as Diderot admiringly stated, the expression of a philosophical position marked by a certain vehemence dictated by "enthusiasm for virtue and horror of vice."[3] Like Voltaire in his *Essai sur les mœurs*, Raynal adopts a global perspective, disregarding the military glories of princes and monarchs, the succession of dynasties, and legal and political traditions to focus instead on social relations and the evolution of his compatriots' mores.[4] But he claims to go further than Voltaire, announcing the emergence of a true "revolution in the manners" of men.[5] Here Raynal's text is not merely descriptive but prescriptive, adopting two approaches: the systematic denunciation of religious fanaticism and its destructive effects and the defense of a civilization of reason based on more moderate customs and the benefits of commerce. The only place where this moderation could be observed at the time was in North America. And, although the possibility of moments of regression or even a return to the barbarism of humankind's early days could not be excluded, Raynal suggested that moderation was here to stay and constitutes a preponderant, observable tendency in both the Old World and the New World.

He describes this new phenomenon as follows:

> Since an intercourse has been established between the two hemispheres of this world, our thoughts have been less engaged about that other world, which was the hope of the few, and torment of the many. The diversity and multiplicity of objects industry has presented to the mind and to the senses, have divided the attachments of men, and weakened the force of every sentiment. The characters of men have been softened, and the spirit of fanaticism, as well as that of chivalry, must necessarily have been extinguished, together with those striking extravagancies which have prevailed among people who were indolent and averse from labour. The same causes that have produced this revolution in the manners, have yet had a more sudden influence on the nature of government.[6]

In a striking formulation, Raynal describes "a revolution of another kind" resulting from two distinct developments, namely modern religion and the progress of navigation: "Luther and Columbus appeared; the whole universe trembled, and all Europe was in commotion; but this storm left its horizon clear for ages to come. The former awakened the understanding of men, the latter excited their activity."[7] The spirit of freedom, a pure product of the Reformation, combined with the expansion of commerce and industry, was destined to improve the "legislation" of modern nations and by extension the "felicity of mankind."[8]

Let us now take a closer look at Raynal's view of the relationship between religion, trade, and the spirit of the Enlightenment. For him, Luther indeed represented a certain progress of reason over religion's "phantoms of imagination."[9] But the effects of religious pluralism in North America were not entirely positive. The chapters on New England in the *Philosophical and Political History* reveal a paradox. "Fanaticism, which had depopulated America to the south, was destined to repeople it in the north."[10] The Puritans who arrived in New Plymouth demonstrated exceptional force of character, the product of years of resistance to persecution by the Anglican Church. Their fanaticism, although unproductive in the Old World, guaranteed their success in the New World at a time when "a severity of manners had the same effect as laws in a savage country."[11] But that fanaticism, while initially useful, led to excesses, which Raynal denounces. For example, Puritan criminal law, derived from a literal reading of the Old Testament, was excessively harsh. Sorcery, blasphemy, adultery, perjury, and idolatry were all punishable by death. Anyone who danced or drank alcohol was whipped in public. The banishment of Quakers, condemned for their immorality and their "impious custom of letting the hair grow"—a custom decried as "very indecent and dishonest" because it "horribly disguises men"[12]—and the atrocities committed against the "witches" of Salem amply demonstrate that the fanaticism transported to North America was just as harmful as the fanaticism circulating in Great Britain at the time of Cromwell and just as inexcusable as that of the conquistadors. The best example is the "villainous" scalp-hunting expeditions undertaken in the White Mountains of New Hampshire, in 1725, by a gang of ferocious men led by the famous rancher John Lovewell.[13] The episode moves Raynal to make this impassioned aside: "After this, have you, ye Anglo-Americans, any reproaches to make to the Spaniards? Have they ever done, or could they possibly ever do, any thing more inhuman? And yet you were men, civilized men, and you boasted of being Christians. No, you were rather monsters, fit to be exterminated."[14] Most shocking to Raynal is that this cruel hunt for "savages" was not just a misstep during the early days of colonization but an event that occurred much later—and one that augured a somber future for the Native Americans.

But the deplorable example of New England does not thwart all dreams of Enlightenment progress, especially the progress of reason over old superstitions. In the same book 17 of the *Philosophical and Political History*, the author proposes a secular remedy for the violence and religious persecutions observed in New England, namely the creation of a neutral state, one indifferent to all churches, which would treat all confessions equally and not grant the least privilege to any. Benefits and favors could be obtained from the sovereign through merit and virtue alone. "Maybe then the differences between churches would be no more than the insignificant differences between schools of thought. The Catholic and Protestant would live as peacefully together as the Cartesian and the Newtonian."[15]

"What should be done?" Raynal asks. How shall the transposition and reproduction of fanaticism from the Old World to the New World be prevented? The best thing would be to intervene sooner, in early childhood, and to remove children from those teachers who make them "suck along with their milk the poison of fanaticism on which they become drunk."[16] It would be best to copy the minimalist religion practiced by the island inhabitants of Ternate in the Indonesian archipelago of the Maluku Islands, whose religious service consisted of simply reading, once a week, the inscription engraved on a pyramid inside a church as it was pointed to by a mute priest: "Worship God, obey all laws, love your neighbor." Could this curious manifestation of an embryonic theism be exported from Asia to Europe or North America? Raynal has serious doubts and concludes, disillusioned, with this question: "Where will one ever find an indifferent clergy, a catechism so short, and a mute priest?"[17]

Religion as practiced in New England inverts the utopia of Ternate. In the former, writes Raynal, the clergy is intolerant, the priests never stop talking, and the catechisms are "complicated." The inevitable result, as one would expect, is a fanaticism that fills the land with calamities.[18] But there is reason to hope, if one considers other, more successful colonization experiments, in Carolina, for example, or—better yet—in Pennsylvania, both laboratories of modern tolerance.

TOLERANCE IN CAROLINA AND PENNSYLVANIA

Carolina (later North and South Carolina) did not become one of the high points of American tolerance by accident. Its constitution, mostly written by Locke, was remarkably inclusive.[19] It defended the religious freedom of nonconformists and Jews and accepted the pagan practices of Native Americans. The English philosopher, as reported by Raynal, was open to all religious faiths: "As the savage inhabitants of America have no idea of a revelation, it would be the height of folly to torment them for their ignorance."[20]

All signs suggest that Locke was opposed to establishing an official church in Carolina, such as the Anglican Church, because he defended a true separation of church and state. As reported again by Raynal in his summary of the English philosopher's position, "the colony had from its origin been open indiscriminately to all sects, which had all enjoyed the same privileges. It had been understood, that this was the only way to make an infant state acquire rapid and great prosperity."[21] But this unprecedented tolerance, Raynal confesses, was short-lived; as soon as the Anglicans arrived in the colony they began to edge out the nonconformists by attempting to "exclude them from government, and even to oblige them to shut up the houses where they performed divine service."[22] The Anglican clergy of the colony behaved as poorly as Catholic priests in Europe: "While, in our countries, the Catholic priests were making a traffic of prayer, the clergy of the Church of England were carrying on, in the other hemisphere, the more odious traffic of the praises of the dead." They thus adopted the custom of pronouncing an *elogium*, indiscriminately, "never in proportion to the actions and virtues of the deceased, but to the greater or lesser reward which they were to receive from the funeral oration."[23]

The first chapters of the *Philosophical and Political History*, devoted to Pennsylvania, most clearly draw their inspiration from Voltaire. The French philosopher, as we saw, admired Quakerism—a religion without priests or sacraments—as well as the impact of this religion on the economic and political development of Pennsylvania. According to Voltaire, William Penn had brought to the land a true "golden age" unknown in the rest of the world.[24] Raynal says much the same thing when he praises the sense of justice and the spirit of moderation that the founder spread throughout the colony. Penn was a "true philosopher" who had earned the support of the Native Americans by refusing to dispossess them of their lands and had facilitated the acquisition of land for new settlers in the colony by instituting fair and impartial laws. Penn's system guaranteed the happiness of citizens by making "toleration the basis of his society." He anticipated the secularism of modern thinkers by instituting state neutrality and the principle of separation between church and state. "He left every one at liberty to invoke the Supreme Being as he thought proper, and neither established a reigning church in Pennsylvania, nor exacted contributions for building places of public worship, nor compelled any person to attend them."[25]

The exceptional economic success of the colony contributed to its burgeoning population, with Pennsylvania attracting people from the Dutch Republic, Sweden, France, and Germany, each as industrious as the next. Since all religions coexisted, the prejudices and theological disputes so frequent in Europe were gradually replaced by a "delightful harmony" particularly favorable to commerce and industry.[26]

Like Voltaire before him, Raynal contributed powerfully to the construction of the notion of the "good Quaker"—a positive image that would be taken up and given mythic status in the writings of Jaucourt, Brissot, Rabaut Saint-Étienne, Volney, Crèvecœur, and Démeunier before being eventually questioned by more skeptical visitors such as La Rochefoucauld-Liancourt, Ferdinand Bayard, and Chateaubriand.[27] In fact, Pennsylvania was an extreme case that did not allow for easy generalizations.

The author of the *Philosophical and Political History* situates the starting point for the "revolution of morals" at the end of the fifteenth century, with the discovery of America, and at the beginning of the sixteenth century, with the Reformation. He cites in particular two fundamental innovations: commercial navigation between "the two hemispheres" and freedom of conscience—in short, the contributions of Christopher Columbus and Luther. Tolerance as practiced in North America greatly facilitated enormous population transfers between Europe and its colonies. But as the example of New England demonstrates, "tranquil manners" introduced by colonial settlers could degenerate into barbaric violence harmful to the innocent native peoples.

Interestingly, the imperial expansion of the European powers had beneficial consequences for the Europeans, too. First, the exportation of religious fanaticism by conquistadors and Puritans relieved Europe of some of its most excessive elements. The most extreme left the Old Continent for the Americas, and word of their excesses as relayed by eminent travelers did much to increase the indifference and even contempt of Europeans toward religion. Furthermore, the North American practice of trade between the "most opposite sects" tended to attenuate religious hatred and resentment.[28] The well-tested regimes of tolerance in North America soon became an object of admiration to be introduced in Europe. Raynal's work even predicted a complete reversal between hemispheres: "It is partly to the discovery of the New World that we shall owe that religious toleration which ought to be, and certainly will be, introduced in the Old."[29]

North American progress in the respect for tolerance and impartiality toward religions was therefore to serve as an example to hasten the decline of dominant religions in Europe. In short, thanks to the American detour, "agreeable commerce," tolerance, and nonbelief were to have a salutary effect on a European continent finally rid of its overwhelming religious obsessions.[30]

Because his approach is too partial and too limited geographically, Raynal's explanations give the impression that tolerance developed spontaneously with the progress of commercial navigation. In fact, North American tolerance emerged gradually from a lengthy struggle for freedom of conscience, followed by an even more difficult battle for the implementation of a true separation of church and state. These struggles, which concerned a vast colonial empire, took place principally in the British Parliament after discussions within the Council of State and the Committee on Foreign Plantations (a kind of Ministry of Colonial Affairs). The solutions adopted for the colonies depended on the political and religious ideas of their

"Proprietors." Intolerance was acceptable in the Puritan colonies of New England. A certain form of tolerance existed in Maryland, founded in 1632 by a noble Catholic family, the Calverts. Later, in other colonies such as Virginia, the Anglican Church became the official church, while other, dissident denominations were poorly treated. In New Holland, a colony of the United Provinces, the "public church," the Dutch Reformed Church, was the only official church. There was no religious uniformity—everything depended on local contexts, on the political and religious regimes of the mother country, and on the place accorded first to Puritans, then to Anglicans and Dutch Calvinists.

The Massachusetts Bay Colony, for example, outright refused the principle of freedom of conscience. Catholics and Protestant dissidents such as Baptists or Quakers were hunted down and subjected to cruel punishments. Anyone who attended a Quaker meeting had to pay a fine, and Quakers accused of proselytizing could be immediately arrested and punished with caning or mutilation of the ear or tongue. If they committed a second offense, a second ear was cut, and, if that was not enough to curb their enthusiasm for preaching, dissidents had their tongue pierced with a hot iron poker. Banished Quakers who returned to Massachusetts were condemned to death by hanging. Three such hangings occurred in 1659.

The first colony really to embrace religious tolerance in North America was Rhode Island.[31] The colony was founded in 1637 by Roger Williams, a Protestant theologian trained and ordained in Cambridge. He accepted a post in Boston in 1631 but was chased out of the Massachusetts Bay Colony in 1635 after being first excommunicated by his peers for espousing subversive ideas. To legitimate the existence of his new colony, Williams needed a royal charter. Thanks to the support of Robert Rich, the Second

Earl of Warwick and head of the Committee on Foreign Plantations, Williams obtained his charter on March 14, 1644, at the
start of the English civil war. The charter created something
new and extraordinary: a civil government established by the
"voluntary consent" of a majority of the residents of the colony.
The charter was vague about religious matters, assuming that
they would be decided by the majority and without the establishment of an official state church. A new charter obtained in
1663 specified that the colonial government could exercise "full
freedom in religious matters." Roger Williams thus succeeded
in implementing what he had defended in his most famous publication, *The Bloudy Tenent of Persecution for cause of Conscience,
discussed, in a Conference between Truth and Peace* (1644), namely
a complete separation of the spiritual from the temporal.

According to Williams, the church and the state are akin to
two ships. On the ship of the church, the clergy alone are in
charge. Their main job is to steer the boat toward its ultimate
goal: eternal salvation. The Christian prince, being a passenger
among others, has no divine right and must accept the rules of
the clergy. On the ship of state, however, the prince alone is in
charge. All the passengers, whether clergy or laity, must obey
him. He alone can steer the community toward the civil goals
of peace and prosperity. The religion of the prince does not matter: "a pagan pilot or antichristian pilot may be just as talented
as a Christian one when it comes to steering the boat toward this
most desired harbor."[32] The fusion of civil and religious powers
was justified for the nation of Israel described in the Old Testament, but it lost its relevance with the arrival of the Messiah,
"because now, under Christ, all nations are purely civil, and have
no outstanding features as was the case for the national church
of Israel; a civil sword may not extend to spiritual matters nor
impose punishments for spiritual infractions. This power only

belongs to the double-edged sword of God's word."[33] Civil persecution for matters relating to an individual's private conscience was unjustified; it could only lead to disorder and anarchy and be disastrous for religion itself because the authority of the prince and his church would lack consistency. One day's heresy could become tomorrow's truth, and vice versa. Constraining an individual's conscience for civil reasons was, to use Williams's metaphor, a rape of the soul—"a spiritual rape, more abominable in the eyes of God than the rape of the bodies of all the women in the world."[34]

In short, the best "radical remedy" against religious persecution was to forbid all official churches and maintain a complete separation between church and state.[35] Only persuasion via the dissemination of the divine word could alter consciences without violence. For Williams, this noble task was of a purely private nature. It belonged solely to voluntary associations of believers, to churches or "worship societies" that functioned like "a collective of doctors in a city, a cooperative, a company or trade group doing business with the East Indies or Turkey."[36] This is why Williams was able to assert on the very first page of the *Bloudy Tenent* that "It is the will and command of God, that . . . a permission of the most Paganish, Jewish, Turkish, or Antichristian consciences and worships, be granted in all Nations and Countries."[37]

Rhode Island thus became, early on, as its founder wished it to be, a place of asylum for all victims of religious persecution. As it was a very small colony, however, the Rhode Island experiment was often openly mocked by Calvinist Protestants in neighboring states as "the receptacle of all sorts of riff-raff people, and is nothing less than the sewer (*latrina*) of New England."[38]

FROM NEW NETHERLAND
TO VIRGINIA

Contrary to the predominant literature on the subject, now contested by historians, New Netherland and its capital New Amsterdam were not the only examples of a quintessentially American form of tolerance.[39] Managed by Pieter Stuyvesant, a hardline Calvinist who was named director general of the colony by the Dutch West India Company in 1645, this new colony practiced tolerance as it existed in the United Provinces, meaning that freedom of conscience was fully recognized. Forced conversions no longer happened, but the public exercise of any religion other than that of the Dutch Reformed Church was prohibited. The proselytizing activities of Quakers, Catholics, Baptists, and Lutherans who arrived from neighboring lands were closely supervised and prohibited as soon as they became too visible—even if they occurred in private. Those who broke the rules were fined and then banished after a repeat offence. The clearest protest against the colony's punitive measures targeting the conventicles (meeting places) of Quakers and other religious dissidents took the form of a solemn Remonstrance signed in December 1657 by some thirty city fathers and citizens of the little town of Vlissigen (in English, Flushing). The signers of this unprecedented document were defending a new conception of freedom of conscience that went well beyond that of the Dutch authorities, who, some months earlier, had condemned Quakers for the illegal practice of a "heretical" religion.[40] The free exercise of religion, according to the petitioners, should not be limited to certain pious acts performed in private. It should extend to the public sphere as well. As for "Jewes, Turkes, and Egiptians," they all deserved tolerance because they were, like the rest of us, "sonnes of Adam."[41] The Quakers should never have suffered the mistreatment the colony imposed on them. The Flushing Remonstrance, though an exemplary defense of religious freedom, did not produce the desired effects. Tobias Feake, the individual who submitted the petition to Stuyvesant, was immediately arrested and convicted for supporting the "sect called Quakers," a "heretical and abominable" group that was not to be "tolerated" or "admitted" into the colony.[42]

Tolerance in the mid-Atlantic states did not fully develop until after the British conquest of the Dutch colonies in 1664, when New Netherland and other territories under Dutch authority become the states of New York, New Jersey, and Delaware. The new tolerance introduced in this part of North America reflected the religious pluralism established at the time of the English Restoration (1660–1685) by the Duke of York (brother of Charles II), the sponsor-protector of the colony, whose official title was James, Duke of York and Albany.

The Dutch Reformed Church ceased to be the official church of the colony after the Dutch surrendered following the naval expedition of the Duke of York (September 29, 1664).[43] From then on, it was simply tolerated along with other competing religions. Dutch residents of New York obtained freedom of conscience and the right to exercise their religion as they pleased. But this right was shared equally with other churches recognized as legitimate under the founding laws of the colony, the so-called Duke's Laws, compiled by the first governors of New York. These laws established a new regime of pluralist tolerance: towns were divided into parishes, and the families in each parish were required to name by majority vote the religious leader who best represented their beliefs. This new territorial arrangement could be applied identically to Presbyterians,

Lutherans, Dutch Reformed, Congregationalists, and Anglicans, but it excluded Quakers, Baptists, and Catholics, who were judged too heterodox. The idea of a hierarchy of churches dominated by an established church, the Dutch Reformed Church, was thus abolished. Once dominant, it was now merely tolerated.[44]

The entry for "Church" in the Duke's Laws defends freedom of conscience and its natural extension, the free exercise of religion in each parish, but it forbids all interference that could disturb a congregation on the Day of the Lord or on official religious holidays or days of thanksgiving. The "affront" would be punished by a fine and prison terms.[45] But what kind of affront did the law intend to prevent? As Evan Haefeli observes, this clause targets Quakers in particular, who often spoke out and proselytized in places of worship or in the public square. Quakers were free to gather among themselves without fear of punishment, but they could not openly pursue their missionary activities as they would later with considerable success in the province of New Jersey (founded in 1665)[46] and in Pennsylvania (founded by William Penn in 1682).[47] Tolerance in the New Jersey territory was greater than in New York because, according to the founding laws of the province, no one could "in any waies [be] molested, punished, disquieted or called into Question for any difference in opinion or practice in matters of Religious concernments."[48] No dissident would be forced to submit to the domination of any established church, as was the case in the province of New York, which explains the high number of Quaker and Baptist immigrants who moved to New Jersey or Pennsylvania.

During the period of the American Revolution (1776–1783), tolerance made great strides, just as it did in Europe around the same time. Travelers were struck by the diversity of religions in North America, dominated in New England by Congregationalists, in the South by Anglicans, in Pennsylvania and New Jersey by Quakers, in Maryland by Catholics and Anglicans, and in Rhode Island by Baptists. This diversity made the establishment of an official religion across the entire continent impossible. But "established" religions proliferated in various states of the union, notably Anglicanism in Virginia and Congregationalism in Massachusetts, where individual parishes could choose their preferred denomination. The Constitution of the Commonwealth of Massachusetts of 1780 repeats almost word for word the principles of tolerance articulated fifteen years earlier in New Jersey. It specifies that the various districts, towns, parishes, and other entities have "the exclusive right" to choose their "public teachers" and "of contracting with them for their support and maintenance." The text further specifies that "no subject shall be hurt, molested, or restrained in his person, liberty, or estate, for worshipping God in the manner and season most agreeable to the dictates of his own conscience; or for his religious profession or sentiments, provided he doth not disturb the public peace, or obstruct others in their religious worship."[49] The free exercise of religion now completed the simple expression of freedom of conscience. However, local authorities could and did suppress the proselytizing activities of Baptists and Quakers who disturbed "others in their religious worship."

Virginia offered, on paper, an expansion of the regime of religious freedom as affirmed in Article 16 of its 1776 Declaration of Rights, which states that "religion, or the duty which we owe to our Creator, and the manner of discharging it, can be directed only by reason and conviction, not by force or violence; and therefore all men are equally entitled to the free exercise of religion, according to the dictates of conscience; and that it is the mutual duty of all to practise Christian forbearance, love, and charity toward each other."[50]

The freedom of conscience affirmed here does not, however, guarantee the complete neutrality of the state on religious matters. In 1784, the Virginia legislature discussed a bill proposing to pay the salaries of all ministers of Christian denominations. Presbyterians and Baptists judged that the old established religion, the Anglican Church (now Americanized as the Episcopal Church), would be the major beneficiary of the law should it be adopted. Petitions against the bill began to circulate, the most famous of them by James Madison.[51] His petition denounced the corrupting effect of public funds on the operation of churches. Paying ministers' salaries, no matter what faith they professed, was a dangerous abuse of power that compromised the integrity of the religion and turned it into a vulgar "engine of civil policy." Such a practice would only encourage the worst instincts of an established clergy, who would be inclined toward "pride and indolence," while the laity would tend toward "ignorance and servility"—the end result being "superstition, bigotry, and persecution."[52] Madison considered it completely necessary to preserve the "great Barrier" separating temporal and spiritual powers.[53] To claim that religions would decline without public financing was illogical and contrary to the history of Christianity, since it had always prospered solely from the voluntary donations of the faithful. Madison's petition proved effective, and in 1786 the Virginia General Assembly adopted a statute, drafted by Jefferson, that separated the religious from the political once and for all. It pushed to its extreme limit the notion of "disestablishment":

> To compel a man to furnish contributions of money for the propagation of opinions which he disbelieves and abhors is sinful and tyrannical; that even forcing him to support this or that teacher of his own religious persuasion is depriving him of the

comfortable liberty of giving his contributions to the particular pastor, whose morals he would make his pattern, and whose powers he feels most persuasive to righteousness, and is withdrawing from the Ministry those temporary rewards, which, proceeding from an approbation of their personal conduct are an additional incitement to earnest and unremitting labours for the instruction of mankind; that our civil rights have no dependence on our religious opinions any more than our opinions in physics or geometry, that therefore the proscribing any citizen as unworthy the public confidence, by laying upon him an incapacity of being called to offices of trust and emolument, unless he profess or renounce this or that religious opinion, is depriving him injuriously of those privileges and advantages, to which, in common with his fellow citizens, he has a natural right, that it tends only to corrupt the principles of that very religion it is meant to encourage, by bribing with a monopoly of worldly honours and emoluments those who will externally profess and conform to it; that though indeed, these are criminal who do not withstand such temptation, yet neither are those innocent who lay the bait in their way.[54]

The bold tone and universal applicability of Jefferson's text did not go unnoticed in prerevolutionary France. The "Bill on Tolerance" passed by the Virginia General Assembly was "so curious"[55] that it was quoted at length in the second volume of Jean Nicolas Démeunier's *Encyclopédie méthodique*, published in 1786. Madison recalled the Virginia experiment when he defended the necessity of adding a bill of rights to the federal constitution—a bill of rights that would protect both "the freedom of the press and the rights of conscience."[56] That Bill of Rights was finally adopted in 1789 and ratified in 1791. It included in its first article (the First Amendment) the provision that "Congress shall make no law respecting an establishment of religion, or prohibiting the free exercise thereof; or abridging the freedom of speech, or of the press; or the right of the people peaceably to assemble, and to petition the Government for a redress of grievances." But it was unclear whether this amendment applied to established religions in individual states. With the exception of Virginia, Pennsylvania, and Rhode Island, state legislatures upheld the privileges that had been acquired by various established churches. But the growing influence of Baptist churches and the pressure exerted by the Quaker movement and the Catholic Church led most of the original thirteen states to abolish those privileges and the taxes and tithes that funded them. The Virginia model of disestablishment was gradually adopted by all the states. By 1833, no church was recognized as being official or benefited from public funds for its religious, philanthropic, or educational activities.

BEYOND TOLERANCE

At the end of the eighteenth century, tolerance lost its narrow, pejorative meaning. It no longer was a matter of tolerating Jews, Quakers, Baptists, Catholics, or other dissenters by according them a few new rights. In a republic, all citizens (except slaves and women) ideally should have full access to civil rights. Tolerance was henceforth considered an integral part of each individual's rights of citizenship; it no longer could be restricted. But such a widespread, almost limitless notion of tolerance was not universally accepted. Political leaders on both sides of the Atlantic still gave a narrow meaning to the concept of tolerance. Tolerance for them, in the prerevolutionary sense of the term, was only granted at will by a sovereign for a limited period of time, and only to certain privileged groups. But full universal rights of citizenship, once acquired after a republican revolution, could no longer be altered. They were "inalienable," beyond the reach of any sovereign or legislature, and they concerned all categories of citizens, including members of ethnic and religious minorities. Tolerance, in that particular, restrictive sense, had become obsolete.

Rabaut Saint-Étienne, a Protestant minister and member of the French National Assembly, thus explained in a speech to the National Assembly delivered on August 23, 1789:

> Gentlemen, it is not even tolerance that I demand, it is freedom! Toleration! Support! Pardon! Clemency! Ideas that will remain supremely unjust toward dissidents for as long as it is true that a difference of religion or of opinion is not a crime. Tolerance! I demand the abolition of this unjust word which describes us like citizens to be pitied, like guilty individuals that ought to be pardoned, like [individuals] who because of their particular education, or just by chance, do not think like we do. . . . Gentlemen, I therefore demand, for French Protestants and all the other non-Catholics of the kingdom, what you demand for yourselves: freedom and equal rights. I demand it for this people torn from Asia, forever wandering, still outlawed, still persecuted eighteen centuries later, but who would adopt our customs and habits if, by our laws, they were incorporated with us.[57]

George Washington, the hero of the War of Independence, made a similar statement in his famous address to the Hebrew Congregation in Newport, Rhode Island, delivered shortly after his inauguration as president in August 1790:

> The Citizens of the United States of America have a right to applaud themselves for having given to mankind examples of an

enlarged and liberal policy: a policy worthy of imitation. All possess alike liberty of conscience and immunities of citizenship. It is now no more that toleration is spoken of, as if it was by the indulgence of one class of people, that another enjoyed the exercise of their inherent natural rights. For happily the Government of the United States, which gives to bigotry no sanction, to persecution no assistance requires only that they who live under its protection should demean themselves as good citizens, in giving it on all occasions their effectual support. It would be inconsistent with the frankness of my character not to avow that I am pleased with your favorable opinion of my Administration, and fervent wishes for my felicity. May the Children of the Stock of Abraham, who dwell in this land, continue to merit and enjoy the good will of the other Inhabitants; while everyone shall sit in safety under his own vine and fig tree, and there shall be none to make him afraid.[58]

The U.S. Constitution and the constitutions of certain states, such as Virginia and Pennsylvania, offered France models to imitate, in a dynamic system of mutual transatlantic emulation. France, with its Declaration of the Rights of Man and the Citizen, was sending a message of liberty to all of Europe, declared Rabaut Saint-Étienne before the National Assembly. And if there was one source of inspiration to be credited, it was "those generous Americans who placed at the top of their civil code the sacred maxim of the universal freedom of religions."[59]

4

TOLERANCE IN THE OTTOMAN EMPIRE

For Locke and Voltaire, tolerance was inextricably linked to philosophical and religious debates about the place of the church in society, the connection between temporal and spiritual powers, and the relationships between official churches and dissident, minority religions. The writings of Locke and Voltaire are important because they anticipated the sweeping political changes that led the United Kingdom, France, the United Provinces, and the young American republic to develop authentic regimes of tolerance. These regimes were difficult to establish given the resistance of political and religious elites, who sought to maintain the privileges of established churches. The idea of real religious pluralism—that is, with no preference given to any one religion and equal rights for all—would not be fully realized until the end of the eighteenth century, at the time of the French and American revolutions.

In this chapter on the Ottoman Empire and the following chapter on Venice, I propose to examine two other models of tolerance. The first was a bureaucratic tolerance that was improvised rather than reasoned and that developed in response to the administrative requirements of an immense empire. The second, a form of mercantilist tolerance, was created to facilitate trade and increase the prosperity of a great republican city-state. In both cases the word "tolerance" should be used carefully because it was not actually the focus of direct, deliberate attention clearly expressed by sovereigns, their political counselors, or representatives of the people. Nevertheless, these improvised regimes of tolerance are remarkable for having stood the test of time through countless local experiments and adjustments during a period when religious wars were rapidly spreading throughout the Holy Roman Empire.

THE SOURCES OF
IMPERIAL TOLERANCE

Ottoman tolerance is not the first regime of imperial tolerance. A certain kind of tolerance and religious pluralism also existed at the time of the Greco-Roman empires. The empire of Constantine I as it existed after his conversion to Christianity on the eve of the Battle of the Milvian Bridge (October 28, 312) probably offers the best example. Although the emperor became convinced that Christianity represented the absolute truth and that paganism was an inferior form of superstition, he took no steps to impose his religious preference on his mostly pagan subjects. Being realistic and pragmatic, and seeking above all to maintain "public tranquility," Constantine authorized the continuation of pagan worship, named pagans to important imperial posts, and continued to finance the activities of pagan priestesses and priests as well as their places of worship. He nonetheless outlawed the cruelest religious rites, such as animal sacrifice and gladiatorial combat. Historians of the empire describe him as a hybrid individual, "both Christian and pagan." Paganism remained entirely legitimate, and Christianity, which was placed under the protection of the emperor, became a licit religion that benefitted from certain "imperial liberalities," notably the possibility of constructing churches with public funds.[1] Constantine I was tolerant out of necessity, at a time when the Christian community represented a small minority of the total population. A less liberal stance would probably have provoked rebellion or a coup d'état.

Did the Ottoman Empire resemble that of Constantine? The answers given by political observers of the seventeenth and eighteenth centuries are contradictory. Some, writing within a tradition that goes back to Montesquieu, believed that "Among the Turks . . . an atrocious despotism reigns."[2] Others perceived it as a pluralist society, characterized by a kind of multiculturalism before its time, in which all faiths were equally protected by a very accommodating imperial power. If one is to believe the statements of Voltaire's fictional character Rabbi Akib, "Your eyes have witnessed with what kindness the Turks have treated the Orthodox Christians, the Nestorian Christians, the papist Christians, the disciples of John, the ancient ignicole Parsis and ourselves, the humble servants of Moses."[3]

The more complex and ambiguous reality is likely situated between these two extremes. Tolerance existed in the Ottoman territories, but it was neither rationally determined nor conceived as a founding principle of a regime seeking to protect religious minorities. It was a bureaucratic tolerance created in response to exceptional historical circumstances, namely the geographic expansion of the Ottoman Empire from Anatolia, where it was founded by the Osman dynasty in the thirteenth century, toward Christian lands in the Balkans, which were conquered in the second half of the fourteenth century.

The founding warriors of the Ottoman Empire, of Turco-Mongolian origin, were not fanatic supporters of Islam. They were open to inter-religious dialogue, encouraging a flourishing debate between Orthodox, Catholic, and Muslim theologians. They favored the construction of a "hybrid state" whose core responsibilities were to be shared by Muslim and Orthodox Christian elites, while also permitting both groups to practice their religion in public. The ethnic and religious diversity of the conquered peoples, particularly in the Balkans but also in Constantinople, which fell in 1453, called for certain arrangements in order to minimize the risk of rebellion or secession. The stability and even the survival of the empire required that ethnic and religious differences be respected. In this context, tolerance was really an imperial "strategy of incorporation": maintaining religious diversity facilitated the consolidation of state institutions founded on a vast bureaucratic apparatus responsible for administering justice and collecting taxes.[4]

To better understand the significance of this strategy, it is worth examining the demographic and theological factors that justified it. From a demographic point of view, the sheer size of the conquered territories and the ethno-religious diversity of the subjugated peoples created a strong imbalance between Muslims and Christians. This was particularly true in Ottoman Europe, where Islam remained a minority faith until the mid–nineteenth century. According to Ottoman census data collected between 1520 and 1535, 82 percent of taxpaying households in Rumelia (the Balkan Peninsula under Turkish rule) were Orthodox Christian, and only 18 percent were Muslim.[5] Three centuries later, a census conducted in 1831 showed that Muslims residing in Ottoman Europe comprised 37.5 percent of the population—a larger proportion, though still a minority.[6] The Ottoman conquest therefore had little effect on the religious balance between different populations, the majority of which remained Orthodox Christian. But in Constantinople, the heart of the empire, the demographic distribution was more favorable to Muslims.

In the capital, the census of 1477 lists 8,951 taxpaying Muslim households (53 percent), 3,151 Greek Orthodox households (19 percent), 3,095 Armenian households and "Latins" (18 percent), and 1,647 Jewish households (10 percent).[7]

In the mid–fifteenth century, this complex ethno-religious balancing act was achieved by instituting a legal system predicated on the concept of *millets*, or confessional communities. The millet system protected non-Muslims while also affirming the superiority of Islam. The balance of relations between Muslims and non-Muslims could thus be summarized—from a Christian or Jewish point of view—as "separate, unequal and protected."[8] The proximity of these millets did not rule out reciprocal influences among them. Different religions often shared the same saints, places of worship, and pilgrimage destinations, although followers of a given religion remained firmly attached to their religious community.[9]

From a theological point of view, the type of tolerance practiced in the Ottoman Empire has a distant source in the Qur'anic doctrine of the *dhimma* elaborated, according to tradition, by the prophet Muhammad and his lieutenants at the time of the conquest of Arabia. Dhimma designates accords or pacts signed between the conquering armies and conquered non-Muslims (*dhimmis*), extending privileges to the latter if they were "peoples of the Book"—that is, Jewish and Christian readers of the Bible. These contractual agreements guaranteed freedom of movement, conscience, and religious practice; the right to own property; and the existence of a separate legal system with its own codes, courts, and methods for resolving conflicts. That said, the dhimmis were not treated as equals. All conquered peoples had to accept their status as subordinate individuals, treat Muslims with deference, and pay a personal tax—the capitation, or *jizya*—or carry out tasks such as road maintenance.[10] In addition to these duties, certain more humiliating prohibitions clearly distinguished non-Muslims from Muslims—the color of clothing, for instance, or other dress codes that varied according to religious affiliation.

In Egypt at the beginning of the fourteenth century, under Mamluk rule, Jews were required to wear a yellow turban, Christians a blue one, and Samaritans a red one. White and black turbans were reserved for Muslims. In other regions of the empire, such as Syria, modes of transportation expressed the inequality between populations. Muslims reserved noble, saddled mounts— that is, horses—for themselves, while non-Muslims had to make do with donkeys and mules. The unequal status of Muslims and dhimmis also extended to places of worship and to certain religious practices. Existing churches, monasteries, and synagogues were allowed to remain inviolable sacred spaces, but it was forbidden to restore a ruined church or construct a new non-Muslim place of worship. Each religious community had a separate cemetery, and all religious processions, icons, bell ringing, and ratchets were strictly prohibited in public places.

This unequal status even applied to the size of one's home. A Christian's house could not be taller than a Muslim's, so as to avoid "indecent, curious glances" into the neighboring courtyard or atrium. Moreover, Christians were required to offer room and board to passing Muslims, and, conversely, they were forbidden to welcome, shelter, or hide any enemies of Islam. Non-Muslims were also prohibited from carrying weapons, especially the broadsword, which symbolized conquest. Hairstyles, turbans, and hats were to bear no resemblance to Muslim head coverings. Muslim dignitaries reserved for themselves the right to wear sable and other luxurious clothing. At public gatherings, dhimmis were to stand in the presence of Muslims as a sign of respect and, when necessary, give up their seats to them. Striking or otherwise attacking a Muslim was severely punished.[11]

All these signs of inferiority created feelings of humiliation,[12] but accommodations and exceptions were so frequent that it was not uncommon to see Jews or other "infidels" going about on horseback in public, dressed in sumptuous clothing, and wearing a white turban (in principle reserved for Muslims).[13] The Jewish and Christian communities also openly defied the prohibition forbidding the construction of new religious edifices. Only in isolated regions, often under Shiite domination, such as in Yemen, was this interdiction strictly enforced. In Morocco, Jews suffered special forms of humiliation. They had to remove their sandals or slippers in the presence of Muslim dignitaries and whenever they walked near a Muslim place of worship.[14]

The list of prohibitions, whether respected or not, reveals much about the occupation of public space. It testifies to the physical proximity of Jews, Christians, and Muslims and the absence of structures partitioning that public space. Neither the ghetto as it was imposed on European Jews in the Middle Ages nor the *mellah*, later reserved for North African Jews, existed at the time of the Islamic conquest or under the Ottoman Empire of the so-called modern period (1451–1807).[15] The borders separating religious communities were more symbolic than physical and were intelligently managed within the framework of the millet system.

THE INVENTION OF THE MILLET SYSTEM: THE THING BEFORE THE WORD

When discussing how the millet system functioned in the first centuries of the Ottoman Empire, one must guard against retroactively applying more recent notions. The ancient term "millet" was used in the Qur'an (9:16) to refer to "the people of Abraham" (*millat Ibrahim*), which was originally taken to mean Muslims. Later, in the Middle Ages, it came to designate non-Muslim communities, the so-called peoples of the book.[16] This unstable, floating signifier did not attain its modern meaning until the nineteenth century. Yet specialists of the Ottoman Empire agree that the actual thing named by the term "millet," so thoroughly described and codified in the nineteenth century, had already been functioning since the fourteenth century.[17] "Millet" refers to a system of interactions between religious communities, all operating under state supervision, that placed great importance on intermediaries (judges, notables, merchants, religious leaders) who facilitated relations between the center and the periphery of the Ottoman Empire. Diversity was managed horizontally rather than hierarchically, everyday policies were somewhat opaque, and much of the stability and legitimacy of the system derived from the fact that it delivered what was expected of it, namely tax revenues.[18] Census data collected in Constantinople in 1477, at the end of the reign of Mehmed II (the Conqueror), made it easier to identify and describe the different millets.

The separation of ethno-religious communities into millets should not be perceived as a mosaic composed of an ethnic majority (Muslims) and other minority groups or as certain dominant groups prevailing over other, subordinate ones (to apply the binary logic particular to nineteenth-century nation-states). These distinctions were rarely used during the classical period of the Ottoman Empire. Certainly, there were Muslims and non-Muslims, each community possessing its religious institutions and legal system, but the borders between territories and legal systems were not sharply delineated. The individuals who functioned as middlemen or courtiers between the central state and local communities were recruited from among the millet's notables.

Certain of these leading figures, such as the ecumenical patriarch of Constantinople, exercised ecclesiastical duties of unquestioned legitimacy; others served in representative assemblies composed of jurists, laypeople, and rabbis, as was the case for the less unified Jewish communities. If a conflict arose between the government of the Ottoman Porte and the millets, these intermediaries co-opted by the central power had to resolve the problem by ensuring, for example, that taxes had been collected and by punishing those who had violated the agreement between central and local authorities.[19] If they acquitted themselves well, these middlemen would receive benefits, including land, monopolies, farm tenancies, honorary titles, or commercial privileges. If they failed, or if violence broke out within the community or with neighboring communities, they would be severely punished, losing "their livelihoods and, more often, their heads."[20]

The degree to which relations between religious communities and the Ottoman state were institutionalized varied from group to group. Formal relations were strong in the case of the Greek Orthodox millet because the patriarchs functioned as tax collectors, answering directly to the accounting services of the Ottoman government. Being granted that authority (*berat*) in turn legitimated their authority over Orthodox Christians. The correspondence of the patriarch Jeremias I for the year 1544 illustrates this type of relationship officialized in the upper echelons of the state: "I took on the engagement to give yearly to the Imperial Treasury as a *mukataa* [a fiscal unit] the sum of 4,000 pieces of gold on the condition of being the Patriarch of Istanbul-the-well-protected and of the dependent domains and the regions and the countries of Moldavia and Wallachia. Accordingly, I was given an imperial *berat*."[21]

As privileged middlemen between the Orthodox community and the great vizier, the patriarchs of Istanbul, Jerusalem, Alexandria, and Antioch were key agents of the administration of the Sublime Porte. Their principal activity consisted of collecting taxes (the capitation) for the Ottoman state, but their power was not limited to tax matters; they also had legal and religious responsibilities. At the time of Mehmed II (1451–1481), following the conquest of Constantinople, the patriarchs and their bishops (the "metropolitans") retained the right to administer the lands of the church, schools, and hospitals and had at their disposal specialized courts for matters of canon law and civil law. Everything relating to family law, as well as questions of inheritance, contracts, and certain aspects of criminal law, also fell under the authority of the Greek millet. Its reach was such that the Orthodox bishop Theophilos affirmed that the power granted to the ecumenical patriarch of Constantinople and to his synod and metropolitans went far beyond that of the leader of the Orthodox Church at the time of the Byzantine Empire. Indeed, before the conquest of the city the patriarch had neither civil nor fiscal responsibilities, his authority being limited to ecclesiastical matters.[22]

The patriarchs of the Ottoman Empire also had the right to levy taxes on their coreligionists to pay for churches and other buildings in their dioceses. Their power extended over all the Orthodox populations in the empire, encompassing not only the Greeks but also Orthodox communities in Romania, Bulgaria, Albania, and Serbia. The Ecumenical Patriarchate of Constantinople had authority over the patriarchates of Alexandria, Antioch, and Jerusalem and over the archbishoprics of Cyprus, Pec, and Ohrid.[23] Management of the empire, therefore, relied on a hierarchy of intermediate networks that linked the central bureaucracy to local oligarchies, religious leaders, and merchants. The central bureaucracy secured the support of local Orthodox elites by offering them titles, jobs, and emoluments; these local elites in turn readily asserted the legitimacy of the imperial power and praised its institutions.[24] The Phanariots, rich Greek merchants from the Phanar quarter in Istanbul who had become the favored administrators of the Ottoman Porte at the beginning of the eighteenth century, did not hide their admiration for the virtues of the millet system. These virtues were described in great detail by the merchant Nikolas Mavrokordatos in a work dating from 1718. Among them, the author underscores religious tolerance.[25]

Nevertheless, it is important not to adopt an overly positive view of a system that could be ruthless if a designated administrator proved incapable of maintaining public order or of collecting the requisite taxes or customs duties. The punishment could be a forced resignation or a loss of acquired privileges but often also imprisonment or even death, in the case of serious fraud or a poorly suppressed insurrection. In 1821, for example, the patriarch Gregory V of Constantinople, surprised by the revolt of Orthodox principalities along the Danube, imposed punitive measures that were judged to have come too late. Against all evidence, he was held responsible for the uprising and later condemned to death by hanging on the order of the sultan.[26]

The autonomy of the Greek millet was possible because the sultans did not consider themselves to be sovereigns by divine right. There was a dominant religion, Islam, but it left a large place for "people of the book"—Christians and Jews. Therefore, these conquered peoples could continue to live their lives freely and maintain their religious traditions. The patriarchate of the Byzantine church had total freedom to continue managing the Orthodox populations of the empire with a minimum of interference from Ottoman authorities. This general tolerance, despite some discrimination (Orthodox Greeks paid more taxes than Muslims and did not have access to all the public offices of the empire), preserved the peace while maintaining true religious pluralism. It offered a practical solution to a complex problem: the administration of an enormous multiethnic and multidenominational empire.

THE JEWISH MILLET

The best example of Ottoman tolerance can be seen in the welcome extended to Jewish immigrants, who were much less numerous than the large Orthodox populations. Fleeing expulsions and persecution in Europe, they found a haven in the large cities of the Ottoman Empire, especially in Salonica, Smyrna, and Constantinople. Jews had been expelled from England in 1290; from France's largest cities, with the exception of Avignon, in the fourteenth century; and from the entire Holy Roman Empire, except for the cities of Frankfurt, Worms, and Prague. Most Jews forced out of cities and states emigrated east toward Poland. The expulsion of the Jews from Spain in 1492 and from Portugal in 1497 led to mass migrations toward Italian cities such as Rome, Naples, Padua, Ferrara, Mantua, and Venice. Others moved to the large trading centers of Ottoman Europe such as Salonica, Edirne, Smyrna, Constantinople, and Bursa in Anatolia.

Because the Romaniote Jews already present in Byzantium lived side by side with Ashkenazi Jews from Germany and Italy and with large numbers of Sephardic Jews expelled from Spain, the Jewish communities of the Ottoman Empire showed tremendous diversity in terms of places of origin, languages, rituals, and social customs. Although the central power favored the arrival of new populations, it had great difficulty finding trusted interlocutors whose authority and legitimacy was comparable to that of individuals serving within the Ecumenical Patriarchate of Constantinople. After the fall of Constantinople, there existed for a while a "metropolitan of Jews," a chief rabbi named Moses Capsali, who represented all Jewish congregations of the empire. But his power was limited—first because some old communities such as the one in Salonica refused to take orders from an Istanbul rabbi and second because the powers accumulated by Moses Capsali over religious, legal, administrative, and fiscal matters proved to be ephemeral. His successor, Rabbi Elijah Misrahi, exercised only judicial and religious responsibilities.

Tax collection was the responsibility of a powerful layperson, the *kethüda* (intendant or commissary), who was appointed by authorities of the Sublime Porte. Other kethüdas were appointed in Salonica, Rhodes, and Smyrna at the end of the seventeenth century.[27] They exercised considerable power over their coreligionists. They could change tax rates, punish fraud, create new taxes, stimulate trade, and obtain commercial monopolies and additional revenues for their own benefit.[28]

In Constantinople the fragmentation of local congregations led to the formation of two rival communities: the Romaniotes and the "immigrants." The first was composed of Hellenic Jews of Byzantium present before the fall of the city and Jews who had arrived soon after from Anatolia and the Balkans and who had been encouraged, and often forced, to settle in the city on the Bosporus after the victories of Mehmed the Conqueror. The other community was mostly made up of Sephardic Jews expelled from Spain following the Alhambra Decree of March 31, 1492. They were urged by Mehmed II to join the first group in order to repopulate the partially destroyed city and thereby bolster its commercial and financial development.[29] Each community possessed influential notables who could negotiate with the central government and independently manage their own schools, courts, and charitable organizations. However, since the members of these two groups often lived in the same neighborhoods, certain courts had the power to resolve conflicts arising in both communities.

By the sixteenth century, the realistic and pragmatic Turkish authority had abandoned the idea of a singular, central representative for the Jewish community. The horizontal fragmentation of local institutions and power structures was accepted because it did not obstruct the vertical relations of these authorities to the central power. In the eighteenth century, however, the Jews of Istanbul finally came to be represented by a single unified structure composed of a triumvirate of rabbis and a central commission of seven laypeople in charge of fiscal and administrative matters. These changes, favored by the Ottoman power, resulted from the breakup of old Jewish congregations and their dispersal into new mixed neighborhoods that soon fell under the dominant influence of the Sephardic rabbinical authority.[30]

In Salonica, the local authority was just as fragmented. The city's ten synagogues, founded at the beginning of the sixteenth century, reflected the extraordinary diversity of the Jewish diaspora. Italiotes, Romaniotes, Sephardim, and Marranos all had their specific traditions, languages, and legal and religious practices. Each Jewish group remained attached to its place of origin—the kingdoms of Aragon, Majorca, and Sicily; Portugal; the Republic of Venice; Provence—and each community constituted a "little republic" in association with a particular synagogue.[31]

The dispersal of places of power and decision making, along with the endless rivalries between diasporic communities, made negotiations with the central government more difficult. That is the reason why in Salonica, and later in Smyrna and Istanbul, the leaders of the Jewish communities decided to join forces and create a supreme body capable of overseeing the interests of the different local congregations. A triumvirate of rabbis, designated as "officers of the holy mission for the collective account," was therefore created.[32] Tax burdens were calculated proportionally to the wealth of each congregation. In addition, a communal house managed by seven members, the Talmud Torah, served as a meeting place to debate and decide questions of general interest.

Payment in kind was the great originality of the tax system in the Jewish community of Salonica. Each congregation was required to submit a certain quantity of wool cloth (the principal industry of the city). Within each congregation, specialized administrators known as dividers established the contribution of each taxpayer according to his wealth.[33] The fact that such trust was placed in administrators nominated by the congregation and approved by the rabbinical triumvirate is evidence of just how decentralized the structures of authority were. Independent decision making did have its limits, however. Defects in the cloth or financial misconduct could cause the Ottoman authorities to intervene and take charge of the "guilty" community, a step that was invariably accompanied by financial sanctions and the appointment of new administrators, new tax collectors, or even new intendants.[34] All administrative posts were revocable. There was no hereditary transmission of offices as in the France of Louis XIV.

Just as with the Orthodox millet, the Jewish millet was a tolerant regime that offered many advantages: the respect of religious traditions and places of worship; the preservation of a local, autonomous justice system; the official recognition of civic and religious leaders from the local community; the distribution of financial and commercial resources; and the free circulation of populations in the empire's large cities. The millet system functioned well thanks to the flexibility of the mechanisms adopted by the Sublime Porte. Each community preserved its singularity and its privileges within a general configuration that was inegalitarian but accommodating. Islam was clearly the dominant religion, and the best-paying and most prestigious jobs, such as vizier or janissary, were held by Muslims. But these inequalities remained largely invisible. The most striking thing for any foreigner passing through Smyrna or Salonica was the great wealth accumulated by the members of different ethno-religious communities, their peaceful coexistence in public space, and the geographic proximity of churches, mosques, and synagogues.[35]

TOLERANCE AND THE GREAT EMPIRES

Viewed within the general framework of the administration of large empires, the millet system was clearly a novel form of bureaucratic tolerance that was designed to facilitate religious coexistence over a vast territory. Even if it did not create formal equality between all subjects, this system offered peace, prevented religious persecution for more than four centuries, and facilitated the incorporation of minority communities into the empire. Civil, economic, and religious rights were never definitive; their acquisition depended on negotiated accords that were open to renegotiation between the leaders of local religious communities and the Ottoman government. The central authority, interested in rationalizing administration of the empire, sought to make interethnic and intercommunity relations more comprehensible by drawing symbolic borders between Muslims and non-Muslims. The domination of Islam was recognized by all, but the millet system institutionalized a relative separation between political and religious spheres. The reasoning of the Ottoman authorities recalls that of Roman administrators: tolerance was useful and therefore should be encouraged. It contributed to maintaining civil peace and consolidated imperial order by providing the resources necessary for its survival.[36]

If one compares tolerance in the Ottoman Empire in the seventeenth century with the widespread intolerance across the Holy Roman Empire at the time of the Thirty Years' War (1618–1648), the contrast is striking. In the former, coexistence of religious communities was encouraged; in the latter, the principle of *cujus regio, ejus religio* made such proximity difficult if not impossible. The triumph of the Counter-Reformation erased religious pluralism and sometimes led to violence against Protestant subjects residing in cities and provinces of the empire dominated by the Reformation, such as the Palatinate and Bohemia. This violence provoked wars and reprisals by the large Protestant powers of the day—Sweden and the United Provinces, notably—which, for geostrategic reasons, were often supported by certain Catholic monarchies.

The Treaty of Westphalia (1648) put an end to these fratricidal wars by recognizing the political and religious autonomy of approximately three hundred German states, cities, and principalities. The inhabitants of the Holy Roman Empire, now split into hundreds of states and principalities, enjoyed complete freedom of conscience. They were both political subjects bound to respect the common law of their state and believers free to "celebrate their religion, accede to (almost) all offices, and call upon the courts with the certainty of having their case heard."[37] Religious coexistence thus gave rise to a new form of tolerance based on the splitting of the subject into two entities: on the one hand the citizen, concerned with the common good and the respect of civil laws, and on the other the believer, who was the sole judge of his innermost conscience. Public authorities initiated at that time an ongoing process of secularization; they guaranteed the general interest by deliberately placing themselves above factions and religious particularism and by avoiding any opinion on theological questions.[38]

Paradoxically, at the turn of the nineteenth century, at the very moment when parts of Europe were encouraging the development of true regimes of tolerance, the Ottoman Empire was dismantling its own by eliminating the particular features upon which the millet system had been founded.[39]

The Ottoman Porte's attempts at modernization, which all tended toward a greater centralization of administrative, legal, and fiscal matters, weakened the system of Ottoman tolerance at a time when ethnonationalist sentiment was increasing in the Balkan region. The extensive changes known as the Tanzimât reforms (from the Turkish word for "reorganization"), adopted between 1839 and 1869, erased the political and civil differences between Muslims and non-Muslims. Citizens were now equal, with no distinction based on status or religion, and all now had the same rights and obligations. The Imperial Reform Edict of February 18, 1856, completely changed the judicial system and even integrated into commercial and criminal law features borrowed from the French penal code. Litigation was now treated in a uniform fashion by interfaith tribunals composed of both Muslim and non-Muslim judges. All these changes threw into doubt the legal autonomy of the millets to the point of rendering them inoperative. The only surviving remnant of the millet system concerned certain aspects of family law, notably divorce and inheritance law; in these specific areas non-Muslims could still use their own religious tribunals.[40] But those "privileges" did not withstand the centralizing changes imposed by the movement of the Young Turks after the destitution of Sultan Abdul Hamid II.

The emancipation of the Balkan provinces in the second half of the nineteenth century and the beginning of the twentieth century led to the arrival of more than five million Muslim refugees into a geographically shrunken empire. This exacerbated interethnic tensions, especially since Christians benefited from the diplomatic protection of Western powers. These events precipitated the rise of Turkish nationalism, which became increasingly intolerant toward non-Muslims. The religious pluralism that was the hallmark of the old millet system had thus lost its justification. Interethnic violence encouraged by Ottoman authorities resulted in the deaths of thousands of Greeks and over a million Armenians. The Armenian genocide marked the end of Ottoman tolerance.

5

TOLERANCE IN VENICE

A t a time when Jews were enjoying great freedom of movement within the Ottoman Empire and obtaining specific rights and privileges within the millet system, their coreligionists living in Christian-dominated Venice were subjected to severe restrictions: the obligation to live together in a confined space known as the ghetto. But the Venetian ghetto should not be confused with recent ghettos such as the Warsaw ghetto. This enclosed neighborhood certainly constrained the community, but it also, paradoxically, produced a vibrant Jewish culture. Moreover, after 1516 the seclusion was only partial. Countless negotiations between representatives from the Jewish community and Venetian authorities resulted in a softening of restrictions placed on inhabitants of the ghetto. Jews were permitted to circulate freely throughout the city during the day and pursue commercial activities outside of the ghetto, and numerous dispensations were granted to circumvent curfews. The ghetto also offered its inhabitants protection against possible reprisals by Christians seeking scapegoats during times of war and economic crisis—and each year during Lent. Overall, the ghetto was appreciated despite its inconveniences because it offered a permanent place of residence to foreigners who in the past had benefited from only short-term visitors' permits and who faced expulsion at any moment for military, moral, or religious reasons.

The exact date when Jews first settled in Venice remains uncertain. Certain Jewish moneylenders from the neighboring cities of Mestre and Padua traveled periodically to the city of Doges beginning in the late thirteenth century to sell their services. The first permanent Jewish presence clearly documented by historians dates from the early 1380s following the War of Chioggia, which pitted Venice against Genoa from 1378 to 1381. To replenish the state's coffers, depleted by military actions, and to address a severe economic crisis, Venice encouraged the establishment of Jewish moneylenders and merchants, to whom the city offered renewable charters of rights valid for five to ten years. These sharply negotiated concessions spelled out in detail the exact banking and commercial activities open to these new arrivals. They regulated the conditions and types of interest that could be charged by moneylenders, the rules of pawnbroking for customers of more modest means, the physical spaces reserved for money lending, the business hours for banks and pawnshops, and so forth. In exchange for these guarantees, the Jewish community agreed to pay a special tax, whose amount varied over time.[1]

Jews were thus tolerated, but their position in Venice remained precarious and the renewal of their charters uncertain. The Venetian senate therefore proposed in 1516 to grant Jews their own separate quarter, reserved for them alone, where they could reside for extended periods—notwithstanding protestations from the mendicant orders, who were always quick to denounce the dissolute morals of "usurers" and call for their expulsion.[2] After numerous discussions about using the islands of Giudecca and Murano, a small area near the city center, the Ghetto Nuovo, was eventually selected. This enclosed space, the first Jewish ghetto in Western history, occupied a piece of land abutting an old military foundry, the Ghetto Vecchio. The name *getto*, or *ghetto* in Venetian dialect, derived from the Italian verb *gettare* ("to cast"), referred to the pouring of liquid metal into a mold.[3]

VENICE'S THREE GHETTOS

With its high walls and shuttered windows and its two cavernous doors opening onto a bridge linking the enclosed grounds to the larger space of the old ghetto, the Ghetto Nuovo symbolized the extreme rigor of the arrangements imposed on Jewish immigrants. Nevertheless, in the context of the time, the enclosure did not represent the total submission of a people to a higher political authority or the abandonment of its religious practices, nor did it signify the absence of freedom of movement or even economic marginalization. The Jews of Venice lost the freedom they had previously enjoyed to come and go in the city day and night, but in exchange they obtained essential political, religious, and commercial rights—the most important being the right to reside in the city for as long as they liked while going about their business.

What were the precise motives that led Venice's senate, the Consiglio dei Pregadi, to decree on March 29, 1516, that all Jews would have to live permanently in the Ghetto Nuovo? First, there was a partly political, partly religious pretext. Since military defeats were thought to be the result of divine anger,[4] it was considered necessary to perform an act of expiation expressing the submission of the people of Venice to God's will.[5] The Jews were the perfect scapegoat. The presence of roughly two thousand Jewish families scattered throughout the city, the multiplication of "illegal" synagogues, the occasional presence in these synagogues of Christians curious to hear Hebrew chants, and intimate relations between Jews and Christians were said to trouble the divine order and threaten the future of the republic. It was therefore decided that

> the Jews will all live grouped together in houses situated in the Ghetto [Nuovo] near San Girolamo; and to prevent their moving about all night, we decree that on the Old Ghetto side where there is a little bridge, and likewise on the other side of the bridge, shall be erected two doors, and they shall be opened at dawn and closed at midnight by four guards hired for that purpose and they shall be appointed by the Jews themselves and paid an amount that our Council considers suitable.[6]

Surrounded by canals, the houses of the ghetto, four to seven stories high, formed an impregnable wall; its few windows here had to be closed at night. The houses encircled a large open space that lay in the middle of this "castle." Two boats circulated at night to patrol the canals and prevent anyone from leaving the ghetto. In the morning, with the ringing of the big bell of Saint Mark's, the Marangona, the doors giving access to the only two bridges that linked the ghetto to the city were opened, thus allowing Jews to go, for example, to the busy commercial district of the Rialto; in the other direction, Christians could enter the ghetto to sell food, borrow money, or conduct other business. The doors were closed again at sundown and remained under the watch of the appointed Christian guards. But respect for the nightly curfew was far from absolute. The smallness of the fines for violating the curfew suggests that compliance was far from absolute, and certain Jews, such as doctors, were given the right to move about at night to tend to their Christian patients or participate in medical assemblies. Even the ghetto's closing time was negotiable. It could be deferred at any time of year in order to extend the business day of Jewish artisans and traders working in the city. Other concessions facilitated "illegal" exits from the ghetto, including the reduction of the number of watchmen to only two and the elimination of the water patrol.[7]

The creation of the Ghetto Nuovo in 1516 revealed the limits of Venetian tolerance. From the perspective of the city's authorities, the ghetto represented a compromise between two extreme positions: freedom of residence for Jews, on the one hand, and expulsion, on the other.[8] The constraints of being shut in were counterbalanced by a stable and enduring right to residency. In addition, numerous accommodations and derogations eased the hardship of being confined. Over time, however, the ghetto became a victim of its own success: a rapid increase in the Jewish population created difficult living conditions, overcrowded dwellings, poor hygiene (even for the time), and a marketplace that was too cramped to be efficient.

To improve living conditions in the ghetto, the senators decided in 1541 to triple the surface area reserved for Jews by allowing the annexation of the neighboring Ghetto Vecchio. This modest expansion of Venetian tolerance was not an act of benevolence or compassion by the political authorities toward a poorly housed population suffering in cramped quarters. It was instead a crudely pragmatic step reflecting the political necessity of multiplying trade relations with former Byzantine Europe (the Balkans), with an eye toward restoring the commercial supremacy of the Republic of Venice, which had been challenged by the neighboring cities of Ancona and Livorno. To do so, the senate decided to welcome new Jewish migrants coming from the European provinces of the Ottoman Empire. These Levantine Jews agreed to relocate on condition that they receive fiscal advantages and, especially, more comfortable lodgings than those of their coreligionists living in the Ghetto Nuovo. The senate agreed, giving them the right to take possession of the empty space of the Ghetto Vecchio, but on condition that this space also be enclosed and that its inhabitants respect a curfew. Only two doors allowed access to the Ghetto Vecchio: one opened onto the bridge that led to the Ghetto Nuovo; the other, at the opposite end, crossed the Cannaregio canal. To avoid overly intense competition between the two Jewish communities and neighborhoods, banking and money-lending activities were reserved for Ashkenazi Jews, while the Levantines primarily dealt in secondhand goods.[9]

A third enclosure, the Ghetto Nuovissimo, founded by the senate in 1633 at the initiative of the Board of Trade of the Republic, also responded to a specific new reality: the arrival in Venice of Iberian Jews and "new Christians"—the conversos or Marranos who had been forcibly converted to Catholicism but who often practiced the religion of their ancestors in secret. The few Marranos who were present in the city in the sixteenth century had been expelled in 1559 under pressure from the Inquisition. But those punitive measures had had little effect. The need for trade, the ambiguous religious identity of the Marranos (Were they Christians or Jews?), and the refusal of Christian merchants to make theological judgments about middlemen who were appreciated as business associates in effect nullified the official exclusions. Since they were considered indispensable for the economic prosperity of the Venetian Republic, the new Christians and other Sephardic Jews came to be accepted and soon gained permanent-resident status like the Levantines. They were openly encouraged to practice the religion of their ancestors and to move into the newly developed Ghetto Nuovissimo, which was linked to the Ghetto Nuovo by a small bridge.

The sizable increase in the Jewish population in Venice, all the more surprising since it coincided with the Counter-Reformation, certainly contradicted Catholic doctrine. One of the notable Venetian "ideologues" of the day, Father Paolo Sarpi, nonetheless found good reasons to justify the presence of "bad" Christians: treating conversos as what they really were—Jews—and facilitating their establishment in the city was the best way to foster commerce and the long-term well-being of the republic and of Christianity in general. The expulsion of the Marranos would have been counterproductive since that risked moving their operations to the Ottoman Empire, thereby enriching the principal adversary of Christian Europe. Moreover, had not certain popes encouraged the presence of Marranos in Ancona by offering them exorbitant privileges? Therefore, Sarpi concluded, everything should be done to encourage this new generation of Iberian merchants. The Ghetto Nuovissimo thus became the focal point of a policy of openness toward these dynamic businessmen whose feigned or dubious Christianity was of little importance.[10]

To summarize, economic interests won out over the theological intransigence of the mendicant orders and their most zealous preachers. Ultimately, it was decided that the segregation of the Jewish population was preferable to its expulsion. The new Sephardic immigrants were thus allowed to develop their activities despite a prohibition against their making and selling new clothes. To circumvent these strict rules, Jews found ingenious ways to produce new clothes for their customers that could pass as used by incorporating small, barely visible defects, such as a discreet stain or an imperfect seam, thereby respecting the letter of the law if not its intent.[11]

Municipal management of the three ghettos depended on a system of bicameral representation composed of a Great

Council (Università Grande) and a Lower Council. An ad hoc banking commission oversaw the management of pawnshops, and a tax commission kept up-to-date taxpayer rolls and evaluated the rates and amounts of taxes to be paid to the Venetian authorities. The choice of councilors was complex: the composition of the councils had to reflect the ethnic diversity of the three ghettos and the relative importance of the Ashkenazi, Sephardic, and Levantine communities.[12] All the decisions of the Great Council were formalized in charters that were periodically renegotiated with the authorities of the republic. The task of the Lower Council was to regulate and supervise the daily functioning of the ghettos, from policing, to bridge repairs, to the granting of food permits to kosher butchers and bakers. The Lower Council was also responsible for tax collection, and it could excommunicate individuals who failed to fulfill their secular or religious obligations. Overall, the ghetto functioned like a little republic within the larger Republic of Venice.[13]

GHETTOS FOR GERMAN AND TURKISH MERCHANTS?

The idea of enclosing foreign residents in a specially designated space did not just apply to Jews. Foreign merchants—German, Greek, and Turkish—were also forced to live together in closed or semiclosed spaces in response to the same politico-religious demands of Venice's leaders: prevent intermarriage, isolate places of worship to avoid unwelcome conversions, and protect foreigners from the rage of Catholic fanatics.

Starting in 1314, German merchants, whose Catholicism posed no problem whatsoever, were nevertheless required to live in a particular building, the Fondaco dei Tedeschi—the German

Exchange House. The main reason for this separation was economic, as it allowed authorities to control the types of business the Germans were doing and to ensure that customs duties were effectively paid. Almost two centuries later, in 1505, Venetian authorities decided to tighten controls, obliging Germans to live in an enormous commercial residence situated on the Grand Canal near the Rialto Bridge. This building had a large interior courtyard surrounded by galleries four stories high whose doors and windows remained closed at night. To prevent the illegal transportation of undeclared goods, Venetian guards patrolled day and night along the interior galleries of the Fondaco, which housed stores, offices, and lodgings. The city government imposed a more rigorous surveillance, this time religious, after the publication of Luther's *Ninety-Five Theses* in 1517 so as to prevent the circulation of texts judged to be heretical. With the commercial danger of fraud inseparable from the religious danger of the Reformation, the Fondaco dei Tedeschi, the premier location for doing business with Germans, became a space of constant and total surveillance.[14]

Though not as numerous as the Germans or Jews, the Turkish merchants who came from various European provinces of the Ottoman Empire lived scattered throughout the city until 1575, when they were encouraged to live in certain residences such as the house of Bartolomeo Vendramin, located in the Rialto quarter near the San Matteo church. The initial presence of the Turks was highly displeasing to certain delicate Christian souls, who complained to Venetian authorities about the loose morals of the Ottomans and the lascivious adventures they were alleged to be having with Christian women and boys. Other religious complaints had an even greater impact. In March 1620, the priests of San Matteo claimed that the infidel Turks, "our enemies . . . and enemies of the Christian religion . . . were laughing and mocking our most sacred rituals" during Lent, even provoking the faithful by shooting arrows at the stained-glass windows of the church on the feast day of Saint Matthew.[15] Such a scandalous incident required keeping the infidels at a safe distance from churches. The Turks, often the victims of theft and attacks themselves, also sought a refuge from the Christian fanaticism stirred up during major religious holidays or when maritime conflict broke out between the Republic of Venice and the Sublime Porte. But some Venetians had reservations about the creation of a Fondaco dei Turchi, judging that it would be too great an honor to treat Muslims like the Germans or Jews by giving them a particular building. According to an anonymous petition from 1602, the reason Jews should receive special treatment was that they did not benefit from the protection of their own sovereign state. After all, they were the perfect example of a meritocracy of foreigners who, with their moneylenders, artisans, printers, doctors, and pharmacists, rendered many services to the city. The Turks, on the other hand, who only exported materials to the Ottoman Empire, did not contribute in the same way to the common good. Viewed in this light, belonging to a ghetto or a fondaco appeared as a privilege that was bestowed upon the most deserving of the city's foreign residents.[16]

City authorities did not resolve the matter until 1621, when they finally decided to grant the Turks their own space, comparable to the Fondaco dei Tedeschi, in the former palace of the Duke of Ferrara, also situated along the Grand Canal near the Rialto. As with the Jewish ghetto and the German business residence, this palace was sufficiently large to offer separate lodgings for Turks from Asia, Albania, and Bosnia. It was also a walled space with one main door that stayed open by day on the mainland side. The waterfront, accessible by day for the delivery of goods, was closed at night. To prevent Christians from peering indiscreetly into the large courtyard where the Muslims went about their business, the city authorities sealed off the windows of adjacent buildings. Guards were charged with ensuring that all windows, large and small, remained closed between sunset and sunrise. After that the Turks could no longer come and go as they pleased in the city; like the Jews and Germans, they became foreigners under surveillance.

Orthodox Greeks enjoyed more freedom of movement, but their religious activities were strictly regulated. Even after the Council of Florence in 1439, which formalized the reconciliation between the Catholic and Byzantine churches, and despite numerous requests, they were never allowed to construct a basilica adapted to their needs. They had to make do with a chapel inside the church of San Biagio, and the patriarch of Venice required that they practice their faith behind closed doors during the Holy Week. From a religious standpoint, the Greeks were less privileged than the Jews, who disposed of eight synagogues in their two main ghettos.[17]

THE GHETTOS OF ROME, FLORENCE, SIENNA, AND PADUA

In the second half of the sixteenth century, the Venetian ghetto experiment was replicated in the large cities of the Papal States on the order of Pope Paul IV (1476–1559). With the papal bull *Cum nimis absurdum* of 1555, Pope Paul ordered the confinement of the Jewish population of Rome in a closed neighborhood called the Saeptus Hebraeorum, which was separated from the Christian quarters and had only one point of entry and exit. The use of the term "ghetto" to mean an urban space for the relegation of a segment of the population appeared in papal documents starting in 1562. Following the Roman example, ghettos were created in Florence in 1571, Sienna in 1572, and Padua in 1582.[18] The generalization of this type of urban segregation began with the Counter-Reformation. It was a response to the pope's injunction to separate Jews from Christians in order to limit the risk of theological "contamination."

This "contamination" seems to have been in one direction only, if one considers the number of conversions to Catholicism recorded in the Venice archives. The priests in charge of the House of Catechumens converted and baptized nearly 1,300 "foreigners" between 1590 and 1670.[19] These unforced conversions reflected the personal choices of Jews and Muslims who wished to integrate into the dominant community of Roman Catholics. Although there is no reason to doubt that their motivations were religious, they most likely also included more prosaic considerations. Converts could enjoy the support of a tutor or sponsor, work as middlemen, join a merchant guild, serve the Venetian republic as colonial administrators, or (for female converts) pursue advantageous marriages. In short, by converting they gained access to all the benefits of full Venetian citizenship.[20]

In the seventeenth century, religious tolerance remained more the exception than the rule. The Dutch Republic was the only European country that was truly pluralistic. The Dutch Reformed Church, known as the Public Church, cohabited with other public and private churches or places of worship that included dissident Protestants, Arminians, Socinians and other non-trinitarians, Anabaptists, Catholics, and deists. Long before France and England, the Republic of the United Netherlands offered exceptionally welcoming conditions to non-Christians and especially to some three hundred Sephardic Jews who were allowed to develop an independent community in Amsterdam at the turn of the seventeenth century—the beginning of the Dutch Golden Age. The new arrivals, mostly conversos, were referred to as "the Portuguese." The independence of the United Provinces proclaimed in 1581 (and definitively attained in 1648 at the end of the Eighty Years' War) put an end to all forms of intolerance inherited from Iberian Catholicism. This allowed many members of the "Portuguese" diaspora to return to their religious traditions without having to fear the torments of the Inquisition. Moreover, conditions improved over time. At first Jews were not allowed to build a public place of worship. They could practice their faith by congregating discreetly in a private home or, starting in 1612, in a rented building unofficially used as a synagogue. The construction of the first officially recognized synagogue dates from 1639. At that time three Jewish communities—Portuguese, German, and Polish—cohabited in Amsterdam. A grander edifice, the "Portuguese Synagogue," was completed some time later, in 1675.[21]

No formal document detailed rules for relations between Jewish immigrants and the municipal authorities of the city. A number of tacit agreements with civic authorities left the Jewish community free to organize and manage its own affairs, so long as its members did not publicly express any "disdain" for the Christian religion or attempt to "seduce any Christian person . . . or have any carnal conversation, whether in or out of wedlock, with Christian women or maidens, not even when such are of ill repute."[22] This relative tolerance was not based on well-established political or religious principles but rather on informal rules of a mercantilist nature. The "Portuguese" possessed exceptional commercial, financial, and linguistic abilities that were well suited to the needs of the Dutch economy at a time when the nation was building a vast empire across Asia, Latin America (Brazil and Surinam, in particular), and North America (with the foundation of the colony of New Netherland, including parts of what is today New York, New Jersey, Delaware, Pennsylvania, and Connecticut). But in the end Jews remained second-class citizens. They were free to move about but only within Dutch territory, and they were excluded from numerous professions. "Dutch tolerance did not accept Jews as equals, but it did accept them as Jews. Sometimes. Some places."[23]

Though later than Venetian tolerance, Dutch tolerance derived from the same mercantilist logic. In both societies, Jews were tolerated but not given all the rights of citizenship, and they were required to live in ghettos (with fewer restrictions in Holland). The loose administrative supervision of the Dutch regime of tolerance differed sharply from the exacting legalism practiced in Venice. This more relaxed attitude fostered the growth and flourishing of the Jewish community during the Dutch Republic's imperial expansion in the eighteenth century. The Netherlands would soon become the premier model of a society that was tolerant by economic necessity but also because its political elites accepted true religious pluralism.

But in the seventeenth century, perceptions were different. Most historians, travelers, and philosophers vaunted the merits of Ottoman tolerance, which they saw as surpassing the Venetian and Dutch regimes of tolerance. According to records by contemporary travelers, Smyrna had more synagogues and Orthodox, Catholic, Armenian, and Protestant churches than either Amsterdam or Venice. In his *Generall Historie of the Turkes* (1603), the British historian Richard Knolles expresses great admiration for Muslims, who, he writes, "converse with Christians, and Eat and Traffick with them freely; yea sometimes they marry their daughters, and suffer to live after their own Religion."[24] Other seventeenth-century authors observed that "the Turks put none to death for Religion" and emphasized that converts to Islam had freely made that choice without force or violence. An influential 1681 British Tory manifesto—Heraclitus Ridens—praised "Protestant Mahometans" who, "according to the Law of the Alcoran . . . are so zealous for Toleration of all Jews, Pagans, Turks, and Infidels; if they have but a Conscience, it is no matter of what colour or size it is, it must have Liberty."[25]

The proponents of widespread religious tolerance such as Roger Williams, John Locke, or Pierre Bayle were inspired in part by Paul Ricaut's major work, *The Present State of the Ottoman Empire* (1668). Accordingly, they thought of Turkey as an exceptionally peaceful and tolerant country.[26] In his *Letter Concerning Toleration*, Locke could not help but comment ironically on the vain, impassioned religious debates opposing Arminians to their Calvinist rivals. Imagining for a moment such disputes transposed to Constantinople, he alleges, as we have said, how surprised a Turk would be to witness such rage of Christians against Christians.[27] Pierre Jurieu, a famous French Calvinist minister living in exile in Holland, judged the tolerance of the "Mahometans" far superior to that of Catholics. Although the "Saracens" sometimes placed restrictions on Catholics, they behaved themselves "more evangelically." The cruelty of Catholics, he writes, "surpassed the cruelty of the Cannibals," as is clear from the Saint Bartholomew's Day massacre (1572)—a tragic day during which more blood was spilled than "in all Muslim persecution of Christians."[28] But it is from a fictional rabbi and a real Jewish historian that we have inherited the highest praise of Ottoman tolerance. The first is Voltaire's character, Rabbi Akib, quoted in the previous chapter, and the second is Eliyahu Capsali, a chronicler of the reign of Sultan Bayezid II (1481–1512), who had the honor of welcoming the Sephardic Jews expelled from Spain.

> Sultan Bayezid, who reigned in Turkey, learned of all the punishments the King of Spain had inflicted on the Jews. He knew

that the Jews were looking for a place to rest their feet (Deuter-
onomy 28:65), and came to look tenderly on them. He sent mes-
sengers and had it proclaimed throughout his kingdom, orally
and in writing (Esdras 1:1), that no city government would be
allowed to turn away or expel Jews; but that instead they were to
be welcomed with goodwill; and that anyone disobeying this
order could be punished by death. . . . The expelled Jews came to
Turkey in countless droves and the country become full of them.
Turkish communities in turn made countless and endless donations to make amends to the outcasts, and money was distributed
as though it were water.[29]

This lyrical praise did not exactly match the reality of the
Jewish diaspora in the Ottoman Empire, but it retained its symbolic significance at least until the end of the nineteenth century: "Before you were banished, now you are welcome," had
declared the authorities of the Sublime Porte four centuries earlier, according to a poem published in an Izmir journal on the
occasion of the four-hundredth anniversary of the expulsion of
the Jews from Spain in 1892.[30] At the end of the nineteenth century, this warm welcome was still fresh in the collective memory of Levantine Jews.

6

ON BLASPHEMY

The preceding chapters focused on new forms of tolerance that appeared in large empires, such as the Ottoman Empire, and in dynamic commercial cities, such as the Republic of Venice, as well as on the emergence of tolerance in the colonies of North America. In these cases, tolerance was not egalitarian: some religions were favored by political authorities, and others were accepted only reluctantly, yet they all ended up peacefully coexisting, serving as models of tolerance for continental Europe. Dissident Protestants, Jews, Muslims, deists, and Native Americans could all exercise freedom of religion and express themselves without fear of censorship. But some forms of speech remained strictly regulated: blasphemy was a crime that was severely punished until the end of the eighteenth century.

This chapter deals first with the existence of antiblasphemy laws in France, England, and the United States and their gradual demise over the course of the nineteenth century and then with the rise of religious fanaticism in the twentieth and twenty-first centuries and the attempt by radical Islamists, often accompanied by calls to violence and terrorist acts, to reintroduce the crime of blasphemy in societies that had abandoned it.

What is blasphemy? The concept derives from the Greek *blasphêmía* (wounding, insulting, or impious words or speech). *Blasphemia* in ecclesiastical Latin adds an explicitly religious meaning to the Greek definition: it is a form of speech that offends God, religion, or the sacred.[1] In France, the crime of blasphemy was always systematically punished under the monarchy. It was implicitly abolished at the start of the French Revolution with the adoption of Article 10 of the Declaration of the Rights of Man and the Citizen, which states that "No one shall be disturbed on account of his opinions, including his religious views." The first revolutionary Penal Code, adopted in 1791, did not even mention the possibility of blasphemy.

To understand better the emergence of free speech in that troubled period, it is important to recall the decisive role played by Voltaire in the struggle against all forms of religious fanaticism. The cruel and anachronistic trial of Chevalier de La Barre, in 1766, is emblematic of that struggle. La Barre was condemned to death—he was tortured and beheaded—for allegedly committing blasphemy against the Catholic Church. His death was particularly shocking because it took place at a time when liberal thinkers were advocating the abolition of the death penalty for precisely this type of crime.[2]

THE CASE OF CHEVALIER DE LA BARRE

What exactly was the young chevalier accused of? According to unverified reports, he was said to have "mutilated" with the tip of a hunting knife a large wooden crucifix located on the Pont Neuf in the town of Abbeville. He was also accused of not removing his hat while standing within thirty meters of the procession of the Holy Sacrament on the day of Corpus Christi.

Furthermore, he was said to have sung "abominable and execrable songs against the Virgin Mary and all the saints"[3] while in a state of inebriation. He was also accused, with a confirming witness, of mocking the sign of the cross by saying "In the name of c[ock]" instead of "In the name of the Father," and so forth. He then continued, ex tempore, reciting Panurge's famous Litanies of the Cock "roughly as one finds them in Rabelais."[4] In the context of the time, his statements might have shocked the devout faction in Abbeville, but the young man was neither a criminal nor a murderer. In his account of the incident, Voltaire emphasizes the shocking disproportion between the actual acts committed, which he calls "secret imprudences" and "light childish pranks,"[5] and the cruelty of the punishment.

For Voltaire, the trial and its aftermath demonstrated a new form of modern "barbarism," one whose effects on European public opinion were both deplorable and counterproductive because they made "our Roman Catholic religion detestable to all foreigners." The philosopher tried unsuccessfully to turn the trial into an "affair" by using legal documents to prove the illegality of the proceedings and the indulgence that is owed to a youth "accused of singing old, blasphemous songs."[6] Voltaire also had reason personally to be nervous because the written accusation of the court of Abbeville linked Chevalier de La Barre to a pocket copy of Voltaire's *Dictionnaire philosophique*, which the young man read fervently. The sentence specified that Voltaire's *Dictionnaire* should be attached to the body of the condemned youth and burned with it. The chevalier's execution was thus inseparable from the "virulent war" waged by the Parlement of Paris against the encyclopédistes and other philosophers. Indeed, Voltaire thought it wise to go into exile for a time in Rolle, a small spa town on the shores of Lake Geneva.[7] In that tranquil setting he had plenty of time to compose his famous *Account of the Death of the Chevalier de La Barre*. He addressed it to Cesare Beccaria, an important Italian jurist known for his writings favoring the abolition of the death penalty and the implementation of judicial reforms to make punishments proportionate to crimes.[8]

The crime of blasphemy was formally abolished in 1791. Later laws, however, were passed sanctioning crimes and misdemeanors of a similar nature, such as "offenses against public and religious morals" (1819) and "sacrilege," or the profanation of sacred objects (1825). In France in the twentieth century, the Pleven law (July 1972) introduced the concept of hate crime and penalized all "incitements to discrimination, hate, or violence" targeting individuals because of their ethnic, national, racial, or religious identity.[9] Another law adopted in 2004 expanded the list of protected persons to include disabled individuals as well as individuals singled out because of their sexual orientation. With this new legislation, the French court system has been overwhelmed with discrimination lawsuits and, in the words of a leading constitutional scholar, has witnessed a sharp escalation in claims of victimhood.[10]

THE CRIME OF BLASPHEMY
IN GREAT BRITAIN

From 1400 to 1612, blasphemy in England was considered by religious courts to be a cardinal sin that warranted, in certain extreme cases, torture and execution by burning at the stake. In 1656, at the time of Cromwell, the Quaker James Naylor, who claimed to be God's equal, was condemned by Parliament and submitted to the following treatment: he was first brutally whipped, then his tongue was pierced with a hot poker, and with a hot iron his forehead was branded with a B for blasphemy. He spent the rest of his life in prison condemned to hard labor.[11] With the abolition of religious courts in 1640, blasphemy was redefined within common law as a political act of high treason. In the famous case of *Rex v. Taylor* from 1676, John Taylor, who was judged of sound mind and body, had dared claim that Christ was, among other things, a bastard, pimp, imposter, and crook. Such statements, according to the Lord Chief Justice, constituted "much more than a crime against God and religion." They expressed "a crime against laws, the state, and the government." He argued that questioning the Christian religion that serves as a foundation for the kingdom's laws amounted to "dissolving all the obligations that bind together civil society" and was therefore tantamount to an "act of treason."[12]

In the eighteenth century, blasphemy was still treated as a common-law offense. But it was also accepted that opinions contrary to Anglican doctrine could be tolerated, in the name of free speech, so long as they were expressed discreetly and avoided all formulations considered harmful or indecent to Christians. Punishment for the offense of blasphemy was generally limited to prison sentences. For example, Thomas Woolstan, a deist, was sentenced to life in prison in 1729 for having published short texts denying the reality of Christ's miracles as described in the Bible.

In the nineteenth century, blasphemy convictions were unusual, but the laws remained on the books. The reasoning of judges retained a theological-political dimension. An offense was "blasphemous" if it was found to be contrary to the teachings of the Church of England and formulated in words that could "shock or offend the feelings of a group of believers."[13] Could blasphemy apply to Christian churches other than the Church of England? Court records indicate that the jurisprudence remained uncertain and contradictory on this point.

In the twentieth century, blasphemy convictions became extremely rare. In 1977, however, a poem by James Kirkup published in the journal *Gay News* was judged blasphemous for describing acts of fellatio and sodomy committed by a Roman centurion on the dead body of Christ and suggesting that Christ had had sexual relations with his disciples. The publisher of the journal received a nine-month suspended sentence and was fined five hundred pounds. On appeal the sentence was reduced, but the conviction for blasphemy was upheld. More importantly, though, the case raised a number of questions. Was the law against blasphemy valid for non-Christian religions? Could a book or a caricature perceived as insulting toward Muslims be deemed blasphemous? The infamous Rushdie affair raises all these questions and more.

The publication of *The Satanic Verses* (1988), a work of fiction, should not have been a problem in England. Peter Mayer, the director of Penguin Press and Salmon Rushdie's publisher, had not anticipated encountering any particular difficulties: Rushdie was, after all, considered one of the great writers of his generation; his novel *Midnight's Children*, an epic satire of postcolonial India, had won the prestigious Booker Prize in 1981. Mayer's professional philosophy was rather straightforward: "If you're a publisher, you will always find people offended by books you publish." In the past he had not hesitated to publish works that could arguably be shocking to Christians and Jews. He accepted the legitimacy of laws that protected minority ethnic or religious groups against racial hatred and discrimination, but he did not imagine that one could prohibit a work of fiction because it was deemed to be offensive to Muslims. After all, a publisher was not a theologian and therefore not in a position to judge the validity of negative opinions or comments expressed about the Qur'an.[14]

The author of *The Satanic Verses* was quickly demonized by critics who had rarely taken the time to read the book. What, then, were they so upset about? The first published review of the book in the newspaper *India Today* was entitled "An Unequivocal Attack on Religious Fundamentalism."[15] Syed Shahabuddin, an Islamist and Indian parliamentarian, published an open letter to the author denouncing his "satanic forethought" in attacking the reputation of Islam and its prophet. Other critics highlighted what they considered to be the book's "vulgar and disgusting language" and perverse self-flagellation, which they viewed as "a malicious attack on his [Rushdie's] ethnic past."[16] In England, the Council of Mosques of the city of Bradford denounced the author for "attacking our beloved prophet Muhammad—peace be upon him—and his wives, by using language more repugnant than any Muslim could tolerate."[17] Criticism came from numerous countries: India, Afghanistan, South Africa, Iran, Saudi Arabia. The endless repetition of accusations against the work for describing the Prophet's wives as "whores" seemed to lend credence to those criticisms, which were then repeated and amplified in other news media. Yet nowhere in the novel is it stated that the Prophet's wives were prostitutes, nor does the author ridicule Islam or show disrespect to its founder.[18] For Rushdie, *The Satanic Verses* was a modern epic set in contemporary India and depicting a new, fictive religion, resembling Islam, which portrayed the Prophet Mahoud and the struggle between Good and Evil embodied by the archangel Gibreel Farishta and the devil Saladin Chamcha. The distance separating Rushdie's work of fiction from actual Islam was clear: the novel's prophet was not Muhammad, and his city was not Mecca but Jahilia. Furthermore, the part of the book devoted to the origin of Islam, Rushdie thought, demonstrated his admiration of and respect for the Prophet. "It treated him as he always wanted to be treated, as a man ('the Messenger'), not a divine figure (like the Christians' 'Son of God'). It showed him as a man of his time, shaped by that time, and, as a leader, both subject to temptation and capable of overcoming it."[19]

These explanations carried little weight for the adversaries of a storyteller who, as they saw it, had made a career out of attacking Islam. Why read it, since it was said by everyone to be a "blasphemous" book? As Syed Shahabuddin put it, "I do not have to wade through a filthy drain to know what filth is."[20] But for radical Islamists, the true crime was something else: Rushdie had tarnished the aura of the Prophet by depicting him as a man like other men, a poor sinner subject to temptation.

Rushdie's interpretation was based on the hadiths, a collection of sayings of the Prophet compiled by his disciples that retains a certain authority even today. One such hadith, composed by Tabari, a famous Sunni interpreter of the Qur'an, discusses a variant of sura 53 of the Qur'an, known as "The Star" (an-Najm). According to the hadith, the first version of the sura refers to three winged goddesses, creatures akin to angels or sacred birds that were well known to travelers. Named al-Lat, al-'Uzza, and Manat, each had its own place of worship at the gates of Mecca. Were the three goddesses angels? Daughters of God? Idols? Were they rival divinities challenging the one and only God? Interpretations diverge, and the first version of the sura maintains a certain ambiguity: "Have you heard of al-Lat, and al-Uzza, and al-Manat, the third, the other one? They are the exalted birds and their intercession is greatly to be desired."[21] The final version of the same sura, described as "expurgated" by the commentators, completely obliterates the influence of the winged goddesses: "Have you heard of al-Lat and al-Uzza, and al-Manat, the third, the other one? They are but names that your forefathers invented, and there is no truth in them. Shall

God have daughters while you have sons? That would be a very unfair division."[22]

The discrepancy between these two versions stems from the historical context of the moment when Muhammad received the first "revelation" from the archangel Gabriel atop Mount Hira. The monotheism vigorously defended by the Prophet stood in opposition to the polytheistic traditions of Mecca's elites. The cult of the three winged goddesses was strongly encouraged by the city's magistrates for financial reasons: merchants who entered the city were required to make an offering in one of the three temples dedicated to the bird-women. This offering, essentially an obligatory tax, benefitted Mecca's wealthy families. The winged divinities, as Rushdie points out, were "at the heart of the economy of the new city, of the urban civilization that was coming into being."[23]

The first version of sura 53 expressed a thirst for recognition, a desire to please the powerful, a compromise that bordered on compromising. The second version showed that the Prophet had come to his senses and overcome the satanic temptation of a possible reconciliation between monotheism and polytheism. In the end Muhammad "both confessed to having been tempted and also repudiated that temptation."[24]

Was it blasphemous to highlight the virtue of a man capable of resisting temptation? By affirming that Mahoud, the fictional version of Muhammad in *The Satanic Verses*, is only a "prophet, messenger, and businessman," a weak, ordinary man ready to accept a few winged female idols to better convert the lowly pagans of the city of Jahilia (an allusion to Mecca in the novel),[25] Salman Rushdie had committed an irreparable crime. Rushdie's novel was particularly shocking to Muslims of the Indian subcontinent who followed the Deobandi tradition that insisted on total devotion to the Prophet and his virtues. In the words of

Zaki Badawi, the president of the Muslim College of London, a school that trains imams and confers degrees in Islamic studies, what Rushdie wrote is "far worse to Muslims than if he had raped one's own daughter. . . . Muslims seek Mohammed as the ideal on whom to fashion our lives and conduct, and the prophet is internalized into every Muslim heart. It's like a knife being dug into you."[26] Other critics, such as the essayist Richard Webster, claimed along the same lines that the atheist author had committed "cultural rape" in the name of a secular and rationalist Western culture that considers itself superior and whose unique goal was to subjugate and belittle new Muslim immigrants. Rushdie's "apocalyptic" provocations were blasphemous because they attacked the most sacred traditions of Islam. The author of *The Satanic Verses* was therefore considered largely responsible for the violence that broke out following the publication of his book.[27] Anglican authorities claimed to "understand" why Muslims' feelings were hurt, according to a much-remarked-upon statement by Robert Runcie, archbishop of Canterbury.[28]

The Satanic Verses was published by Penguin on September 26, 1988. It was banned in India at the beginning of October and later the same month by the South African and Saudi governments out of a desire, they said, to uphold public order. In other words, the stated motive was not yet blasphemy. The work was simply declared to be in poor taste, likely to shock not only Muslim sensibilities but also those readers "who value decency and culture."[29] In India, the main motive for the ban was political: Rajiv Gandhi's ruling party was preparing for legislative elections in November, and there was no wish to trouble the faith of Muslims likely to vote for his party. The first public accusation of blasphemy was made in November by the grand sheikh Gad el-Haq Ali Gad el-Haq—an antiquated name worthy of the *Arabian Nights*, according to Rushdie—one of the hard-line, conservative theologians at Cairo's Al-Azhar University.[30]

The first and most spectacular public burning of *The Satanic Verses* took place two months later in January 1989, in the northern English city of Bradford, in Yorkshire. Thousands of demonstrators, most of them Muslim, gathered in the city center to attend the public burning of the blasphemous book. "A copy of the novel had been nailed to a piece of wood and then set on fire: crucified and then immolated."[31] One month later, as the book was being published by Penguin's Viking Books in the United States, a protest march in front of the American Cultural Center in Islamabad turned violent, and five demonstrators died. Similar violent incidents occurred in Kashmir, where one protester was also killed.

THE FATWA OF AYATOLLAH KHOMEINI

It was in this context rife with anti-Americanism and the hysterical denunciation of the Indo-British author for blasphemy and apostasy that the Ayatollah Khomeini issued his famous fatwa. It is worth citing in its entirety:

> In the name of Him, the Highest. There is only one God, to whom we shall all return. I inform all zealous Muslims of the world that the author of the book entitled *The Satanic Verses*—which has been compiled, printed and published in opposition to Islam, the Prophet and the Qur'an—and all those involved in its publication who were aware of its contents, are sentenced to death. I call on all zealous Muslims to execute them quickly, wherever

they are to be found, so that no one else will dare to insult the Muslim sanctities. God willing, whoever is killed on this path is a martyr.

In addition, anyone who has access to the author of this book, but does not possess the power to execute him, should report him to the people so that he may be punished for his actions.

May peace and the mercy of God and His blessings be with you. Ruhollah al-Musavi al-Khomeini, 25 Bahman 1367.[32]

From that date—February 14, 1989—the author was forced to live in hiding and under the protection of the Special Branch of the London Metropolitan Police. A bounty of three million dollars was put on his head, and the book's publishers and translators around the world received death threats. The Italian and Japanese translators were stabbed. William Nygaard, the Norwegian publisher, survived gunshot wounds. The Turkish translator, Aziz Nesin, narrowly escaped the fire set at his hotel in Turkey; the fire killed thirty-seven people. Many booksellers were threatened, including the owner of the famous Berkeley bookstore Cody's Books, who was the target of a homemade bomb. Other bookstores were also bombed, including Collets and Dillons in London and Abbey's Bookshop in Sydney. As a precaution, *The Satanic Verses* was pulled from the shelves in the 430 bookstores of the W. H. Smith chain in England. The author had become a pariah, and his publisher, Penguin, decided not to take the risk of publishing a paperback edition.[33]

To understand the scope and significance of Khomeini's fatwa, it must be placed in the geopolitical context of the time. The great rival of Shiite Iran was Sunni Saudi Arabia. The Saudi kingdom had chosen a discreet but effective method for denouncing Rushdie's "perverted" work, creating the United Kingdom Action Committee on Islamic Affairs, directed by the Saudi diplomat Mughram al-Ghamdi and an imam from London's Balham mosque, Iqbal Sacranie. The committee's mission was to promote Wahhabism and cleanse public discourse of all Islamophobic statements, and it used its influence to block or discourage sales of *The Satanic Verses*. This relatively low-key Saudi committee contrasted with the Muslim Institute, a foundation for Islamic studies closely allied with the Tehran regime. Its founder, Kalim Siddiqui, constantly asserted the greatness of the Iranian revolution and its leader Ayatollah Khomeini and considered the fatwa "one of the greatest acts of leadership of the *umma* by any political or religious leader in the history of Islam." As the embodiment of a universal revolution, Khomeini was qualified to speak "on behalf of the one thousand million Muslims of the world" and to make the claim that "virtually every Muslim man, woman and child agreed Rushdie should die."[34]

The denunciation of Rushdie for blasphemy was not only a religious matter. It epitomized the eschatological combat that opposed Saudi Arabia and Iran "to conquer the hearts and souls of Muslims."[35] To a greater extent than the backroom diplomacy of the Saudis, the fatwa kindled the imagination of new Muslim immigrants to the United Kingdom who were seduced by radical Islam and saw themselves as "crusaders in reverse."

The Saudis, faced with the extreme action of the Iranians, refused to be outdone, as revealed by the sensational declaration made by Imam Iqbal Sacranie, the future secretary general of the Muslim Council of Great Britain: "Death, perhaps, is a bit too easy for him [Rushdie]."[36] In other words, the fate of Chevalier de La Barre—torture followed by decapitation—was implicitly being countenanced by this modern holy warrior.

Since the English law against blasphemy was still on the books, it was only to be expected that some Muslim defense organization would attempt to bring Rushdie to trial. And this is precisely what Abdul Hussain Choudhury did on behalf of the British Muslim Action Front. The strategy he pursued was classic. He asked a local court to enforce the law and arraign Salman Rushdie and his publisher for blasphemy. The court refused to summon the accused, maintaining that the law against blasphemy only protected the Christian religion. Choudhury then appealed to a district court, which affirmed the lower court's decision: "In our judgement, where the law is clear it is not the proper function of this court to extend it. . . . It is in that circumstance the function of Parliament alone to change the law."[37]

Attempts were made, backed by Labour Party MPs from districts with sizable Muslim populations, to change the blasphemy law and extend its application to non-Christian religions. Those attempts failed, however, on the grounds that broadening the criminalization of blasphemy would create an untenable situation wherein even an insignificant remark could be interpreted as "blasphemous" by members of a church whose doctrine was unfamiliar to the public at large. One logical solution would have been to apply the blasphemy law to the leading religions of the kingdom, but that idea was not in keeping with evolving mores and with the progressive secularization of public life in a modern-day monarchy. When James Kirkup's "blasphemous" poem was resurrected in 2001 and read aloud on a show broadcast by the BBC appropriately entitled *Taboo*, no court was asked to prosecute the matter, notwithstanding the numerous complaints received by the show's producers. In response, BBC executives published a soothing statement pointing out that the topic had been treated responsibly, without violating any existing law. Opinions and beliefs had changed since 1970, thereby justifying an "enlargement of the sphere of tolerance" applied to the channel's broadcasts for the general public.[38] The evolution of public opinion had rendered the blasphemy law obsolete, and, on March 5, 2008, Parliament abolished the common-law offense of blasphemy.

But the elimination of the crime of blasphemy was not as sweeping as first thought. Other laws were passed to protect believers from particularly acrimonious displays of hate. The Racial and Religious Hatred Act of 2006 stated that an offense was committed if threatening words or materials (documents, theater performance, film, and so forth) were used with the intention of deliberately causing harm and provoking hateful reactions. The notion of "threat" is the operative distinction; statements or texts that are simply "rude" or "insulting" are not considered to be incitements to religious hatred. Finally—and this further restrains the scope of the law—legal action can only take place with the explicit approval of the minister of justice.[39]

BLASPHEMY IN THE UNITED STATES

In America, the crime of blasphemy was severely punished in Puritan times. Four Quakers were executed for blasphemy in the Massachusetts Bay Colony in 1659 and 1660, and numerous "witches" were condemned and burned alive for the same reason at the infamous Salem trials in 1690. The common-law tradition inherited from Great Britain forbidding blasphemy remained in force in all American states even after the country gained its independence. Although the First Amendment prohibited the institutionalization of religion and guaranteed freedom of speech, blasphemy could and was still prosecuted in a number of states at a time when judges did not hesitate to proclaim "We are a Christian people." In the 1811 case of *People v. Ruggles*, the condemnation of a young man who, in a drunken state, had declared outside a tavern that "Jesus Christ is a bastard and his mother a prostitute," was upheld by the New York State Supreme Court in the name of a Christian culture perceived as dominant in North America.[40] Ruggles's lawyer unsuccessfully argued that Christianity had no legal status, since the state constitution defended "free toleration to all religions and all kinds of worship." But according to Judge Kent, who heard the case, it was out of the question to defend foreign religions such as those of Muhammad or the Great Lama, "for this plain reason, that the case assumes that we are a Christian people, and the morality of the country is deeply ingrafted upon Christianity, and not upon the doctrines or worship of those impostors."[41] Furthermore—still according to Judge Kent—allowing blasphemous statements to stand would amount to compromising the very integrity of official oaths that require witnesses before the court to "place their hand on the Bible and embrace its contents."[42]

But the rapid progress of religious skepticism and nonbelief changed the situation starting in the 1830s. By that time, a young Abraham Lincoln could, with no cause for worry, read in public from the deist works of Voltaire, Thomas Paine, and Volney—even going so far as to proclaim aloud during a debating-society meeting of young lawyers in New Salem, Illinois, where he had recently moved, that Jesus was a "bastard."[43] No legal proceeding resulted from these shocking statements, although we know that a pamphlet written by Lincoln on "religious infidelity" was destroyed by friends who sought to protect the political career of a young lawyer whose future looked so promising.[44]

Blasphemy prosecution at the state level "rested on the understanding that attacks on Christianity were anything but protected speech."[45] Punishing blasphemy was tantamount to defending an official religious doctrine against impious or insulting statements. Blasphemy ceased being constitutional as soon as the Supreme Court extended to the states the fundamental rights guaranteed by the Bill of Rights, starting with freedom of speech in 1925 and followed by the Free Exercise Clause of the First Amendment in 1940 and the Establishment Clause in 1947.[46] As a consequence, the notion that Christianity was a privileged religion gradually disappeared. Christians were no longer shielded from the insults of atheists, deists, or non-Christians; freedom of speech took precedence, and the religious diversity of the New World could no longer favor one religion over another. This was explained by Justice Roberts in a famous 1940 court decision: "In the realm of religious faith . . . the tenets of one may seem the rankest error to his neighbor." The affirmation of these principles, "in spite of the probability of excesses and abuses," is essential if citizens are to develop "enlightened opinion and right conduct."[47]

Today, freedom of religion and freedom of speech are viewed as expressions of the free market of ideas, which must be protected at all cost, since truth emerges from the unrestrained clash of ideas. Although free speech and religious liberty are deeply anchored in American constitutional law and tradition, one can still find remnants of old illiberal habits at the state level. At the end of the twentieth century, for example, certain religious groups successfully lobbied state legislators to pass antiblasphemy laws intended to protect believers from public statements judged to be scandalous. Perhaps the most remarkable case was a civil suit brought by George Kalman, a film producer, against the state of Pennsylvania in June 2010. Kalman had boldly named his production company I Choose Hell Productions, LLC. This positive reference to hell was judged to be in violation of a 1977 state law forbidding company names from incorporating "words that constitute blasphemy, profane cursing or swearing or that profane the Lord's name." The state law had passed the Pennsylvania House of Representatives by a vote of 193 to 1. It had been proposed in response to protests that had occurred some years earlier in the small town of McKeesport, where citizens had been incensed by the name of a local business, the God Damn Gun Shop, which they viewed as unacceptable and blasphemous. The antiblasphemy law was designed to prevent such names on signs displayed in public. But since the bill's drafters provided no precise definition of blasphemy, the agency charged with registering company names used a classic reference work, the eighth edition of *Black's Law Dictionary*, which gave the following definition of the word: "Irreverence toward God, religion, a religious icon, or something considered sacred. Cf. Profanity: Obscene, vulgar, or insulting language. Profanity is distinguished from mere vulgarity and obscenity by the additional element of irreverence toward or mistreatment of something sacred."

Was the use of the word "hell" blasphemous? That was evidently the conclusion of the employee responsible for registering names, who had even compiled a list of inappropriate words, including "Christ," "damnation," "God," "hell," and "Jesus." The agency therefore refused to register Kalman's production company. Kalman filed suit in a district court and, after a long procedure, the case was decided in his favor on grounds that the antiblasphemy law violated the Establishment Clause and the Free Exercise Clause of the First Amendment. "To choose hell," explained U.S. District Judge Bayslon of the Eastern District of Pennsylvania in his sixty-eight-page opinion, is perhaps an irreverent choice for a company name, but it is fully compatible with the type of "uninhibited, robust, and wide open debate and discussion" protected by the First Amendment.[48] The judge also reminded those present that they were, after all, in the state of Pennsylvania, a republic founded by the Quaker William Penn, the inventor of a new form of religious tolerance whose precepts anticipated the major principles of the First Amendment. He could have added, even more persuasively, that Quakers had been the first American victims of antiblasphemy laws and that Pennsylvania's founder would most likely never have consented to such attempts to criminalize blasphemy.

While antiblasphemy laws were making a comeback, well-known artists were deliberately provoking their most devout fellow citizens by producing works of art that, in another era, would have been condemned for blasphemy and burned publicly. The American artist Andres Serrano, who claimed to produce "beautiful objects from unorthodox materials," displayed color photographs of a crucifix submerged in a tank filled with his own urine. The work, *Piss Christ*, was first shown in 1987 at the Stux Gallery in Manhattan, then at the Los Angeles County Museum of Art (LACMA) and the art museum of Carnegie Mellon University in Pittsburgh, and, finally, in 1989, at the Virginia Museum of Fine Arts in Richmond. The first exhibitions provoked no organized reaction; the Virginia show, on the other hand, was opposed by the American Family Association, an evangelical lobby created in 1977 under the name the National Federation for Decency. Its founder and director, Reverend Donald Wildmon, sent to every member of the U.S. Congress a personal letter denouncing the scandalous nature of a work of art that in his view constituted "blasphemy," an "insult," a total "lack of respect," and worst of all "the desecration of Christ." Certain senators, including Jesse Helms of South Carolina and Alfonse D'Amato of New York, joined in the protest by publicly ripping up reproductions of the sacrilegious work. But these angry outbursts were not followed by legal action. The *Piss Christ* photographs, printed as a limited edition, continued to be displayed in museums. The only sanction imposed was monetary. To punish this outrage to Christ, Congress cut funding to the

National Endowment of the Arts by $45,000, citing the fact that this federal agency had formerly subsidized the artistic pursuits of Serrano.[49]

Abroad, reactions were more violent. When shown at the National Gallery of Victoria in Melbourne, Australia, in 1997, *Piss Christ* was vandalized with a hammer; the work met with the same fate in Avignon in 2011 when it was displayed as part of the Yvon Lambert collection. The French iconoclasts were responding to the appeal of an ultraconservative Catholic group, the Institut Civitas, which had called for protests: "For the honor of the cross, let us demonstrate our indignation at this profanation of Christ's image."[50]

Many other examples of "sacrilegious" works can be cited, such as *Holy Virgin Mary* (1996), a painting by the Nigerian British artist Chris Ofili representing a black Virgin Mary surrounded by a pornographic collage of female genitals, glitter, and elephant excrement. The work was shown without incident in London and Berlin as part of an exhibition of works by a group known as the Young British Artists. When it traveled to the Brooklyn Museum of Art, however, *Holy Virgin Mary* provoked loud protests from New York's mayor at the time, Rudy Giuliani, who tried unsuccessfully to have the show canceled by cutting municipal funding to the museum. A lawsuit initiated by the city in federal court also failed when Judge Nina Gershon ruled that banning the show would violate freedom of expression as protected by the First Amendment. The controversial work thus remained on display, and the New York mayor was left to rail against the judge's decision: "There is nothing in the First Amendment that supports horrible and disgusting projects!"[51]

Other photographic and cinematographic works, including *I.N.R.I.* by Serge Bramly and Bettina Rheims (1997), *Je vous salue Marie* by Jean-Luc Godard (1985), and *The Last Temptation of*

Christ (1988) by Martin Scorsese, have provoked scandal but not censorship. Less tolerant than their American and British counterparts, French ultraconservative Catholics set fire to a cinema in central Paris and vandalized movie theaters in Paris and Besançon that were showing the Scorsese film.[52] Although works of art considered blasphemous by devout believers can no longer be banned outright, they can still incite strong political and religious feelings, result in financial pressures, and occasionally provoke uncontrolled acts of violence.

THE TRIUMPH OF SELF-CENSORSHIP

While the crime of blasphemy has lost all legal standing in liberal democracies, censorship still exists as an anachronistic, unacknowledged punishment for behavior judged to be "sacrilegious." The refusal to fund a Swiss theater's October 12, 1993, performance of Voltaire's tragedy *Le fanatisme ou Mahomet le Prophète* was justified in budgetary terms, but it was in fact an act of censorship. The director, Hervé Loichemol, an enthusiastic reader and admirer of Rushdie, wanted to test the limits of free speech in the former Republic of John Calvin. He proposed a production of Voltaire's play to the Geneva Office of Cultural Affairs as a way of celebrating both the tricentenary of the philosopher's birth and the city's commitment to the principle of free speech.

Voltaire's tragedy is much more critical of Muhammad than Rushdie's *Satanic Verses*. Voltaire portrays Muhammad as a cruel and bloodthirsty "false prophet"[53] who exploits the naïveté and religious faith of Zaphna to convince him to murder Muhammad's great rival Alcanor, the sheikh of Mecca. In Voltaire's tragedy Alcanor is in fact Zaphna's true father, and therefore the crime to be carried out is an act of parricide—a fact of which Muhammad is perfectly aware. Act 3 of the tragedy contains this unkind portrait of the prophet exchanging words with his faithful lieutenant Mirvan:

> MIRVAN: Now, Mahomet's the time to seize on Mecca,
> Crush this Alcanor, and enjoy Palmira.[54]
> This night the old enthusiast offers incense
> To his vain gods in sacred Caboo:
> Zaphna, who flames his zeal for heaven and thee,
> May be won o'er to seize that lucky moment.
> MAHOMET: He shall; it must be so; he's born to act
> The Glorious crime; and let him be at once
> The instrument and the victim of the murder.
> My law, my love, my vengeance, my own safety,
> Have doom'd it so—but, Mirvan, dost thou think
> His youthful courage, nursed in superstition,
> Can e'er be work'd —
> MIRVAN: I tell thee, Mahomet,
> He's tutor'd to accomplish thy design.
> Palmira too, who thinks thy will is heaven's,
> Will nerve his arm to execute thy pleasure.
> "Love and enthusiasm blind her youth:
> They're still most zealous who're most ignorant."
> MAHOMET: Didst you engage him by a solemn vow!
> MIRVAN: I did, with all the enthusiastic pomp
> Thy law enjoins; then gave him as from thee,
> A consecrated sword to act thy will.
> Oh, he is burning with religious fury![55]

Loichemol's proposal to perform the play was at first warmly received by Geneva's city councilors, including one elected member from the city's executive branch, Alain Vaissade. But the local Muslim community considered the play scandalous and discreetly voiced its opposition. Hafid Ouardini, the rector of the Geneva mosque, asked for the play to be banned out of respect for Islam. Tariq Ramadan, an influential and highly controversial Islamic scholar, took a more subtle approach by publishing an "Open Letter to Monsieur Hervé Loichemol" in the *Tribune de Genève*. In his letter Ramadan called for respect to be accorded to the beliefs of those in the Muslim community who would inevitably find shocking Voltaire's depiction of a "bloodthirsty, stubborn, jealous, hypocritical, and 'fanatic'" Muhammad. Playing skillfully on the reader's feelings, Ramadan was careful not to denounce the play as blasphemous or call for censorship. He asked the city's Office of Cultural Affairs not to stage Voltaire's tragedy: "You may call that 'censorship,' I see it as sensitivity." He also let it be understood that if the production were allowed to go forward it could result in a breach of public order and perhaps even a dangerous "*dérapage*" (loss of control) with devastating "emotional consequences." "It will be another brick in the wall of hate and rejection behind which Muslims feel they've been enclosed." Such reasoning left little room for tolerance or open criticism of religious ideas. This self-appointed leader of the Muslim community took it upon himself to establish the limits of tolerance, asserting that tolerance must "stop at the edge of the intimate and sacred spaces" that define the Muslim identity.[56] But since no one knows exactly what the contours are of these "intimate and sacred spaces," one can only conclude that tolerance is unacceptable to a Muslim like Tariq Ramadan.

Ultimately, Ramadan's convoluted quasi-theological argument carried the day. Voltaire's tragedy was not performed on stage in Geneva, the city's administrative council having decided not to grant the promised subsidy. Disillusioned by the whole situation, the director, Loichemol, left Switzerland, complaining that "One cannot celebrate Voltaire by banning one of his plays; it's perfectly contradictory!" After moving to the village of Saint-Genis-Pouilly, in eastern France, the director managed to overcome yet more hurdles and, with the support of the mayor and the local prefect, organized a small public reading of Voltaire's play. No public disorder seems to have occurred, and Voltaire's *Muhammad* was finally heard in December 2005—twelve years after the Geneva fiasco.[57] After several more years of exile, Loichemol was named managing director of the Comédie de Genève in 2011, but he has prudently avoided staging any of Voltaire's plays, preferring instead the work of G. E. Lessing, Denis Guénoun, Olivier Py, and Hanokh Levin.

Other artists, painters, sculptors, photographers, and directors have also carefully avoided provoking the "Islamic sensibilities" of their countrymen, as though they felt themselves to be under the same threat as Salman Rushdie. No sculptor, for example, has taken the risk of building something analogous to *Piss Christ* but directed at Muhammad. Examples of self-censorship abound. In 2005, London's Tate Gallery refused to exhibit a sculpture by John Latham entitled *God Is Great*, comprising a large plate of glass from which the Bible, Qur'an, and Talmud protruded, for fear of shocking certain Muslim visitors. In 2006, the Berlin opera canceled a performance of Mozart's *Idomeneo* because one of the stage sets (admittedly of questionable taste) displayed the decapitated heads of Jesus, Buddha, and Muhammad. In 2007, the head curator at The Hague's Gemeentemuseum decided to interrupt a photography exhibition by the Iranian artist Sorreh Hera that showed homosexuals wearing Muhammad masks to avoid offending "certain people" who might find the photographs hurtful. The same year, London's Royal Court

Theatre canceled a new production of Aristophanes's *Lysistrata* that was to be set in a Muslim "heaven." And the list goes on. It would seem that Ayatollah Khomeini's fatwa had been extended to all artists who might dare impugn the image of the Prophet or his holy book.[58]

And then came the Muhammad cartoons. This controversy started on September 30, 2005, when the well-established Danish newspaper *Jyllands-Posten* published twelve caricatures of Muhammad, the most famous of which showed the Prophet wearing a turban in which is nestled a bomb with a lighted fuse. Flemming Rose, the paper's culture editor, had asked permission from his director to solicit caricatures from a syndicate of newspaper illustrators who were prompted to draw "Muhammad as you see him."[59] This invitation may seem surprising coming from a large-circulation, conservative newspaper that has more in common with *Le Figaro* or the *Wall Street Journal* than with a satirical publication like *Le Canard Enchaîné*, *Charlie Hebdo*, or the *Onion*. The editors thought it important to fight against what they considered to be the "growing political correctness that treated Muslims with exaggerated respect" and prevented so many Danish artists from depicting Muhammad as they wished.[60] The decision to publish the caricatures was motivated in particular by the impasse encountered by the author of a children's book entitled *The Qur'an and the Life of the Prophet Muhammad*, for which no illustrator could be found. Likely candidates for the job all declined, fearing they might offend readers strongly opposed to any figurative representation of Muhammad.

In reaction, the editors of *Jyllands-Posten* sought deliberately to provoke their readers by subjecting them to "democratic electroshock therapy"[61] designed to jolt them out of their torpor by means of a few clever cartoons—a modern version, if you like, of Voltaire's call to crush religious fanaticism (*Écrasez l'infâme*).

Flemming Rose also justified publishing the caricatures as a radical defense of free speech. In a democratic society, he wrote, "everybody must be willing to put up with sarcasm, mockery, and ridicule."[62] The Danish prime minister, Anders Fogh Rasmussen, expressed a similar sentiment in his reply to a delegation of eleven ambassadors representing Arab and Muslim countries who demanded an official apology. "The Danish society," he told them, "is based on respect for . . . freedom of expression, on religious tolerance and on equal standards for all religions. The freedom of expression is the very foundation of the Danish democracy . . . and the Danish government has no means of influencing the press."[63] Relations between the Danish government and these Arab-Muslim countries soured when Saudi Arabia imposed an embargo on Danish imports. Out of solidarity with their Danish counterpart, many European media outlets, including *Charlie Hebdo*, *France Soir*, and *Le Monde*, reprinted the caricatures from *Jyllands-Posten*. The dissemination of these caricatures over the internet and on cable television unleashed a storm of violence. Danish embassies in Tehran, Damascus, Beirut, and Islamabad were attacked.[64] Hundreds of thousands of protesters demonstrated against the cartoons in Pakistan, India, Egypt, Syria, Lebanon, the Palestinian territories, and Nigeria. More than 250 people died in clashes with the police. Death threats were made against Kurt Westergaard, the artist who drew Muhammad with the turban bomb, leading to the arrest of two Tunisians and a Dane of Moroccan origin. And all this because a few artists had dared to make fun of the Prophet.[65]

The attack against the Parisian headquarters of the satirical weekly *Charlie Hebdo* (January 7, 2015) and the assassination of eight artists and editors showed yet again the violence of an extremist Islam promoted by al-Qaeda in the Arabian Peninsula. For the French perpetrators of the attack, the Kouachi brothers, *Charlie Hebdo* had committed two crimes. It had reprinted the *Jyllands-Posten* caricatures, including the infamous one of Muhammad with the turban bomb, and it had continued to print numerous other caricatures of the Prophet, some of which could be regarded as obscene. Since Western courts tolerated "blasphemers," it was up to the jihadists to settle the matter once and for all by physically eliminating the offenders. But the much-anticipated clash of civilizations did not come to pass. *Charlie Hebdo* still exists, and its circulation continues to increase (the first issue after the attack sold more than eight million copies, and three million copies of the controversial cartoons could be seen on Google as of March 2015). The large public demonstrations of support that took place on January 10 and 11, 2015, in Paris and throughout France showed that freedom of speech was not an empty platitude, even if most of the demonstrators were hardly regular readers of *Charlie Hebdo*. It was surely no coincidence that the route of the massive demonstration in Paris went from place de la République to place de la Nation via boulevard Voltaire.

The publication of the cartoons that mocked Islam and Muhammad raised important legal questions. As noted by Basile Ader, a legal expert on freedom of the press, "Cabu, Wolinski, and other [artists from *Charlie Hebdo*] were the first to push the limits of good taste with drawings that had previously been considered too vulgar to publish. They were the founding fathers of a new genre of humor and libertarian expression, and they inspired all those who came after, from Coluche [a comedian] to Canal+ [a popular TV channel]."[66] The works of these satirists took full advantage of a new right to shock and disrespect—a right that was reaffirmed in a key court case of March 2007 concerning *Charlie Hebdo*'s anti-Muslim caricatures. Several organizations for the defense of Islam initiated a lawsuit against the satirical journal for "public offense against persons on account of their religious identity."[67] The Tribunal de Grande Instance de Paris (TGI) dismissed the case on March 22, 2007, arguing that the controversial drawings did not seek "to directly and gratuitously offend *all Muslims*" but instead were intended to mock a small group of fanatics who promoted a radical, violent brand of Islam. The court emphasized that "in France, a secular and pluralist country, the respect of all beliefs cannot be separated from the freedom to criticize all existing religions and to freely represent subjects or objects of religious veneration," adding that "*blasphemy* that is offensive to a divinity or religion" is not prohibited in France, "unlike *insults* which constitute a personal, direct attack against a person or *group of persons* on account of their religious affiliation."[68] In other words, the right to be offensive and blasphemous is not without limits; it all depends on the context.[69] As explained by the court, considered in isolation the cartoon representing Muhammad wearing the turban bomb might appear outrageously shocking to Muslims. Replaced in its context—a special issue of *Charlie Hebdo* dedicated to religious fanaticism—the cartoon did not constitute an injurious offense punishable by law; it was simply drawn to illustrate "a *debate of ideas* on the excesses of certain followers of radical Islam."[70]

As could be expected, the publication of the first issue of *Charlie Hebdo* after the January attacks—a caricature of Muhammad carrying a sign that read "Je suis Charlie" (I am Charlie)—provoked a violent reaction: skirmishes during demonstrations in Niger left five people dead and forty-five injured; bombs exploded at the French cultural center in Gaza; and thousands of protesters denounced the "insult to the Prophet" in Amman, Algiers, Bamako, Dakar, Khartoum, and four cities across Pakistan. These protests were accompanied by angry slogans such as "We are Kouachi!" and the public burning of effigies of the artists of the satirical journal. On February 14, 2015, a new attack occurred in Denmark at a cultural center during a lecture on free speech. The French ambassador and Lars Vilks, one of the illustrators of the Muhammad caricatures for *Jyllands-Posten*, were both present. The attack, which killed one person and wounded three others, was generally considered to be a smaller, copycat version of the Paris violence.[71]

Contrary to a widespread belief, it is only recently that the portrayal of Muhammad has been considered blasphemous. For over five hundred years Persian and Ottoman miniatures regularly represented the Prophet's face. The prohibition on representing Muhammad was introduced only at the end of the eighteenth century by devout Wahhabi Islamists.[72]

In diplomatic circles around the world, the Danish drawings scandal triggered a series of initiatives to punish countries that "insulted" Islam. These efforts were spearheaded by the Organization for Islamic Cooperation (OCI), a fifty-seven-member bloc of Muslim-majority nations. To ease tensions and prevent the repetition of similar incidents, the OCI in 2005 attempted to introduce into international law the new and highly questionable notion of "defamation of religion." The idea was to sanction countries that permitted acts of "defamation" against Islam, as though they were equivalent to racist insults or acts of discrimination in violation of human rights. For most Western countries, the introduction of such a notion into international law was unacceptable because it threatened the fundamental rights enshrined in the Universal Declaration of Human Rights of December 10, 1948—namely freedom of expression, freedom of religion, and freedom of conscience. To punish the "defamation" of a religion—in this case Islam—was nothing but a veiled attempt to revive the old notion of "blasphemy." Moreover, it would be a double blow to liberty because it would limit free speech (openly criticizing a religion would become much more difficult), and it would endanger the existence of minority religions whose beliefs could be considered "defamatory."[73]

After several inconclusive votes in the UN General Assembly, the OCI decided in 2011 to moderate its demand. The consensual solution adopted by the Council on Human Rights and the UN General Assembly was to recognize that religions were not "persons" and that international law already offered ways to protect individuals against racial hatred, insults, and discrimination. The UN member states were exhorted to take effective measures to punish "any advocacy of religious hatred that constitutes incitement to discrimination, hostility or violence."[74]

Leaving aside the specter of "religious defamation," which is no longer an issue, what remains is the fact that the threats, fatwas, and other Islamist interventions against the "crime" of blasphemy have left their mark. The most perceptible and saddening consequence of these interventions is the self-censorship of Western media. Neither the *New York Times* nor the *Boston Globe* dared reprint the drawings from *Jyllands-Posten*; worse yet, the publishers of the most scholarly treatment of the Muhammad caricatures controversy proved "too cowardly"—in the words of Salman Rushdie—to include the drawings in the work devoted to them.[75] The twelve Danish drawings that were supposed to illustrate Jytte Klausen's book *The Cartoons That Shook the World*, as well as earlier images such as Gustave Doré's famous print representing the torment of Muhammad in Dante's *Inferno*, were expurgated by the director of Yale University Press. The reason given was that reprinting the caricatures presented "a serious risk of incitement to violence."[76]

In the aftermath of the *Charlie Hebdo* controversy, major newspapers such as the *New York Times* and the *Washington Post* in the United States; the *Times*, *Guardian*, and *Financial Times* in England; and *Jyllands-Posten* in Denmark all refused to publish the caricatures—even as a gesture of solidarity with their colleagues or as a way to better inform their readers. The excuses put forward sometimes turned on "decency" or on a certain notion of civility and sometimes on the necessity to ensure the safety of their employees. The caricatures were most often reproduced in online media such as the *Daily Beast*, *Slate*, *Buzzfeed*, and the *Huffington Post*—probably because, without any physically identifiable headquarters, such outlets were less exposed to the risk of terrorist attack. These strategies of evasion, although sometimes legitimate as in the case of *Jyllands-Posten*, which had received numerous threats, appeared less so when publishers made hypocritical assertions about decency or respect for readers. Asked about his refusal to reprint a selection of the caricatures from the French satirical paper, one of the editors at the *New York Times* explained that he wanted to protect "the Muslim families of Brooklyn." But the same newspaper had not shown the same concern for decency toward the Christian families of Brooklyn when, some years earlier, it had printed a reproduction of Chris Ofili's *Holy Virgin Mary*. In similar fashion, the Associated Press refused to publish any of the caricatures, claiming that its policy was to never publish "deliberately provocative" images; in the past, however, the AP had both printed and sold reproductions of Serrano's *Piss Christ*. These acts of self-censorship thus reflected a decided bias in favor of Muslim readers.[77]

"To print or not to print? Publish or perish?"[78] These are the dilemmas of our time and of every Western democracy. Shall we soon censor our literature classes and cut out the verses of the *Divine Comedy* that are found to be too critical of Islam? Shall we soon have to give up reading Voltaire's *Mahomet* and his other antireligious texts? Shall we, following the same logic, censor Rabelais, expurgate La Fontaine, forget Renan's *Vie de*

Jésus and Molière's *Tartuffe*, shelve Thomas Jefferson's *The Life and Morals of Jesus of Nazareth*, and ban countless other works that dare to represent as "all too human" the lives of Jesus, Muhammad, Buddha, and other great religious figures? There is legitimate cause for concern. The self-imposed censorship by publishers, authors, and film and stage directors has had lasting effects. At the start of the 1970s it seemed as though blasphemy had become an anachronism in a time of rising secularization of Western societies. This is clearly not the case today. As certain non-Western countries have attempted to reactivate the criminalization of blasphemy in France, England, and at the UN General Assembly, the subject has once again become a topic of heated debate. Terrorist organizations such as al-Qaeda and ISIS have chosen to pursue their own brand of justice by recruiting jihadists ready to perpetrate the most horrific massacres to eliminate "blasphemers." The Rushdie affair, the Danish cartoons, and *Charlie Hebdo* have given rise to a new phenomenon: the globalization of religious fanaticism and the exportation, beyond sovereign borders, of sentences and punishments decreed in the name of divine justice, that of radical Islam. Only Rushdie managed to escape the curse of Khomeini's fatwa. He had become a free man again long before the controversies provoked by the Muhammad caricatures. His example shows that a single courageous person can withstand the morality police and survive the threats of fanatics.

7

MULTICULTURAL TOLERANCE

ulticultural tolerance privileges the group over the individual and values the preservation of traditions and rituals considered essential for the identity of the group. This identity is presumed to protect the group in a hostile environment and to guide its destiny.[1] The defense of the group may require certain guarantees, exemptions, or accommodations in order to ensure the survival of strongly held religious, linguistic, or cultural values. To what extent and according to which criteria should certain religious groups be exempted from the application of facially neutral, general laws?

Labor laws forbidding work on Sunday are an obvious example. This type of prohibition is generally well accepted because it applies equally to all. But such laws may conflict with ethnoreligious minorities whose religion imposes another day of rest. This is the case notably for Jews and Seventh-Day Adventists, for whom Saturday is the day of rest. Other laws forbid businesses from opening on Christmas or Easter out of respect for the dominant religion, and the same is true for public schools: they close for important Christian holidays but remain open over Jewish and Muslim holidays. These laws are therefore not completely neutral; they reflect the preferences of a majority of citizens and the continuation of old Christian traditions. Should the laws be changed to accommodate the preferences of a particular minority?

The accommodation or its refusal—beyond questions of fairness and social justice—typically reflects the power relationships between dominant and dominated groups. A religious minority that considers itself discriminated against by certain "unjust" laws will have to demonstrate that the demand for an exemption is both just and reasonable.[2] But what is a reasonable exemption? What degree of deviation from the ethical, political, and social norms of the dominant society is acceptable? Clearly, physical violence such as female genital mutilation or the stoning of an adulterous spouse is unacceptable in liberal democracies. But what about other "deviant" practices, such as polygamy? The question arose in the United States at the end of the nineteenth century, at a time when most residents of the Utah Territory wished to join the Union in order to benefit fully from the advantages of American citizenship.

TOLERATING THE INTOLERABLE? THE CASE OF MORMON POLYGAMY

Mormon "plural marriage," or polygamy, as practiced in the early 1830s by Joseph Smith, the founder of the Church of Jesus Christ of Latter-Day Saints, only became legitimate in 1852. The "Prophet," as Joseph Smith became known to his followers, justified the practice with a biblical explanation: the patriarchs of the Old Testament had many spouses, and it was time to revive this ancient tradition in order to create a "primitive Church." Contrary to a widely held belief at the time, plural marriage was not about libertinage or harems. The new wives of the prophet

Joseph Smith lived in their own homes or with their parents, that is, outside the marital home, and DNA analysis of their male descendants has proved that their children were not fathered by Smith. Most Mormon husbands had no more than two or three wives, who bore many children and shared the husband's attentions. The practice of plural marriage became gradually more common among Mormons in the second half of the nineteenth century—43.6 percent had formed polygamous families by 1860. Although polygamy conformed to official church doctrine, it nevertheless declined in the 1880s after the prohibition of polygamy by the U.S. Congress and its official abandonment by the Church of Jesus Christ of Latter-Day Saints. In 1900, only 7 percent of Mormons had founded polygamous households.[3]

Could federal authorities tolerate a practice that so openly violated the social norms of the time? What were the limits to the "free exercise of religion," in theory protected by the First Amendment of the U.S. Constitution? To challenge the constitutionality of the federal law prohibiting plural marriage, the Mormons encouraged one of their own, the bigamist George Reynolds, to defend his "plural" marriage in federal courts. The case was appealed to the Supreme Court, which decided against Reynolds in *Reynolds v. U.S.* (1878). This decision offered a curious mix of legal precedents and a history of Western civilization. Polygamy, according to Justice Waite's majority opinion, was "an offense against society" that could not be tolerated. In the common-law tradition, polygamy was punishable in the civil courts during the reign of James I, and the penalty was death in England, Wales, and all the colonies. From a political point of view, according to Waite, polygamy was a form of "despotism" based on a "patriarchal principle." Monogamy, on the other hand, favored the development of republican ideas because it required the mutual consent of the spouses, treated as equals at the time of their marriage. Polygamy belonged to the world of Oriental despotism; it was "almost exclusively a feature of the life of Asiatic and of African people" and had "always been odious among the northern and western nations of Europe."[4] The West had always been monogamous, even before the introduction of Christianity, according to the German historian Francis Lieber, cited at length by Justice Waite.[5] Lieber's argument was based on his reading of the Roman historian Tacitus, who had lavishly praised the virtues of monogamy as practiced by the ancient Saxons.[6]

From a legal perspective, polygamy was also unacceptable because it disturbed the rule of law. Accepting polygamy would render "the doctrines of religious belief superior to the law of the land, and in effect . . . permit every citizen to become a law unto himself," thus destroying the very possibility of a social compact.[7] In a context where polygamy was denounced as barbaric, there was no room for compromise: the practice had to be eradicated in the interests of civilization.

The only author to my knowledge who defended polygamy in the name of freedom of conscience is John Stuart Mill, who held that polygamy, as retrograde as it might be, was a voluntary arrangement freely consented to by the parties to a plural marriage. It was therefore not advisable to destroy through punitive means reminiscent of medieval crusades a practice widely accepted by the Mormons. There was no need for a "civilizade," and, concluded Mill, "I am not aware that a community has a right to force another to be civilized."[8]

Torn between their belief in the truth of the prophet Smith's revelations and the fact that the practice was now prohibited by law, Mormons had few options. They could practice polygamy either in secret or in exile, in Mexico for example, as was the case of the polygamous ancestors of Mitt Romney, the unsuccessful 2012 Republican presidential candidate. At the end of the nineteenth century, thousands of Mormon polygamists were arrested and sentenced to prison terms of a year or more. Faced with the massive disobedience of Mormons, federal authorities multiplied sanctions against the rebels by taking away their right to vote, serve on a jury, or run for office. But it was not until Congress began to seize Mormon property that the leader of the church at the time, Wilford Woodruff, decided in 1890 to put an end to the doctrine of plural marriage by refusing to allow such marriages to take place. The doctrine was still mentioned in the sacred texts of the Mormon Church, but the practice was gradually abandoned, thus opening a path to statehood for the rebel territory of Utah in 1896.[9] From then on, the citizens of the new federal state could elect their own representatives. Mormonism survived, after having abandoned its most controversial theological principle. It no longer was the patriarchal countersociety imagined by Joseph Smith; it had become a "normal" religion coexisting with other legitimate religions.

THE AMISH AND
MANDATORY SCHOOLING

The most famous example of preferential treatment given to a religious group concerns the Old Order Amish. The U.S. Supreme Court granted the Old Order the highly unusual right to limit mandatory schooling to the age of fourteen, on grounds that the full-time contribution of young people to farm labor was essential for the survival of the group. Descended from Anabaptists who rallied around the preacher Jakob Amman, the Amish suffered frequent persecution in Switzerland, Alsace, and Holland in the seventeenth and eighteenth centuries. They arrived in the United States in two successive waves in the eighteenth and twentieth centuries. Although numbering only about five thousand at the beginning of the twentieth century, there are today nearly a quarter million Amish in the United States thanks to their economic success and high birth rate.

For religious reasons the Amish reject modern industrial society, including the use of cars and machinery. Their farming practices require substantial manual labor, and the laborers, recruited exclusively from within their own community, include numerous teenagers. Without the latter's participation, it is unlikely that the deliberately archaic Amish way of life could survive amid the constraints of contemporary American industrial and postindustrial society. The Amish gave three reasons for their objection to high-school education. They first argued that their particular way of life was entirely dictated by religious considerations because of their "fundamental belief that salvation requires life in a church community separate from the world and worldly influence." They then claimed that school attendance limited to the eighth grade was sufficient for the apprenticeships and employment opportunities that awaited the young members of their faith. Finally, they pointed out that the Old Order's political and civic involvement was exemplary despite the group's limited level of formal education.

The Supreme Court accepted all three arguments. In particular it agreed with the notion that longer studies could lead to skepticism and an abandonment of the religious values promoted by the Old Order. The only ambition of the Amish was to live "the simple life of the early Christian era." Reading, writing, and arithmetic were enough for that purpose. Furthermore, prolonging the school experience in a hostile or unsympathetic environment could only result "in great psychological harm to Amish children."[10]

Unlike the Mormons, who were stigmatized for their religious deviance and for the ten-year standoff that had pitted their local militias against federal troops, the Amish community demonstrated that "its members [were] productive and very law-abiding members of society."[11] To justify its decision to exempt the Amish from respecting Wisconsin's requirement of school attendance until age sixteen, the Supreme Court delivered an extraordinary history lesson:

> We must not forget that, in the Middle Ages, important values of the civilization of the Western World were preserved by members of religious orders who isolated themselves from all worldly influences against great obstacles. There can be no assumption that today's majority is "right," and the Amish and others like them are "wrong." A way of life that is odd or even erratic but interferes with no rights or interests of others is not to be condemned because it is different.[12]

Mormon polygamy had been rejected by the Supreme Court because it did not respect the norms of Western civilization. The Amish way of life was more acceptable because it did not challenge the justices' concept of Western civilization. Yet the comparison of the Amish way of life to that of a medieval monastic community, a comparison defended by Chief Justice Burger, is questionable for several reasons. If the Amish are a community of monks, they are uneducated monks more adept at farming than at engaging in intellectual pursuits. It is therefore a stretch to claim that they, like the learned monks of the Middle Ages, are preserving "important values of the civilization of the Western World." As for embodying the democratic spirit, there is less evidence for this than suggested by the Supreme Court. The

Amish refuse to do jury duty, fight in the American armed forces, pay Social Security taxes, wear helmets on construction sites, or vaccinate their children. They also avoid taking legal action to punish cases of rape and incest, preferring instead to impose sanctions prescribed by their church. Rather than model patriots respectful of the laws of the republic, the Amish are instead reluctant citizens who only respect the law because they have been able to exert pressure on public authorities to obtain special exemptions to preserve their way of life.[13]

THE SIKH TURBANS

In pluralist and multicultural societies, the clothing choices of new immigrants can provoke tensions, especially if their attire is invested with a religious significance that seems to challenge existing social norms and customs. A classic example of this is the refusal of British Sikh motorcycle riders to wear a helmet, as required by law since 1972. In addition, Sikh construction workers also refused to wear safety helmets, despite the existence of new regulations requiring helmets at construction sites. In refusing to remove their turbans, British Sikhs asked for an exemption based on religious grounds. They argued that turbans, although affording less protection than helmets in case of accident, offered enough padding to justify an exemption and that, should they be injured at work or on the road, they would take full responsibility for the consequences. All that mattered to them was retaining the right to wear a head covering imposed by a sacred rule of Sikhism, namely never to cut their hair. British Sikhs also had another, patriotic argument at their disposal to justify their demand for an exemption: they reminded their fellow citizens that thousands of them had served in the British army during both world wars without ever having been required to wear military helmets. An exemption that had been valid at a time of war should remain valid in peacetime.

In Canada, the prestigious Royal Canadian Mounted Police (often considered a living symbol of Canadian nationalism), in keeping with federal law, refused to hire Sikhs wearing turbans. The distinctive wide-brimmed hat of the Mounties was the only authorized head covering, and it allowed an officer of the Mounted Police to be recognized at a distance. In 1990, however, the federal government changed the rule, thus making it possible for a Sikh both to abide by his religious principles and serve his nation by becoming a member of its national police. He can now express his patriotism in his own way, by keeping his traditional head covering.[14]

In the United States, the question of the Sikh turban was evoked in a Supreme Court decision concerning military dress code. Was it proper to ban discreet religious articles such as the yarmulke or less discreet items such as the turban of Sikh recruits or the dreadlocks of Rastafarians? The court's decision was uncompromising: there would be no exemption to the dress code, not even for an unobtrusive yarmulke. To accomplish its mission, the military requires uniformity of appearance, "instinctive obedience, unity, commitment and *esprit de corps.*" Any other decision would produce a dangerous rivalry between ethnic groups favoring this or that head covering, with unacceptable results. However, according to Justice Brennan's dissent, the majority of the court had been too easily impressed by the government's argument, which "dangle[d] before the Court a classic parade of horribles, the specter of a brightly colored, 'rag-tag' band of soldiers."[15]

Other societies with a colonial legacy, such as the United Kingdom, were more tolerant. They accepted Sikh soldiers in their ranks and allowed them to grow beards and long hair.[16] In France, regiments of Spahis wore the *guennour*, a headpiece resembling a turban, and recruits in the Foreign Legion have always been allowed to grow a beard, a tradition that goes back to 1844, when King Louis-Philippe tolerated this practice in recognition of the valorous service of a regiment led by the Duc d'Aumale.

In 2003, members of France's Stasi commission, which had been asked to make recommendations about the presence of religious symbols in public schools, skillfully ignored the question of the Sikh turban. French Sikhs, less numerous than their British counterparts, lacked influence, and their sense of patriotism had never been tested in French wars. As a result no exemption was ever accorded to the French Sikhs, whether in schools, on construction sites, in the army, or on a motorcycle.[17]

JEHOVAH'S WITNESSES AND BLOOD TRANSFUSIONS

Certain religions prohibit the transfusion of blood for theological reasons, maintaining that it violates a divine interdiction. For Jehovah's Witnesses, for example, blood is sacred and must not be "eaten," according to their own reading of the Old Testament.[18]

In the United States, most states have passed laws obliging parents to provide basic health care to their children despite possible religious objections. Regarding the prohibition of blood transfusion, state courts have not hesitated to intervene to ensure that health-care providers are able to carry out certain procedures, sometimes against the express wishes of the parents. Generally the reason given is the survival of the child, but it can also be "to prevent substantial harm or suffering."[19] In less urgent medical cases, such as a parent's refusal to allow mandatory vaccination, courts have been known to grant exemptions provided that the parents "hold genuine and sincere religious beliefs." A simple "medical or purely moral" opinion is not sufficient to justify a derogation.[20]

In Canada, the medical beliefs of Jehovah's Witnesses cause the same problems as in the United States. Blood transfusions are prohibited for religious reasons, and parents of minors pressure hospitals to prevent medical personnel, and especially emergency-room workers, from giving transfusions. A battle of conflicting rights is inevitable: on the one hand the right to life of the young child, on the other the parents' right to act according to their religious beliefs. Such rights cannot be reconciled when a patient is in urgent need of a blood transfusion. In response to these conflicting positions, the Canadian Supreme Court has decided in favor of the medical profession and against the will of the parents. In a 1995 decision, the justices stated that a parent's freedom of religion "does not authorize him or her to impose religious practices on a child that would threaten that child's safety, health, or life."[21] In this case, as Jocelyn Maclure and Charles Taylor point out, "respect for the parents' rights was obviously too great an infringement on the right to life of a minor, namely, their child."[22]

In France, the Kouchner law of March 4, 2002, offers a clear distinction between the rights of adults and those of minors. With adults, "no medical procedure and no treatment can be carried out without the free and informed consent of the person."[23] Case law from the Council of State (Conseil d'État), France's highest administrative court, formalized patients' rights in an August 16, 2002, decision concerning the refusal of a blood transfusion by a Jehovah's Witness. The court stated that "the right of the patient to accept or refuse treatment has the character of a fundamental liberty."[24] But in the case of an underage patient, the experienced judgment of the doctor outweighs the opinion of the sick child or the parents. In the latter case, the doctor must consider the consequences of nontreatment and is obliged to provide all vital care.[25] In short, a minor has the right to express a preference, but the child's health takes precedence over the religious objections of parents.[26] An adult's right to refuse treatment is not, however, as absolute as it may seem. According to the French court's decision, a doctor has the right to override a refusal of treatment if there is "an extreme situation that is life-threatening" and on condition that there is no therapeutic alternative. The medical consensus in France is that surgeons and anesthesiologists can "do everything" to avoid a blood transfusion out of respect for the religious convictions of their patient but that "in the case of absolute necessity and as a last resort, they will perform a transfusion." They have no other choice, because in France "the failure to provide assistance to a person in danger" is a punishable offense.[27]

As one might expect, religious traditions have a cost: an American study of 134 Jehovah's Witnesses who refused a blood transfusion reveals a mortality rate 37 percent higher than the rate observed among other patients who received a blood transfusion for the same medical condition.[28] This extreme example about the limits of tolerance raises ethical questions that have been resolved in similar ways in countries as different as France, Canada, and the United States. The child's right to life is protected in France, the United States, and Canada against the explicit wishes of the parents, but an adult may place his life in jeopardy if his religion prohibits all medical treatment. Only French doctors may be required, in rare circumstances, to transfuse an adult patient against his or her explicit wishes.

THE SABBATH: A DAY OF REST?

Since observing Shabbat or Shabbos is a religious obligation for Orthodox Jews, should an Ontario businessman who does not work on Saturday be allowed to open his business on Sunday? Should an exemption be granted to those who, scrupulously respecting the dictates of their faith, assume a heavy financial burden by having their businesses closed two days a week—Saturday and Sunday? In the case of *Edwards Books and Art v. The Queen*, the Canadian Supreme Court refused to grant the requested derogation. The Retail Business Holidays Act of Ontario already granted exemptions to small retail businesses. However, extending exemptions to all businesses, including those with a large number of employees, risked having a deleterious effect on the labor market.[29] The law was on its face secular, egalitarian, and noncompetitive. Its goal was to guarantee a common day of rest for all workers. The exemptions granted to owners of small businesses seemed to be sufficiently accommodating to satisfy the most devout among them. The compromise position endorsed by the court—exemptions, yes, but only for small businesses—was consistent with the Canadian Charter of Rights and Freedoms, which states that essential freedoms such as freedom of conscience and freedom of religion can be restricted "within reasonable limits."[30] For similar reasons, the Canadian Supreme Court refused to grant an exemption to drivers belonging to the Hutterite community of Alberta, who refused to have a photo ID on their driver's license. For a Hutterite, to display one's photograph constitutes an act of idolatry, a clear violation of the Second Commandment—"Thou shalt not make unto thee any graven image." The court's refused to grant an exemption based on a balance of interests—Hutterite interests versus those of the general public. It concluded that "the harm done to freedom of religion was outweighed by the beneficial effects of the norm in question." For the court, the absence of a driver's-license photo was unacceptable because it could facilitate the fraudulent use of an official document.[31]

THE RITUALISTIC USE OF MESCALINE

This last case study on the limits of tolerance involves a small community of Native Americans affiliated with the Native American Church, whose members make ritual use of peyote—a cactus containing mescaline—to attain a state of religious ecstasy. The central issue in the case of *Employment Division v. Smith* is similar to that of the *Wisconsin v. Yoder* case about the Amish, but this time the court adopted the opposite view. Do the interests of a small community of individuals outweigh those of society at large if that community's unlawful actions are motivated by religious convictions? Should the minority group be exempt from obligations imposed on the rest of the population in the name of the free exercise of an unusual religious practice?

The Smith affair concerns two employees of a drug-rehabilitation center who were fired for taking mescaline at work, a serious criminal offense under Oregon law. As a result, the two Native Americans not only lost their jobs but were also denied unemployment benefits. They challenged their employer's decision, arguing that their use of mescaline was purely ceremonial and in conformity with their religious beliefs. They based their claim on the Free Exercise Clause of the First Amendment. The Supreme Court's response was of a practical nature: contrary to an older precedent, the public authority, in this case the State of Oregon, need not prove the existence of a "compelling interest" to justify banning a religious practice that violated a neutral and generally applicable law. Doing otherwise would be complicated, difficult, and completely unwarranted; it would, in fact, "be courting anarchy."[32] The great diversity of American society requires keeping things simple. Justice Scalia argued: "Precisely because 'we are a cosmopolitan nation made up of people of almost every conceivable religious preference,' and precisely because we value and protect that religious divergence, we cannot afford the luxury of deeming *presumptively invalid*, as applied to the religious objector, every regulation of conduct that does not protect an interest of the highest order."[33]

Multiplying exemptions for religious reasons would amount to calling into question most American civic obligations: from compulsory military service to paying taxes, from protecting children's health to prohibiting cruelty toward animals. Granting exemption after exemption "contradicts both constitutional tradition and common sense," affirmed Scalia.

> Laws . . . are made for the government of actions, and while they cannot interfere with mere religious belief and opinions, they may with practices. . . . Can a man excuse his practices to the contrary because of his religious belief? To permit this would be to make the professed doctrines of religious belief superior to the law of the land, and in effect to permit every citizen to become a law unto himself.[34]

For these reasons, and to avoid the risk of disorder that would result from an endless stream of exemptions, the court ruled that the religious use of a hallucinogenic drug was not protected by the Constitution. Democracy comes with this price: it favors the religious practices of the majority to the detriment of the esoteric rituals of smaller, lesser-known sects and churches.

Exemptions are not ruled out from the start, but it is up to law-makers to decide each case.[35]

The latitude given to small religious communities is therefore extremely variable. It is generous whenever the survival of the group is at stake, as we saw in the case of the American Amish, or if the group is considered to be "patriotic" and well integrated, as in the case of the Sikhs in Canada and the United Kingdom. But civil liberties are more constrained for groups whose requests for exemptions, however sincere and grounded in religious con-victions, appear eccentric, difficult to implement, or contrary to dominant mores. The Mormons, after all, survived the abolition of polygamy, Orthodox Jews from the state of Ontario did not go out of business, and the Native Americans of Oregon con-tinue to ingest mescaline because the state legislature later granted them the exemption that the Supreme Court had denied. Hutterites, however, did not get what they wanted: their mobil-ity remains limited, although they still can be driven by others or take public transportation.

THE MIRAGE OF PERFECT FAIRNESS

All the decisions discussed here have been debated and contested by philosophers, lawyers, judges, and public-policy experts. For the most conservative among them, refusing an exemption is jus-tified in the name of a Hobbesian approach to political debate: the only way to put an end to religious conflicts is to impose a supreme arbiter, the sovereign, who alone can decide on the legit-imacy of this or that derogation. No belief, no religious practice can be put forward in opposition to the will of the sovereign on the grounds that it comes from some higher divine authority, natural law, or transcendental truth. Today the sovereign is the

legislator, the only interpreter of the general will, the only authority capable of preventing the anarchy produced by unlimited
religious freedom. The judge must therefore defer to the authority of legislators, especially if they pass reasonable laws that are
neutral and universal on their face.[36]

Seen from a more progressive standpoint, the specter of the
chaos that would be unleashed by a proliferation of exemptions is
greatly exaggerated. After all, no law is truly neutral, and nothing
prevents a judge from weighing the pros and cons of an exception
by examining the intentions motivating the request—is it based
on a sincere religious or philosophical conviction?—and by antic-
ipating its consequences for the society as a whole.

In the delicate search for a satisfying balance between what
is permitted and what is prohibited in the realm of religious freedom, it is best to avoid "the mirage of perfect fairness."[37] A generally applicable law will necessarily run counter to someone's
particular interest, and religious liberty cannot always be systematically defended when it encompasses unacceptable forms of
violence or domination such as the criminalization of blasphemy,
forced marriage, the refusal of medical care, or female genital
mutilation.

Not all forms of religious freedom are defensible, even if they
are unassuming or peaceful, as we saw in the Hutterite example.
Judges and legislators, not being theologians, should abstain from
evaluating the legitimacy of an esoteric belief. At the same time,
both must also be mindful not to adopt the bias of the majority.
Why prohibit the sacramental ingestion of mescaline when the
liturgical consumption of wine has always been permitted for
Catholics and Protestants, even during America's Prohibition
era? This suggests that when it comes to public morality in a pluralist society there is no absolute truth about good exemptions
and bad exemptions. What matters is finding a reasonable

balance between what is suitable for the public good and the needs and expectations of small religious communities.[38]

Let's delve deeper into some of the cases discussed above. Was it reasonable, for example, to prevent Amish children from going on to high school and perhaps higher education? One of the key elements of freedom of conscience and freedom of religion in a democratic society is that the person belonging to a particular faith—church, sect, or system of meditation—always has a right to leave.[39] Being trapped for life within a church, sect, or any religious order is not acceptable. Keeping that in mind, is the limitation on schooling akin to preventing, or at least rendering extraordinarily difficult, the independent decision to leave the Amish world? How is an individual to make his or her way outside the group if he or she is unequipped or too old to take up new studies? Is the apostate doomed to misery? These questions are not idle musings but urgent matters, since 20 percent of Amish will at some point in their lives leave their community.[40] Is the option to leave really being honored if a young person, for lack of an education, does not have the means to make a clear, thoughtful, and autonomous decision about his or her educational and professional future? As Justice Douglas stated in his dissenting opinion, an Amish "may want to be a pianist, or an astronaut, or an oceanographer. To do so he will have to break with the Amish tradition. . . . If a parent keeps his child out of school beyond grade school, then the child will be forever barred from entry into the new and amazing world of diversity that we have today."[41]

These questions raise a still broader issue: Are we not perhaps idealizing the charm of Amish communities? Do we not tend to whitewash the dynamics of domination that, in a rural and patriarchal setting, lead to the oppression of young women whose sole function in society is to help the men? And what about young people of both sexes, deprived of the liberty to choose a path other than the one set out for them by their parents? The Old Order Amish is not tyrannical enough to prevent a member from exercising his or her right to leave, but that right of exit may be exercised too late or in circumstances that are far from ideal.[42]

Finally, is it acceptable to say that the Amish deserve preferential treatment because the survival of their group depends on it? A religious community that had five thousand members in 1900, 130,000 in 2001, and more than 280,000 today is manifestly not in danger of extinction. In any case, using the rationale of "group survival" to justify exceptions to social norms might open the door to justifying forced marriage, polygamy, child labor, and the use of a dangerous drug.

The policies of religious accommodation raise challenging questions about fairness that are often overlooked by those who favor a form of ethno-religious pluralism. A good case in point is the permission granted to Sikh motorcyclists not to wear helmets. Is it fair to refuse the same exemption to a nonreligious motorcycle rider who dreams of traveling across a country as an "easy rider," free of all constraints and without a helmet? The answer for a proponent of multicultural tolerance such as the Canadian philosopher Charles Taylor is that this is indeed unfair and should be corrected by public authorities. What truly matters is an "ideal of authenticity," that is, deeply held personal values, for example, a sense of communion with nature, which may affect a nonreligious rider as much as a deeply religious individual.[43]

The same is true for conscientious objectors who were released from their military obligations for religious reasons. Should this type of exemption only be given to Quakers or Jehovah's Witnesses, whose religions are truly pacifist? What about a pacifist who has no religious affiliation? Should he not benefit from the same exemption? The difficulty for a judge or a legislator is to assess the sincerity and depth of conviction of the individual making such a request.

Finally, it should be kept in mind that even the most valid exemptions have costs and that measuring those costs complicates to no small degree the job of the decider. If we accept that wearing a helmet substantially reduces the risk of death or serious injury in the case of an accident, is that reason enough to require everyone to wear helmets, including those who object on religious grounds? Many will say it depends on the social cost of the objection. A true liberal would maintain that if Sikhs want to take the calculated risk of riding without a helmet and accept full responsibility for that decision, then so be it. But this stance is inadequate in the context of a social democracy where taxpayer money covers most of the medical costs incurred in major road accidents. It then becomes perfectly reasonable for taxpayers to refuse to bear the cost of excessively risky behavior individuals engage in for exclusively religious reasons. In this case the public good—including the solvency of the state—outweighs what some may view as a religious whim. But the exemption for this or that group may be justified if the social cost of enforcing a universal one-size-fits-all rule is itself excessive. That is the argument put forward by Brian Barry in the case of Sikh construction workers who refused to obey Britain's mandatory helmet law. The Sikhs in this job sector number forty thousand skilled workers; barring them from entering construction sites for not respecting this regulation would amount to firing half the Sikh male population. In this particular case, refusing to exempt Sikhs for safety reasons would arguably have a higher social cost than doing away with helmets altogether in this industry, where accidents are in fact relatively rare. Here a rigorous and pragmatic cost-benefit analysis supports bending the obligatory helmet rule.[44] Multicultural tolerance takes on its full meaning when the well-being of a particular group outweighs other less essential considerations. Demands for exemption from the application of general laws cannot be ignored in a liberal democracy. The only risk is that such requests may provoke an escalation of demands from competing groups.[45]

8

OF VEILS AND UNVEILING

If we view tolerance broadly as a way of "living well together" (*bien vivre ensemble*) in a diverse society,[1] how does this *vivre ensemble* work in societies as diverse as France and the United States, where there is no consensus on the extent to which diversity can be tolerated?

In the French case, the "neutrality" of public space is often invoked to justify the prohibition of religious symbols in the public sphere. The principle of neutrality is justified by the notion of *devoir de réserve* (obligation to exercise discretion). A civil servant, teacher, or judge is not permitted to state his or her political or religious beliefs publicly. It is forbidden, for example, for a priest wearing his robes to teach in a public school or even—following a famous decision by France's highest administrative court, the Council of State (Conseil d'État)—to sit for a state teacher's exam. Similarly, a public-school teacher may not wear a hijab. This is the price of public service in France: the secular state (*l'État laïque*) does not allow the conspicuous display of religious convictions.

But why not? Where is the harm so long as a teacher wearing religious garb behaves in a strictly impartial way in his teaching and his relations with students? Clothes do not make the man, and proselytizing can take place in even the most ordinary clothing. But, as the philosophers Jocelyn Maclure and Charles Taylor point out, having a teacher wear a burka or niqab in a primary-school setting, where nonverbal communication is essential for language acquisition and socialization, could be problematic.[2] On the other hand, they defend a teacher's right to wear a hijab, arguing that this will expose young children to the "diversity" they will inevitably encounter in the real world outside of school. But if the hijab does not itself represent a proselytizing gesture, one could be concerned about the signal it sends to a young girl who, out of sheer admiration for her teacher, might think she should dress the same way, independently of her or her parents' religious convictions. Maclure and Taylor also recognize that an "appearance of impartiality" is essential in certain other professions, such as judge, police officer, or prison guard.[3] But their notion of neutrality does not apply to all government employees, and it only applies on an ad hoc basis. In contrast, the French concept of *devoir de réserve* is simpler and easier to implement in that it offers a uniform rule any person in a position of authority can apply. Naturally, this requirement does not prevent civil servants from expressing political opinions or religious convictions outside of the workplace.

But how should the duty to remain neutral apply to schools, which are, after all, a public service? Should students be subject to the same obligations as their teachers? The question was raised in relation to the Islamic headscarf, or hijab, and the responses formulated by French administrative authorities were neither clear nor consistent. Wearing the hijab was first accepted by the Council of State in a 1992 decision, but that decision was overturned twelve years later by lawmakers following guidelines imposed by France's executive branch.

To recapitulate the main facts of the case: three girls were sent home from their middle school in Montfermeil, an eastern suburb of Paris, because they were wearing "Islamic headscarves" in violation of the school dress code. They were brought before a disciplinary committee, which decided to suspend them for violation of internal regulations. A local tribunal rejected their parents' request to overturn the school suspension, but they won on appeal before the Council of State.

In its decision, the Council of State attempted to define more clearly religious rights and their limits.[4] One such limit was to be found in Article 10 of the Declaration of the Rights of Man and the Citizen (1789): "No one shall be disturbed on account of his opinions, including his religious views, provided their manifestation does not disturb the public order established by law." Transposed to the school context, "public order" refers to normal teaching activities, respect for regulations, and conformity to dress codes. Provocative speech in the form of political propaganda or religious proselytizing is not permitted.[5] A second limit to religious rights can be found in the notion of "human dignity." A third limit is based on the key notion of secularism as defined in Article 1 of the French Constitution: "France shall be an indivisible, secular, democratic, and social Republic." In a secular republic based on a strict separation of church and state, civil servants—and these include public-school teachers in France—are expected to remain "neutral" in matters of politics and religion. The same principle of *devoir de réserve* applies to judges, who are not permitted to take a stand on the true meaning of religious symbols, customs, or practices. The judge's position is thus particularly delicate, especially if the observed religious practice comes into conflict with competing rights. For example, should the hijab be banned at school because it can be perceived as contrary to women's rights? Perhaps, but such a ban could be challenged, on religious grounds, by Islamic scholars more qualified than a judge. After all, what do French judges know about Islam? Nothing, or next to nothing. And it is not their job as neutral civil servants to distinguish true from false, the worthy from the unworthy, the *halal* from the *haram*.[6] A judge can, however, prohibit certain religious practices that produce bodily harm, such as female genital mutilation. The red line here is physical violence.[7]

After considering all these factors, the Council of State decided to invalidate the school's headscarf ban, for three reasons. First, they regarded a blanket ban as excessive because it did not take into account local realities that may vary from school to school. Second, students are not state employees bound by some "obligation to discretion" but autonomous subjects "endowed with rights," among them the right "to display their religious beliefs inside school buildings."[8] Third, the hijab, as worn by the pupils of the Montfermeil middle school, did not represent a threat to public order. Only the wearing of a religious symbol that could be considered a provocation or accompanied a proselytizing activity was judged unacceptable by the Council of State.[9]

The principal outcome of the court's decision was to shift the burden from the legal sphere to the schools; teachers and school administrators were now responsible for weighing the meaning and consequences of religious signs and symbols. This task was burdensome in understaffed schools, especially those in troubled suburbs where teachers were already overworked and not properly trained to take on disciplinary questions. But these practical considerations did not enter into the Council of State's decision.

For those opposed to the Council of State's ruling, accepting the headscarf at school was playing directly into the hands of Islamic fundamentalists, who, they argued, were using all available means to subvert the secular neutrality of France's public schools in order to replace it with a dangerous system of "communitarian domination." For these critics, permitting Islamic headscarves was opening a Pandora's box. Soon students would be requesting exemptions from biology class or gym class or might even interrupt their studies "to enter into a forced marriage"—all in the name of some inherent "cultural right."[10] In most cases, according to the same critics, the girls were presumed to be covering their heads against their will, in direct violation of the International Convention on Women's Rights signed by France in 1984. As for the teaching faculty, overwhelmed by multiple demands for exemptions and under pressure from Islamist groups, they would endure an impossible situation, "abandoned by rectors and the education ministry and left to fend for themselves against local pressures."[11]

While certain Salafist groups did indeed encourage acts of insubordination against headscarf bans, the consensus among sociologists who interviewed many hijab-wearing girls is that the decision to cover their heads was in fact their own free choice based on a mix of religious and cultural considerations. Muslim women politically engaged in the defense of laïcité, as well as activists from the feminist movement "Ni putes ni soumises" ("Neither Sluts nor Submissive"), were a minority; so, too, were the women who used the hijab as a symbol of their attempt to "Islamize modernity."[12]

Wearing a hijab can be a sign of submission—the result of pressure exerted by fervent Muslims who claim that young women who do not cover their heads are "bad Muslims" or even "whores" who must be put back on the right path.[13] But wearing a headscarf can also express positive values such as belonging to a cultural community or affirming individual religious beliefs within an agnostic family environment. It is, in reality, perfectly possible to wear an Islamic headscarf and to belong to a feminist organization.[14] The mistake is to assume that "all veiled women are submissive women."[15] How, then, shall the distinction be made between what derives from abusive domination (by older generations, peers, older brothers, or the local imam) and what embodies true freedom of expression with no proselytizing subtext? Who can judge the sincerity of girls with covered heads?

THE OBLIGATION TO REMOVE HEADSCARVES AT SCHOOL

On March 15, 2004, twelve years after the nuanced and accommodating ruling of the Conseil d'État, the French National Assembly completely changed the discussion by passing a coercive law banning from all public primary and middle schools "the wearing of signs or clothing by which students conspicuously manifest a religious affiliation."[16]

To grasp the reasoning of French legislators, let us consider the debate that preceded this decisive vote. It is revelatory of a certain difficulty in France when it comes to thinking about tolerance and reasonable compromises. Rather than continue to resolve headscarf-related issues locally and amicably, on a case-by-case basis, teachers and their representatives preferred, in the finest French Jacobin tradition, to call on the highest state authority—the president of the republic—to "clarify" the principle of laïcité at school. In appointing a "commission to reflect on the application of laïcité in the republic," President Jacques

Chirac expressed his worry about the risk of "communitarian tendencies"; he wished to see concrete measures taken to ease tensions and better define "the obligations implicit in the principle of laïcité."[17] This somewhat puzzling request hid a categorical imperative: draw a red line through the vast field of religious symbolism and tell us once and for all what is permitted and what is forbidden when it comes to expressing one's religious beliefs in schools.

This strong message was addressed to members of the commission chaired by the mediator of the republic, Bernard Stasi. It was followed by hearings and interviews with teachers, principals, union representatives, and local elected officials. All those interviewed expressed their uneasiness about dealing with religious signs; they asked political authorities to provide a clear framework by establishing universal norms applicable throughout France's public schools.[18] The report prepared by the members of the Stasi Commission comprised the draft of a bill stating the limits of tolerance: "Prohibited religious clothing and signs include *conspicuous signs* such as large crosses, headscarves, or kippot. Discreet signs, such as medallions, small crosses, stars of David, or hands of Fatima are not considered to be signs expressing a religious affiliation."[19] To justify these interdictions, the members of the commission invoked the classic argument of a latent threat to public order coming from Islamist groups whose identity politics troubled the "silent majority" of girls whose parents or grandparents were North African immigrants.[20]

The Stasi report had two major weaknesses. First, it refused to grant middle-school students the same freedom of expression and dress code that it conferred on university students. It was necessary, according to the terms of the report, to protect young teenagers from the "savagery of the world" by transforming school into a haven of peace and perfect neutrality and by forbidding any visible expression of political or religious opinions. Female university students, on the other hand, since they were legally adults, had the right to attend a "university open to the world"; these young women, therefore, had the possibility of expressing their religious or political sensibilities as they saw fit. Headscarves were permitted as long as they did not run afoul of any internal university regulations. For younger students the central government was imposing a simple and universal norm; for older ones, university authorities were free to draw up the rules on an ad hoc basis. Less sure of their rights than university professors, middle- and high-school teachers preferred to have political authorities step in to settle disciplinary conflicts on their behalf.

The other limitation of the Stasi report had to do with a lack of analytic rigor. The report's conclusions were based on a superficial investigation and hearings that were conducted too quickly to make the case convincingly that a "majority" of veiled girls had been subjected to inappropriate pressure to wear headscarves. Jean Baubérot, the only member of the Stasi Commission who refused to approve the proposal to ban the *voile*, emphasized the amateurism of the whole enterprise: a report prepared at the last minute, only one week after wrapping up hearings; a lack of scientific objectivity; and, especially, a timid consensus based on a vague idea of laïcité that did not effectively challenge the prejudices of school authorities.[21] The commission avoided making waves by simply delivering the decision that was expected of it: the ban of "conspicuous" religious signs. The law adopted on March 15, 2004, borrowed the same language used in the Stasi report, insisting on the "conspicuously" visible character of the suspect items of clothing.

To hide the discriminatory character of a law that, in fact, specifically targeted the Islamic *voile*, French lawmakers followed the recommendation of the Stasi report by also forbidding the kippah and crosses of exaggerated size.[22] This in turn led the minister of education to denounce, for good measure, the appearance, as surprising as it was improbable, of "large Assyro-Chaldean crosses" worn by middle schoolers.[23]

With the law of 2004, French secularists had won the fight, but were they right? It is doubtful. Banning the veil gave an outsized role to a paternalistic state desirous of being the sole judge of the true meaning of religious symbols. The girl "emancipated" by the 2004 law could no longer exhibit her freedom of conscience, nor could she physically manifest, through a means more cultural than religious, a critical attitude toward contemporary forms of sexualization of the female body. The Jacobin logic of educators—Thou shalt not wear religious symbols in school!—ran counter to the more inclusive logic of accommodationists, for whom wearing an Islamic headscarf was akin to "allowing the private sphere into public space."[24] A genuine emancipation of women cannot be brought about by force or by ultimately excluding them from school in the name of an uncompromising secularism. Expulsion is none other than an educational death sentence. The best way to prevent that outcome and its corollary, namely a community that turns inward upon itself, is to allow a girl to gain independence without forcing her to repudiate Islam.[25] In this perspective, republican tolerance would privilege "educating for independence." Teachers are in no position to judge the beliefs of their pupils; instead, they are expected to educate their students in such a way as to encourage them to think critically and, if necessary, resist "strategies of domination" by their family and acquaintances.[26]

Was this ideal of republicanism—tolerant while remaining critical of systems of domination—even possible in early-twenty-first-century France? It seems highly doubtful given

166 of 292 OF VEILS AND UNVEILING

the political climate at the time. Beginning with the first "affair of the scarf" at a middle school in Creil in 1989, the media went into a frenzy about headscarf conspiracies, the rise of alternative Qur'anic schools, forced conversions to Islam, and the Islamization of France. Noted intellectuals denounced the peril of radical Islam in categorical terms and described French school-teachers as the last rampart of a besieged republic.[27] "Teachers, don't surrender!" was the title of an open letter signed by writers and university professors that appeared in the popular magazine *Le Nouvel Observateur* on November 2, 1989. The letter's first sentence set the pessimistic tone of this call to action: "Time will tell if this bicentenary year [of the French Revolution] will have been the 'Munich' of the republican school." The signers worried about the damage that could result from even the most well-meaning concessions in school curricula, thereby opening the door to the censoring of Rushdie, Spinoza, Voltaire, Baudelaire, Rimbaud, and other denouncers of "infamy" in order to satisfy the demands of devout believers.[28] The Rushdie affair fueled widespread anxiety, which was then further inflamed by the terrorist attacks of September 11, 2001. In this particularly heated context certain teachers even thought it helpful to launch a campaign to liberate the "lost territories of the Republic."[29]

In a country with such a robust Jacobin tradition, it is not easy to foster local solutions and to manage on a day-to-day basis the conflicts that can arise from the violation of dress codes. The kind of tolerance advocated by the Council of State, what sociologists call a "laïcité of recognition"—a form of laïcité that is open and welcomes diverse religions—was too subtle and too difficult to implement at a time when French political elites felt threatened by the recent electoral successes of the xenophobic National Front party.[30] The 2004 law banning headscarves in public schools had the advantage of being simple. It lifted the burden from school teachers and did so in the name of republican values and public order. But it did not facilitate the development of an ethic of personal responsibility.

TOLERANCE FOR THE HIJAB AND THE KIPPAH IN THE UNITED STATES

In the United States one cannot find an exact counterpart to the French example because neither the Supreme Court nor legislators have faced this type of situation. The subject has been debated on a local level, notably in 2004, in the case of a young convert to Islam, Nashala Hearn, who chose to wear a hijab to her public school, the Benjamin Franklin Science Academy in Muskogee, Oklahoma, in violation of the dress code imposed by the school district in this small city. It prohibited wearing "hats, caps, bandannas, plastic caps and hoods on jackets" in school buildings. The reason given was that these types of headwear were often worn by gang members as identity markers among themselves and therefore risked troubling public order and the safety of students. When Nashala Hearn refused to remove her headscarf despite repeated orders to do so from school authorities, she was suspended from school for eight days. Her parents, aided by a Christian organization for the defense of civil rights, the Rutherford Institute, filed a lawsuit that was heard in federal court. The parents demanded the immediate reinstatement of their daughter, citing the fundamental freedoms protected by the First Amendment of the U.S. Constitution. They also requested financial compensation for emotional distress.[31]

The civil rights office of the U.S. Department of Justice also decided to file a brief to defend the rights of this student, who considered herself to be the victim of religious discrimination. The DOJ observed that wearing an Islamic head covering posed no threat to public order. A scarf was not threatening, whereas a baseball cap could be if it signaled membership in a gang. Certain students may have been shocked by the presence of classmates wearing headscarves on September 11, 2003, the second anniversary of the terrorist attacks of 2001, but their discomfort alone was not sufficient cause to warrant banning the hijab. It would have been necessary for the school to show a "compelling interest" to forbid such an item. In fact, the school's dress code was fairly lax—various unusual types of headwear were already permitted, notably around festive occasions such as Halloween or theatrical productions. In addition, headscarves were specifically permitted for medical reasons, for example to cover hair loss resulting from the effects of chemotherapy. Furthermore, nothing in the school rules forbade wearing more or less discreet religious symbols such as crosses or even T-shirts printed with Christian messages.

The U.S. government intervened to file a motion in favor of Nashala's position in a federal district court. It based its complaint on "a denial on account of religion of equal protection of the laws under the Fourteenth Amendment."[32] The motion was granted, and the school was obliged to modify its dress code to allow for exemptions in favor of the hijab and all other clothing or accessories of a religious nature. Satisfied by this compromise in favor of religious freedom, Alexander Acosta, the assistant attorney general for civil rights, was quick to inform the press that "no student should be forced to choose between following her faith and enjoying the benefit of a public education."[33] The decision was applauded by both Christian and Muslim associations, as well as by one of the most prestigious Jewish defense organizations, the American Jewish Congress.[34]

Since that ruling happened to come only two months after the passage of the French law banning the wearing of conspicuous religious signs, many predictably seized on the incident to criticize the excessive rigidity of the French secular model.[35] These criticisms were implicit in President Obama's famous Cairo speech of June 4, 2009. In an allusion to the Muskogee case, the president affirmed that "Islam and America are not competing identities" and that the American government would not hesitate, as it had in the past, to use the courts "to protect the right of women and girls to wear the hijab and to punish those who would deny it."[36]

The only American case that vaguely resembles the Islamic-headscarf controversy in France is the one alluded to in the previous chapter. It concerns a certain Captain Goldman, an Orthodox Jew and a commissioned officer in the U.S. Air Force, who wore a yarmulke in violation of the regulation dress code. Simcha Goldman was no ordinary soldier. He was a psychologist and ordained rabbi and had a clinical practice in a U.S. Air Force base in Riverside, California. Sanctioned by his superiors for this infraction, Goldman believed he had been treated unfairly and therefore sought official permission to "wear a yarmulke while in uniform" in accordance with the Free Exercise Clause of the First Amendment. The case went before the Supreme Court in 1986 and raised a question of general importance: Should an exemption be granted to an individual whose headwear in no way threatens the proper functioning of the U.S. Air Force? The court decided in favor of the Air Force, arguing that "the military need not encourage debate or tolerate protest to the extent that such tolerance is required of the civilian state by the First Amendment; to accomplish its mission, the military must foster instinctive obedience, unity, commitment, and esprit de corps." The only sartorial distinctions permitted are those related to military hierarchy and performance. No exemptions were to be granted, although discreet signs (medallions, rings, bracelets) were tolerated.[37] Thus respect for military discipline overrides freedom of religion. In a concurring opinion, Justice Stevens went further, employing in his analysis the classic slippery-slope argument: If we accept that wearing a yarmulke in no way impedes the proper exercise of military duties, since one can always wear a helmet or a service cap over a yarmulke, it could be argued that such a reasoning applies to members of other religious minorities—a Sikh demanding to wear his turban, a yogi his saffron robe, a Rastafarian his dreadlocks. The consequences, he claimed, would be disastrous for public opinion and military morale. It is not the business of the army to create fallacious distinctions between individuals based on their beliefs or ethnic origins.[38]

In the American context, military personnel must behave in the same way as a civil servant or a teacher in the French context. As with the French government employee, the American soldier must adhere to a certain *devoir de réserve*. In the American case, however, the neutrality of public service is not the determining factor but rather the discipline and uniformity required for forming a military esprit de corps.

Interestingly, it is the U.S. Congress that later stepped in to relax the military dress codes. One year after the Goldman ruling, Congress authorized uniformed military personnel to wear "a piece of cloth" with a religious connotation, on condition that it be "clean and discreet" and in no way compromise the duties of military service.[39] The details for the implementation of the new law were left to the Department of Defense and the chief of staff of the three military divisions (Army, Navy, Air Force). In fact, while not stating so directly, the law was creating an exception for Orthodox Jews while excluding the less discreet headwear of Sikhs and Rastafarians.[40]

The different cases examined in this chapter highlight the distance that separates France from the United States. In France, an administrative judge favored the principle of tolerance in regard to the Islamic headscarf, whereas the French Parliament defended a stricter, less tolerant secular tradition. In the United States, on the other hand, federal judges are reluctant to tolerate religious signs in public space, while lawmakers, influenced by religious lobbies, have encouraged individuals to wear religious symbols in that most secular of institutions, the military.[41] Comparisons, however, do not tell the whole story. For many, the question of the headscarf was about French identity. In France, therefore, it took on the importance of a full-fledged political incident, while the American kippah debate remained largely anecdotal and marginal.

9

NEW RESTRICTIONS, NEW FORMS
OF TOLERANCE

One of the theses of this book is that the limits of tolerance are constantly shifting depending on the country and on historical circumstance. Tolerance may
expand at certain times—one may recall, for example, the France
of Henri IV—or shrink dramatically at others, as happened during the reign of Louis XIV. The same phenomenon is occurring
today, albeit in a form whose consequences are far less brutal.
The question now is not whether to multiply or restrict the number of permitted religions but rather how to address the regulation of religious symbols. At the end of the twentieth century in
France, the United States, Germany, Italy, Great Britain, and
elsewhere, young Muslim women were permitted to wear a
headscarf (the hijab) in all public places, whether for reasons of
cultural identity or religious devotion. This is no longer true in
France, where, as we have seen, everything changed with the
2004 law that proscribed wearing conspicuous religious signs.
But the French prohibition had a limited scope, only targeting
public primary and secondary schools. Another law passed six
years later, in 2010, banned the full-face veil (the niqab and burka)
from all public places, marking a new contraction of the country's territories of tolerance.

To understand the significance of these bans, it is useful to consider different "spaces of tolerance." There are basically four different types: private space (the home), sacred space (places of worship and prayer), public space in the broadest sense (streets, public parks and gardens, beaches), and institutional space (government offices, city halls, public schools, hospitals, airports). Each of these spaces is subject to a different level of regulation. Private space—the home—is first and foremost a place of personal liberty free of all regulation (except in the case of proven violence). Sacred space obeys the rules and rituals of the relevant church and falls outside of regulatory authorities except when it comes to financing the construction of places of worship, as in France. Public space open to all is traditionally a place of freedom with few rules. Individuals must of course obey traffic lights, park rules about pets, regulations in stadiums or movie theaters about food and drink, and so forth, but the public remains free to come and go as they like and for the most part dress as they wish; only nudity is forbidden. Institutional space, more frequently and directly regulated, is intended to be neutral, and every measure should be taken to ensure that it remains so. It is here that a secular government imposes its rules on both civil servants and the users of public services.

THE BAN ON THE BURKA

The burka ban adopted by the French National Assembly in October 2010 regulated public space in a new and discriminatory way. Ways of dressing that had gone unregulated up until then came under the strict control of the state: "No one may, in public space, wear anything intended to cover the face."[1] This general injunction applied to "public thoroughfares" as well as to all "places open to the public or designated as public space." How did the French come to forbid a piece of clothing that, at the time the law was passed, was worn by approximately 1,630 women in Metropolitan France?[2] Are there precedents for this sort of prohibition? The only noteworthy example would be the August 18, 1792, law banning "ecclesiastical dress" for all people working in schools or hospitals. That radical interdiction reflected the extreme hostility of lawmakers to priests, who were loath to accept the French Revolution. But it also had another meaning. Religious attire was unacceptable because it signaled an affiliation with a particular body of citizens—a religious community or a corporation—within a republic that French revolutionaries had envisioned as homogeneous and indivisible: "A well-organized state recognizes no corporation other than the general community of its citizens."[3] The law prohibiting priests' robes in public, abandoned as soon as Robespierre fell from power (July 1794), was reintroduced a century later by a deputy as an amendment to the 1905 law on the separation of church and state. Aristide Briand, the law's principal sponsor, quashed this initiative, stating that such a measure would expose the government to "the reproach of intolerance" and to "a much worse danger—ridicule."[4]

The 2010 law hoped to avoid ridicule by not specifically targeting Muslims. Indeed, the neutral and universal letter of the law applied to all types of face coverings, both religious and non-religious. But this ploy fooled no one; it was clear that the true goal of the law was to ban the burka and niqab from public space. To understand this ban, one must consider the political context of the time. The center right had been in power since 2007, but the electoral successes of the far-right National Front party were perceived as a threat to the parliamentary majority led by Prime Minister François Fillon. With the xenophobic far right channeling discontent about the immigration question, he felt obliged to take a strong stand. For those who supported the successful integration of immigrants, the existence in France of the niqab, though rare, was surprising and worrisome. It seemed to signify the submission of women to a patriarchal order that sought literally to imprison them in a bizarre type of clothing. In her famous "Address to Those Who Voluntarily Wear the Burka," the writer and feminist Élisabeth Badinter chastised women who choose to be fully veiled:

> Are you going to continue to completely hide your face? Concealed as you are from the gaze of others, you must realize that you cause mistrust and fear in children and adults alike. Are we so contemptible and impure in your eyes that you need to reject all contact with us, any connection, even the complicity of a passing smile?. . . I can't help but wonder: Why not move to Saudi Arabia or Afghanistan where no one will ask you to show your face, where your daughters will also be veiled, and where your husband can have multiple wives and be free to repudiate you at will?[5]

Badinter's solution to the problem of the burka, this "prison for women," this "terrible sign of incivility,"[6] was extreme: rescue democracy by deporting the troublemakers. But what did the veiled women have to say? A recent sociological study offers a complex and mixed portrait of the main motives of the *niqabistes* (niqabi) who so fascinated French intellectuals and the media in the 2000s. They are young, mostly born in France, and their parents are generally of African origin, in particular North African. Their motives can be genuinely religious and reflect the discovery of a rigorous strain of Islam encountered through friends, Salafist imams, or radical Islamist websites. Whether newly converted or reembracing their Muslim heritage, their religiosity tends to owe more to a personal, improvised understanding of Islam than to any form of indoctrination imposed from outside. Their approach is most often individual and subjective, and it reflects an ascetic ideal. This ideal may have a therapeutic function, allowing them to cope with a chaotic or violent family situation or distance themselves from a dissolute lifestyle, drug problems, dropping out of school, or some other psychological vulnerability. Those who wear the niqab, like many born-again Christians, often seek to distance themselves from painful events.[7] Paradoxically, the fact of being wrapped in a niqab—often denounced by critics as a "walking cloister,"[8] a "signal of female inferiority," a form of "sexual apartheid"[9]—has sometimes been described by others as liberating. Wearing the niqab can earn a certain respect for women who live in dangerous neighborhoods and may protect them against male violence and sexual harassment.[10]

Contrary to the fears often expressed at the time the law was passed, the same study revealed that the niqab is not imposed by a male authority against the wishes of allegedly submissive women.[11] The subjects of the study used "language related to well-being, personal development, and privacy: a lexicon that conveys the idea of a 'culture of the self' typical of Western modernity."[12]

Was banning a practice relevant to only a small minority of Muslim women a good policy? One can understand why, for purposes of identification and recognition, the full-face veil would be banned in institutional spaces such as government offices, at bank windows, in city halls, at employment offices and other social-service agencies, and perhaps also in airports. But in the street, in public gardens, in the most openly public spaces? Yet this was the path chosen by the French Parliament against the recommendation of the Council of State (Conseil d'État) and in spite of reservations voiced later by the Constitutional Council (Conseil Constitutionnel). The principle of equality between men and women, supposedly violated by this antiquated practice, prevailed over two other fundamental rights: the freedom to express one's religious views and the freedom to come and go as one pleases in public places. However, critics of the full-face veil were not content to invoke the principle of equality. They also based their argument on another fundamental principle guaranteed by the French constitution, namely secularism (*laïcité*), which in this instance was transformed into the curious notion of "transparent communication." This transparency, a key source of social bonding, could only be found in the face, according to the philosopher Emmanuel Levinas, who was abundantly quoted in the report produced by the National Assembly. "I'm not just looking at another man's face," wrote Levinas in *Totality and Infinity*: "I feel an obligation to him, derived from the essential nudity of his face exposed to all types of violence."[13] But what is the relevance of such a comment for the daily reality of women wearing the full-face veil? Are they less human because they hide their faces while revealing their eyes? Are they deprived of speech? After all, they have not taken a vow of silence like Carmelite nuns, nor are they physically confined behind the gates of a convent. Are they condemned to be forever treated as objects of curiosity or a projection of some dark medieval fantasy? Is their desire to be seen without being observed the manifestation of some "perverse enjoyment" that violates the sacrosanct principle of republican *fraternité*? Does wearing the full-face veil amount to "a sort of civil self-mutilation through social invisibility"?[14] These severe criticisms are perhaps not entirely unwarranted. The full-face veil is not pleasant to see. It conjures up images of premodern times and discourages socializing, although communication remains possible. A comparison might be made to motorcyclists and skiers who, despite their faces being hidden, are capable of interacting and communicating with others using words and gestures.

France's prime minister asked for a report from the Council of State, which affirmed that the legal basis for banning the full-face veil was questionable. It pointed out that the principles invoked by the government were either fallacious or improper and denied rights already recognized in decisions of the European Court of Human Rights (ECHR). The Council of State argued that the principle of secularism is not an absolute that can justify a repressive policy. In French public law, secularism is "inseparable from freedom of conscience and religion, and the freedom of every individual to express his or her religion and convictions."[15] These freedoms are guaranteed by the French Constitution and by the European Convention for the Protection of Human Rights and Fundamental Freedoms, better known as the European Convention on Human Rights. Certain freedoms can be regulated in schools and other public institutions but certainly not in all public spaces, which up until then had been lightly regulated. Other rights invoked, such as the right to dignity, according to the report, did not provide sufficient justification, because this right conflicts with another, equally fundamental principle, namely "individual freedom," which includes the right to choose one's own clothing. In both European and American law, the principle of individual autonomy places extreme limits on what can be prohibited: "Every individual may lead his life according to his convictions and personal choices, including putting himself physically or morally in danger, so long as that attitude does not harm others."[16] This is similar to the meaning of Article 4 of France's Declaration of the Rights of Man and the Citizen: "Liberty consists in the freedom to do everything which injures no one else." This personal freedom may lead a woman to accept a position of inferiority to a man—either real or perceived as such by others—"so long as her physical person is not harmed."[17]

Banning the veil therefore remains legally tenuous, all the more so since the European Union's Charter of Fundamental Rights, ratified on December 7, 2000, recognizes the principle of nondiscrimination and applies it to all persons regardless of religion, political opinions, disability, age, or sexual orientation.[18] This principle of nondiscrimination would be clearly violated if the ban targeted only or primarily Muslim women, who could reasonably claim to be unjustly stigmatized.

To avoid this difficulty, French lawmakers took the hard line of imposing a general ban on all forms of face covering, whether religious or not. But they admitted that a number of exemptions would have to be provided for certain sports (such as skiing, ice hockey, and fencing), certain occupations (welding, painting, police forces), certain professions (doctors, nurses, dentists), motorcycle riders wearing a helmet, and certain festive activities (parades, festivals, carnivals). It was unclear whether the ban on face covering would also apply to the hoods of religious penitents in southern France or the tinted windows of "official" cars, hiding the identity of government ministers, business leaders, and entertainers. It took a full year for government officials to clarify the meaning and scope of the law, adopted on October 11, 2010. Implementation guidelines published in March 2011 in a special document (*circulaire*) attempted to define more clearly the vague notion of public space. Included in this vast expanse were all public thoroughfares, beaches, gardens, walkways, train and bus stations, airports, cinemas, city halls, courthouses, prefectures, hospitals, post offices, schools and universities, national health-insurance offices, museums, libraries, and employment agencies. The guidelines did not attempt to distinguish between open spaces used for circulating and enclosed institutional spaces; the two spheres were indiscriminately thrown together. Furthermore, numerous exemptions reduced the universality of the law. Face coverings were permitted "for health or professional reasons," to practice sports, or to ride two-wheeled vehicles. An individual was allowed to wear a full-face veil inside a private vehicle—judged a "private space"—whereas the same mode of dress would be prohibited in public transportation (subways, trams, buses). It could also be worn inside an airplane belonging to a private airline.[19] Finally, hoods would be tolerated for "religious processions so long as they have a traditional character," although the term "traditional" was left undefined.[20]

Reading this document, one grasps the approximations and even incoherencies of a law that attempts to distinguish arbitrarily private from public transportation, public thoroughfares from the private vehicles that use them, and traditional religions from the less traditional and that lumps cinemas, libraries, and places of worship together as public space. One can see why the police would be reluctant to impose fines for breaking this law. Their mission is to ensure public order against likely disturbances, not to bother the few passersby who might be excessively veiled. By turning a municipal police force into a morality police and certain habits of dressing into reprehensible practices, lawmakers in effect weakened the legitimacy of these keepers of the peace. Police officers expressed their reluctance to detain niqabi when there were so many more urgent priorities, including managing unruly protests, regulating traffic, and pursuing thieves and other criminals.[21]

In its October 7, 2010, ruling, France's Constitutional Council (Conseil Constitutionnel) declared the law banning the burka constitutional. However, it expressed a significant reservation concerning places of worship open to the public. Banning the veil in such places, the court affirmed, would violate Article 10 of the Declaration of the Rights of Man and the Citizen, which states: "No one shall be disturbed on account of his opinions, including his religious views, provided their manifestation does not disturb the public order established by law."

In other words, any veiled person, including a Muslim woman, may enter a mosque, church, temple, or synagogue without having to remove the burka. Since the law is supposed to be neutral and universal in its application, no one can deny a fully veiled woman's desire to visit the Cathedral of Notre-Dame, for example.[22]

ACCESS TO PLACES OF WORSHIP

The Constitutional Council's 2010 decision generated a new difficulty: how should a veiled woman be guaranteed free access to a place of worship? Should she be allowed to leave her home fully veiled to go there? Was such an exception acceptable? How should the authorized distance between the woman's home and her place of prayer be measured? Other implementation guidelines simply recommended that police officers avoid "any intervention in direct proximity to a place of worship" or in its immediate surroundings.[23] "Proximity"? "Surroundings"? The borders between legal and illegal, between acceptable and unacceptable distances are surprisingly vague—the main objective being to guarantee the individual's right to exercise her religion freely.

The French law remains too imprecise, too punitive, and too general in its purpose to be consistently applied. While pretending to be neutral, it targets and stigmatizes adult women practicing a pietist form of Islam. The law's principal aim was to instrumentalize religious questions for political ends. The president at the time, Nicolas Sarkozy, hoped that, by taking a firm stand against the most visible signs of a certain radical Islam, he would slow the progress of the far-right National Front party, thereby increasing his chances for reelection in 2012. In reality the law was often poorly enforced or not at all, as Nadine Morano, one of Sarkozy's former ministers, lamented during a trip to Paris:

> I got off my train at the Gare de l'Est, and I saw a figure, a silhouette, advancing toward me—who knows who was underneath—wearing a black niqab, fully veiled, with rectangular openings for the eyes. . . . I confronted her, saying that her dress was forbidden in France and that she must uncover her face in public. . . . It was provocation, they know full well that it's forbidden!

Her efforts did not produce the desired effect. Instead of arresting the niqabi, the police officer asked Morano to produce her ID. The minister, reported by the press as "very irritated" and "extremely aggressive" toward the police officer, exclaimed: "What? You don't recognize me? This is unbelievable! Don't you watch television? I am a minister, I'm a deputy, I am Madame Morano!" From this incident, the former minister concluded that the police officer "didn't want to do his job" or, worse perhaps, was revealing his political allegiance "to the other side" (that is, the Socialist Party).[24]

Five years after passage of the law, the total number of women required to pay a fine for wearing a burka was low and included numerous repeat offenders. The Interior Ministry reported 332 cases in 2012, 383 in 2013, and 397 in 2014. The police are not "burka hunters"; they have shown discernment and are not exclusively focused on the arrest of delinquent niqabi.[25] As noted by French critics of the burka ban, the law risked being overturned by the European Court of Human Rights (ECHR). In a recent case involving the wearing of the Turkish turban in public, the court had ruled in favor of protecting the right "to manifest [one's] religion or belief," in public, in conformity with Article 9 of the European Convention. In that case—*Ahmet Arslan and Others v. Turkey* (February 23, 2010)—the ECHR considered that the members of a Turkish religious sect, the Aczimendi tarikatÿ, whose dress comprises a turban, black tunic, and wide, flowing pants (saroual), could not be legally punished for violating a Turkish law forbidding such accoutrements. Since members of the sect were not acting as representatives of the Turkish authority but were instead "simple citizens," they were not bound by "a duty of discretion in the public expression of their religious beliefs."[26] As long as they were circulating in public spaces "open to all," they did not have to remove their turban as they would be required in a public institution, a school, or a courthouse. No matter how bizarre or old-fashioned their clothing might be, it did not constitute a "threat to public order," and their behavior did not reveal a proselytizing intent. In no way did they exert "undue pressure" on innocent passersby.[27] The Turkish law known as the "Hat Law" was therefore invalidated for having violated Article 9 of the European Convention.

The same argument was made in the case of *S.A.S. v. France* (July 1, 2014). The claimant, a young Frenchwoman who was a practicing Muslim, filed a suit with the ECHR to denounce the burka ban on the grounds that it violated several articles of the European Convention. She declared that she wore a burka or niqab, depending on what she felt like, "in accordance with her religious faith, culture, and personal convictions"—and she asked for these reasons that the law be declared invalid.

In this case, however, the majority of the judges decided against her after examining the objections introduced by the French government to justify the total ban of the full-face veil.

These objections were based on the safety and security of the public, the protection of equality between the sexes, respect for human dignity, and respect for the notion of "living together" (*vivre ensemble*). The first three arguments were rejected by the court. Wearing the full-face veil, according to the judges, could be prohibited if there was a specific need to identify the claimant, but intermittent identity checks in no way justified a general ban. Wearing the full-face veil did not violate the principle of equality between the sexes as long as it had been freely chosen by the claimant "to express her religious, personal, and cultural faith." Nor was the full-face veil a violation of human dignity, since it expressed "a cultural identity which contributes to the pluralism that is inherent in democracy."[28]

A majority of the judges, however, accepted the legitimacy of the fourth reason invoked by the French government to ban the full-face veil, namely the "fundamental requirements of 'living together' in French society." Hiding one's face, the court reasoned, was indeed "contrary to the ideal of fraternity" and to "the minimum requirement of civility that is necessary for social interaction."[29]

What is "living together"? The judges admitted that the term was imprecise and that its content and scope deserved further examination. But since the matter of "living together" relates to the general policies of the French government, the court refused to address the matter in giving national decision makers "a wide margin of appreciation in deciding whether and to what extent a limitation of the right to manifest one's religion or beliefs is 'necessary.'"[30]

Critics of the *S.A.S. v. France* decision pointed out the circularity of the court's reasoning and the "far-fetched and vague" character of the notion of "living together." Banning the full-face veil, these critics claimed, produces the opposite of the stated goal. In practical terms, the ban displayed a "selective pluralism and restricted tolerance" by violating well-established judicial precedents according to which the role of authorities "is not to remove the cause of tension by eliminating pluralism, but to ensure that the competing groups tolerate each other."[31] True tolerance, according to this body of case law, consists in protecting a small, vulnerable, and unpopular minority against the restrictions imposed inappropriately or disproportionately by the majority.[32]

Following this argument, public space (as opposed to institutional space) ought to remain fundamentally free and open. In a liberal democracy all forms of expression, even the most bizarre, should be tolerated in public. I may cross paths on the street with an oddly dressed man or woman with dyed-red hair, vulgar tattoos, and disfiguring piercings, perched on towering stiletto heels . . . I may not like it, but the street is a free place that belongs to everyone, and I have no right to voice an objection unless my safety or public order is directly threatened. Am I required to communicate with those whose values and sartorial style I do not share? No, because public space is not a place of absolute transparency. I may exercise the right to remain silent or even behave as a misanthrope, should I wish. Fraternity may be desirable in a republic, but it is not an obligation.

In this sense, the freedom to display one's religion is no different from freedom of expression itself. Ways of dress, whether religious or nonreligious, are symbolic discourses and must be treated as such. Moreover, according to a consistent line of cases from the ECHR, "the demands of pluralism, tolerance, and broadmindedness . . . without which there can be no democratic society" require that all opinions be allowed public expression, including those that "offend, shock, or disturb." In other words, "there is no right not to be shocked or provoked by different models of cultural or religious identity, even those that are very distant from the traditional French and European lifestyle."[33]

There was abundant testimony produced by an investigative committee of the French National Assembly that the full-face veil causes unease and fear. But public malaise alone is not sufficient to ban the full-face veil; other, more compelling motives are necessary to justify such a measure. But the motives so far given, as we have seen, are ambiguous because they bring into conflict certain fundamental rights: equality between the sexes, on the one hand, and freedom of conscience on the other. These civil liberties overlap, and the challenge is to find a satisfactory balance between them without jumping to a priori theological judgments, which are clearly beyond the responsibility of secular courts. The only motive retained by the European Court of Human Rights to justify the ban on the full-face veil—protection of the notion of "living together"—is too vague to be accepted without critical examination. Perhaps it is necessary to return to the origins of the notion of *vivre ensemble* as defined by Ernest Renan in *What Is a Nation?*, his famous Sorbonne lecture published in 1882. The French definition of a nation, as posited by Renan, differs significantly from the German definition, which considers the nation as founded on a common language, German, and a founding people, the Saxons. A true nation, Renan explains, is a "spiritual principle" that hinges on two key elements: "a long past of endeavors, sacrifice, and devotion" and an equally demanding present founded on "consent, the clearly expressed desire to live together" and to perform "great deeds together." In short, a nation is "a large-scale solidarity constituted by the feeling of the sacrifices that one has made in the past and of those that one is prepared to make in the future." Thus, the desire to live together comes at a high price. It requires the "abdication of the individual" for the benefit of the national community that encompasses it.[34] But who today would place the bar so high by advocating for such sacrifices? Therein lies the challenge: how does one satisfy the "desire to live together" without crushing other existing rights, including the right to manifest one's religious singularity in public? The secularization of the notion of "living together" proposed today by French lawmakers is unsatisfactory because it infringes on the free exercise of religion while at the same time refusing to clearly distinguish public space, open to all, from institutional space occupied and managed by civil servants. Everything would be clearer if the burka were permitted in public spaces and prohibited only in more closely supervised institutional spaces, as is the case today in Germany.[35]

RELIGIOUS MONUMENTS IN THE PUBLIC SQUARE

Beyond certain specific cases related to the armed forces and military discipline, there are no restrictions in the United States on permissible types of religious clothing. Wearing Islamic headscarves is permitted in public schools at all grade levels, and neither the burka nor the niqab are banned from the public sphere. The reason for the difference between the United States and France probably has to do with the multicultural habits of a country of immigrants.[36] Yet not all religious symbols are permitted in public spaces in the United States. Religious markers such as the Ten Commandments, large crosses, nativity scenes, and the like are generally not allowed in public schools, courthouses, military cemeteries, or in the proximity of state capitols. The frequent display of these religious symbols gives rise to countless legal battles at the local and federal levels.[37]

Why is there such a difference between the French and American ways of regulating the public display of religious monuments? It could stem from the fact that French public spaces are filled with crosses, statues, Stations of the Cross, and roadside shrines—many dating back to the Middle Ages. Nowadays, it is out of the question to limit the presence and visibility of such a significant religious heritage. In the United States, a younger country with no ancient architecture, historical monuments of a religious nature are rare and do not benefit from any particular conservation measures. Just as with prayer in public schools or sports arenas, the Ten Commandments and other religious symbols erected in public places have generally been prohibited by federal courts or the Supreme Court, on the grounds that they violate the fundamental principle of the separation of church and state guaranteed by the Establishment Clause of the First Amendment.

The Latin cross is the oldest, most visible, and most sacred of all the symbols of Christianity. Should it be accepted as the expression of an old and venerable heritage? Should its presence in public space be forbidden or regulated? These questions are hotly debated in countries with Christian roots that have become secularized over the last two or three centuries.

In France, as we have seen, wearing the Islamic headscarf, the yarmulke, or a "cross of clearly excessive size"[38] is forbidden in public schools, but *discreet* religious signs and symbols are considered perfectly acceptable. Moreover, the construction, display, or erection of a new cross (or any other "religious sign or emblem") in a public place or on a public monument is forbidden by Article 28 of the 1905 law separating church and state, with the exception of cemeteries, funerary monuments, and museums or exhibitions.[39] However, carrying large crosses and other religious symbols is clearly permitted in demonstrations, processions, parades, and other gatherings of a religious nature. In principle, the organizers of these events must apply in advance for a permit, which can be refused if the event risks troubling public order. Traditional religious processions can take place without a permit.[40]

In the United States it is mainly the judicial branch that exercises control over religious symbols in the public square. A recent case decided by the U.S. Court of Appeals for the Ninth Circuit, *Trunk and Jewish War Veterans of the USA v. City of San Diego* (2011), is a good illustration of the American way of distinguishing between legal and illegal uses of public space. The contested object was a large white cross erected on the summit of Mount Soledad in La Jolla near San Diego in southern California. Visible from a great distance and situated near a heavily traveled highway, its location raised numerous important questions: Did this cross, on public land, violate the principle of separation of church and state affirmed in the U.S. Constitution? Was the monument primarily religious in nature? Was it a cultural symbol accepted by all or instead the manifestation of a tradition so old that it had become secularized with time? Were the uses of the park where the cross is located mainly religious, secular, or a mixture of both? How was the monument perceived by members of civil society, especially those who are not Christian?[41]

Basing her opinion on longstanding legal precedent, Judge McKeown began by questioning the intent of those who had built the widely visible cross.[42] She observed that the monument, originally erected in 1913 on private land, symbolized the triumph of Christianity: it was described in various religious ceremonies as "a gleaming white cross" that served "as a reminder of God's promise to man of redemption and everlasting life." But the cross took on another meaning starting in 1954, when it was dedicated to veterans of the Korean War. After becoming federal land in 2006, the site of the cross, Mount Soledad, was renamed "The

Mount Soledad Veterans Memorial," whose purpose is to honor all American war veterans. The "park" of Mount Soledad is managed today by the Navy, which is part of the U.S. Department of Defense. It therefore functions like a military cemetery in addition to having a patriotic function. Can it be concluded that the white cross that dominates this war memorial acquired little by little, by force of association, a secular character? This was not the view of the two plaintiffs in the case, Steve Trunk and the association of Jewish War Veterans of the United States of America, for whom the symbol of Jesus's crucifixion remained exclusively associated with the Christian tradition; they therefore maintained that the cross could not symbolize the patriotic virtue of *all* Americans.

In this highly charged context, Judge McKeown developed a minute analysis of the significance of crosses in general and their use in military cemeteries more particularly. She first observed that the Latin cross is not a universally recognized religious symbol. Its presence atop Mount Soledad and its immense size near an urban center encircled by highways give the impression that only the dead of a certain religious faith are being honored.[43] Furthermore, with the exception of a few Civil War–era cemeteries, American military cemeteries do not feature large Latin crosses. The flag is the dominant symbol; crosses, stars of David, and Muslim crescents, when present, are small, individualized signs engraved on the headstones of fallen soldiers. Monuments erected to honor the dead from the First and Second World Wars are predominantly secular places of remembrance. One thus cannot claim that the cross on Mount Soledad is the embodiment of a "civil religion," as claimed by one historian consulted by the Department of Defense. The cross, unlike the Ten Commandments or other vague deist symbols such as the motto "In God We Trust," remains an exclusively Christian symbol. Indeed, the cross on Mount Soledad is venerated each year at Easter by Christian ministers who gather there to celebrate the resurrection of Jesus Christ. Such practices may trouble non-Christians, especially in a district of San Diego (La Jolla) known in the past for its anti-Semitism.

Within this context, the cross is probably perceived by the Jewish war veterans of southern California as a "monument of alienation." It is therefore unconstitutional, as it implicitly signals to "non-adherents [of Christianity] that they are outsiders, not full members of the political community."[44] For all these reasons, Judge McKeown decided in favor of the plaintiffs: maintaining the cross on Mount Soledad as it stands, immense and solitary, constituted a violation of the Establishment Clause. The Supreme Court refused to hear the case on appeal. The solution finally adopted was inelegant but consistent with the First Amendment: the part of the hill where this Christian symbol triumphantly stands was reprivatized. The Department of Defense sold the land for 1.4 million dollars to a private association that now manages the site.[45] The cross was saved because it no longer was part of a publicly owned war memorial.

The management and regulation of religious signs in Europe is particularly delicate given the extraordinary diversity of national experiences. Certain countries, such as Denmark, Sweden, the United Kingdom, Ireland, Greece, and Bulgaria, maintain one or more official religions. Others, such as France, Italy, and Spain, are officially secular. Still others, such as Germany, have chosen to implement flexible arrangements that provide for official cooperation between political institutions and churches.[46] In all these various configurations, religious beliefs and nonbelief are respected, as are freedom of education and the parents' right to send their children to the school of their choice. Confronted with a plethora of national experiences, the European Court of

Human Rights has attempted to find new solutions reconciling a state's desire for neutrality with the public display of religious symbols.

The most famous case concerns the presence of crucifixes in the classrooms of Italian public schools. Should they be removed, as requested by some parents, who considered these devotional objects incompatible with the secular values they wished to transmit to their children? The obligation to hang a crucifix in each primary-school classroom goes back to a royal decree of the Kingdom of Sardinia-Piedmont adopted on September 15, 1860. This obligation, carried over when Italy was unified as a nation in 1861, was no longer enforced after the capture of Rome by the Italian army in September 1870. It was revived during the Fascist period by a royal decree (April 30, 1924), which ordered that "each school must have the national flag and each classroom must have a crucifix and a portrait of the king."[47] The Constitution of the Italian Republic ratified in 1948 did not challenge this symbolic practice. But a later law passed in 1985 overturned the principle that "the Catholic religion is the only State religion," thus radically changing the nature of the relationship between the Catholic Church and the Italian state.[48]

But why, many asked, should classrooms retain an old symbol inherited from the times of Italian fascism and a moribund monarchy? The ruling of the European Court of Human Rights in the 2011 case *Lautsi v. Italy* declared that school crucifixes had nothing to do with those historic events. The court affirmed that "a crucifix on a wall is an essentially passive symbol" devoid of any influence over students, and, as an Italian government representative explained, it perpetuates a tradition that is not only cultural but also integral to the Italian "identity."[49] According to the decision handed down by an Italian administrative tribunal, the cross is a strong symbol of Italian identity that it is "indispensable to reaffirm . . . even symbolically" at a time of confusion about cultures and values. The cross is acceptable because of its supposed universal range:

> The cross, as the symbol of Christianity, can therefore not exclude anyone without denying itself; it even constitutes in a sense the universal sign of the acceptance of and respect for every human being as such, irrespective of any belief, religious or other, which he or she may hold. . . . It is hardly necessary to add that the sign of the cross in a classroom, when correctly understood, is not concerned with the freely held convictions of anyone, excludes no one and of course does not impose or prescribe anything.[50]

The argument, one may claim, is rather Jesuitical: it can also be affirmed that the Italian identity is just as much a product of the philosophy of the Enlightenment. From a strictly political point of view, "secularism is a supreme principle" of the Italian constitutional order, even if the Italian word for secularism, *laicità*, does not appear in the country's founding document.[51] The *Lautsi* decision is particularly interesting because it goes beyond the old debate between believers and nonbelievers, clerics and laypeople. In more general terms, it demonstrates that there is no "hermetic border"[52] between a historic tradition that accords importance to Christian religious symbols and a legal tradition that recognizes and enshrines the principle of secularism. The overlapping of these two spheres, religious and secular, is facilitated by the deployment of a new principle of neutrality described by a Belgian jurist as a "neutrality of compensation."[53] Traditionally, historians and jurists distinguish two opposing conceptions of state neutrality: an exclusive conception forbidding all public display of religious symbols outside of places of worship and an inclusive conception that allows public space to be filled with a pluralist array of symbols belonging to different religious traditions or to the secular sphere. The neutrality of compensation offers a third, intermediate path. In the Lautsi case it functions this way: the Italian government has the full right to invoke an old tradition that is not only religious but also "identity-linked" as justification for maintaining crucifixes in classrooms; nor is it wrong, given the majority rule of a democracy, to give a "preponderant visibility" to the country's majority religion.[54]

This argument is only acceptable, however, because the cross, this eminently Christian symbol of Christ's resurrection, is not linked to any proselytizing activities, and especially because the religious pluralism of Italian society is fully respected within its public-school system. In other words, the religious connotation of the cross is tempered in two ways: first, because the school does not impose catechism or other religious teaching, and second, because the school space is in fact "open to other religions." The ECHR noted that students in Italian public schools are permitted "to wear Islamic headscarves or other symbols or apparel having a religious connotation," that events such as the beginning and end of Ramadan are "often celebrated" in schools, and that optional religious education is offered for "all recognised religious creeds."[55] As for nonbelievers, nothing suggests that they are being discriminated against by school authorities. As a result, the ECHR ruled that maintaining crosses in the classrooms does not violate Article 9 of the European Convention of Human Rights. But the judges reserved judgment about the future. For instance, what should be done if a town opens a new school? Should classroom walls be decorated with the same Christian imagery? Would it not be wiser, out of fairness toward new generations of students and recent immigrants beginning to attend school, to leave the walls bare or else vary the symbols, alternating between crosses, crescents, Jewish stars, and other secular symbols?[56] This is the price of true pluralism: no single religion should have a monopoly on symbolic representation. Even the most well-established traditions begin to lose their legitimacy if they do not change with the times.

10

SHOULD WE TOLERATE THE ENEMIES OF TOLERANCE?

W hat is tolerance?" asks Voltaire in his *Philosophical Dictionary*. He answers, surprisingly, "It is the prerogative of humanity. We are all steeped in weaknesses and errors: let us forgive each other's follies, it is the first law of nature."[1]

With this eminently Socratic approach ("I know that I know nothing"), Voltaire reveals the fundamental meaning of tolerance: beyond simply tolerating a rival or adversary, it is about preserving a position of radical openness. We are all fallible and subject to error; we ought to admit, as a matter of intellectual honesty, that we can make mistakes and that the "other" across from us may be right. Tolerance, therefore, presupposes a reasonable understanding of the other and an open-mindedness based on respect and reciprocity. In a sense, tolerance establishes a "regime of hospitality" by breaking down the borders between the self and the other, between my convictions and those of a stranger. But I also expect this other person to be as open and welcoming to me when I am in her home. Tolerance is not compatible with a closed, biased, or absolute point of view: the stronger my conviction is and the more convinced I am of being right, the more I risk becoming a fanatic and tipping into intolerance.

The philosopher Karl Popper, whose reasoning I am following here, identifies in Voltaire's definition of tolerance the principle of *fallibilism*: what I believe to be true may be false, or, rather, truth exists, but it is difficult to arrive at it without a critical approach. Hence the importance of questioning my prejudices and listening to those who think differently from me.[2] Popper offers a rewording of Voltaire's statement: "I may be wrong and you may be right; and by talking things over rationally we may be able to correct some of our mistakes and we may perhaps, both of us, get nearer to the truth, or to acting in the right way." But what happens if certain individuals refuse the very principle of open, mutual, reciprocal tolerance? What happens if, within our society, certain groups, parties, churches, or minorities repudiate tolerance and advocate violence to impose their ideas? "Shall we or shall we not tolerate these minorities?" asks Popper. "If we do not tolerate them, we seem to deny our own principles: we seem to make concessions to intolerance, and so become hypocrites. If we do tolerate them, we may become responsible for ending democracy and toleration."[3]

This is the crux of the question: Should one tolerate the enemies of tolerance? But who is the real enemy? It is never easy to distinguish between a party with a radical or revolutionary discourse but that eschews violence, a more moderate party that threatens to use violence, and a supposedly moderate party that takes advantage of the openness of the democratic contest to destroy democracy once it has gained power. For Popper the answer is simple: "We need not tolerate even the threat of intolerance; and we must not tolerate it if the threat is getting serious."[4] Popper had in mind Goering's threat of using violence against his enemies, after the Nazis' legal accession to power in

1933. In more recent times we may think of the electoral successes of Islamists in Algeria or of the Muslim Brotherhood in Egypt. Was it wise to tolerate intolerance or, in any case, what seemed likely to trigger intolerance? We know the outcome, and it is dismal: canceled elections in Algeria and a military coup in Egypt. But those episodes of violence do not close the door on the possibility of a democratic future.

How should one evaluate threats of this kind in a liberal democracy? What constitutes a serious menace to the public order? Let us take the example of demonstrations that could become violent. The risk of violence is assessed differently from country to country. In France, the right to demonstrate is a fundamental liberty, although the government can take preventive measures if the safety of people and property is thought to be in danger. Such was the reasoning when the minister of the interior, on July 19, 2014, decided to stop a pro-Palestinian demonstration from taking place in Paris. At a time when the Israeli army was intervening harshly in Gaza in response to rocket and missile attacks launched from Palestinian territory, the government feared anti-Semitic violence. The organizers of the march could have appealed the decision to forbid the demonstration. Although they did not, hundreds of demonstrators nonetheless turned out in the streets. Some were arrested and convicted of throwing rocks at police and for attempts to attack synagogues while shouting "Death to Jews." In Germany, the anti-immigrant movement Pegida was forced to cancel a demonstration planned in Dresden on January 19, 2015, for similar reasons: fear of violence against an ethnic minority, in this case Muslim immigrants from Turkey or the Middle East. To justify the ban the German police cited "a concrete risk of terrorism."

Intolerance and fanaticism are certainly present in our societies, but they remain contained because the freedom to demonstrate is not unlimited: the enemies of tolerance will not be tolerated. Yet the threshold of tolerance varies widely from country to country. Certain countries condemn the incitement to racial hatred; others go further and have made denial of the Holocaust or the Armenian genocide illegal; still others persist in considering blasphemy a crime. Certain countries criminalize attacks against the honor of a head of state; others prosecute harm based on ethnic origins, nationality, religion, or sexual orientation.

LET NAZIS MARCH FREELY!

The most remarkable case of freedom of expression pushed to its extreme limits occurred in Skokie, Illinois, in 1978. This suburb north of Chicago was home to forty thousand Jews out of a total population of seventy thousand, many of whom were survivors of Nazi concentration camps. The leader of the National Socialist Party of America (NSPA) planned to organize a march there of neo-Nazis who, he announced, would wear uniforms with swastikas and carry posters affirming "Free speech for white persons." The stated purpose of the march, scheduled for June 25, 1978, was to protest a "freedom-killing" ordinance passed by the town of Skokie that required the organizers of the march to subscribe to a $350,000 property-damage insurance policy. Another city ordinance banned "the dissemination of material that incited racial or religious hatred with intent so to incite." The ordinances were declared unconstitutional by a U.S. district court in a decision that was affirmed by the court of appeals. On further appeal, the U.S. Supreme Court declined to review the case.[5] The march was authorized despite its openly pro-Nazi character and even though more than a dozen anti-Nazi groups had already announced their intention of holding a counterdemonstration.[6]

How does one justify such expansive freedom of expression? For some, the survival of democracy presupposes the possibility of a vigorous public debate, which can include "insults and even outrageous speech," particularly if that speech is heard in a public forum, "on a matter of public concern," and in a peaceful manner. For others, abusive or hurtful speech should not be permitted if it intentionally inflicts emotional distress on individuals, "on matters of purely private significance."[7] The courts have determined that the following are expressions of freedoms protected by the First Amendment: neo-Nazi marches; the public burning of the American flag; public displays by the Ku Klux Klan (including cross burning in front of the home of an African American); open distribution of racist films such as *The Birth of a Nation* by D. W. Griffith or "blasphemous" films such as *The Last Temptation of Christ* by Martin Scorsese; and, more recently, at the funeral of a soldier killed in Iraq, picketing by members of a small homophobic Baptist sect brandishing signs that read "Thank God for the death of this soldier!" and "Fags Will Make Nations Disappear!"[8] This symbolic profanation of the death of a hero was offensive in the extreme, but it too fell within the purview of legitimate free speech. According to the majority opinion written by Chief Justice Roberts in *Snyder v. Phelps*, "the government may not prohibit the expression of an idea simply because society finds the idea itself offensive or disagreeable."[9]

Let us imagine for a moment the same logic of free speech existing in France: Holocaust denial, the theatrical performances of the comedian Dieudonné, the racist and anti-Semitic quips of Jean-Marie Le Pen (the former head of the National Front), and provocative declarations such as "I am Kouachi" and "I feel like 'Charlie' Coulibaly" (expressing sympathy for terrorists) would all be permitted in the name of a robust public debate.[10] Yet such utterances are rarely tolerated for historical reasons, some of which are fully understandable, while others remain harder to justify. Needless to say, a country such as France that was occupied by Nazi Germany and whose collaboration facilitated the extermination of some seventy thousand Jews cannot permit displays of racial hatred such as those in Skokie, Illinois. But does a negationist discourse or a comedian's hate-driven performances merit censorship? Would it not be more effective to accept them in the name of a strong attachment to freedom of expression, just as in fact was done with the publication of the provocative and hurtful caricatures in *Charlie Hebdo*? Freedom of speech is not complete unless there is a free marketplace of ideas, from the most pleasant to the most repulsive. There can be no double standard whereby we (or the powers that be) accept what we find pleasant while systematically refusing what displeases us (or those in power).

This challenging level of freedom is not without limits, but those limits, to be fully acceptable, must be clearly defined and justified. In the United States, certain utterances are forbidden because they risk provoking a violent reaction and therefore represent a clear and present danger to the public order. The classic example is yelling "Fire!" in a crowded theater, an act that could provoke chaos or even the death of spectators crushed by a panic-stricken crowd.[11] The burning of a cross by the KKK can be punished as hate speech deemed unacceptable in a democratic society, but only if this symbolic act contains a "message of intimidation" destined to scare a potential victim and make that person fear the imminence of a violent attack. The same act is permitted if its purpose is only "ritualistic," for example as part of an initiation ceremony that does not target a particular person or group.[12]

In the final analysis, American case law does not seek to balance or reconcile the principles of freedom of expression and those of human dignity. Except in a few rare cases, the censorship of hate speech is considered incompatible with America's First Amendment, even if the speech stigmatizes a category of citizens defined by their race, religion, gender, or place of origin. The typical reflex of an American defender of free speech is to say, "Personally I hate what the racist says, but I will defend to the death that person's right to say what he or she wishes to say." Critics of the American legal tradition, sympathetic to a more European perspective, emphasize the need to ensure that the dignity of groups defamed by racist or injurious messages is upheld. Facilitating hate speech creates a hostile environment that harms the principles of justice and dignity that an orderly democratic society is supposed to guarantee for its citizens.[13]

GERMANY AND FRANCE

In Germany, the right of free speech is much more limited than in the United States. The very concept of a marketplace of ideas is foreign to the German legal culture. Freedom of expression is "subject to government control" and to higher principles related to "dignity, community, and support for democratic self-government." No individual, group, or party is authorized to advocate the "overthrow of the existing constitutional order."[14] When it comes to symbols, brandishing a swastika to express nostalgia for the Third Reich is considered hate speech, prohibited and punishable by law. The same goes for certain caricatures that defile a person's "honor," such as a cartoon published in the magazine *Konkret* that represented the Bavarian prime minister, Franz Joseph Strauss, as a pig humping other pigs.[15]

Still, these restrictive measures have not prevented the proliferation of offensive statements by members of far-right groups.

Prohibitions and acts of censorship often produce the opposite of the desired outcome: they offer publicity to extremists who violate censorship, they turn the perpetrators into martyrs or heroes of free speech, and they amplify their hate speech at little cost. By claiming to be breaking taboos, these individuals, like Dieudonné and his admirers in France, become celebrity victims of a political system deemed unjust and discriminatory.[16]

In France, freedom of expression is less protected than in the United States and less rigorously regulated than in Germany. The French position offers an intermediate stance with a partly free "marketplace of ideas." Article 11 of France's Declaration of the Rights of Man and the Citizen states, "The free communication of ideas and opinions is one of the most precious of the rights of man. Every citizen may, accordingly, speak, write, and print with freedom but shall be responsible for such abuses of this freedom as shall be defined by law." The 1881 law on freedom of the press, updated in 1972, 1990, and 2014, does impose certain limits on free speech. It prohibits insults, defamation, calumny, or speech in favor of war crimes or praising acts of terrorism. Also punishable is speech that calls for discrimination, hatred, or violence toward persons because of their national origin, racial identity, religious affiliation, sexual orientation, or physical disability.[17] Finally, French jurisprudence recognizes that satire, parody, and caricature entail excess, outrageous exaggeration, disrespect, and even insult; these are tolerated on condition that these excesses do not deliberately seek to offend a sexual, racial, or religious group taken "as a whole."

The Paris Court of Appeals engaged in some curious hair-splitting between the whole and its parts in its decision of March 12, 2008, confirming the ruling of a lower court about the Muhammad cartoons reprinted in the satirical weekly magazine *Charlie Hebdo*.[18] The court specified that publishing "these caricatures, which clearly target *a fraction and not the entire* community of Muslims," did not constitute a punishable offense. In this context at least, it was decided that the permissible limits of freedom of expression had not been exceeded.[19] But what happens if, short of the "entire" community of Muslims, a "majority" considers that they have been hurt by these images? Should the judge simply ignore the weight of public opinion? And, in an age when words and images reach every corner of the globe via the internet, should judges also ignore the opinion of Muslims living outside France? The upsetting caricature is tolerated if it targets a small group of fanatics but forbidden if the target is an entire religious community. But, then, isn't this injunction a subtle way of reintroducing the notion of blasphemy? And isn't it a little too easy to say, "This satire is not a punishable insult because it's only targeting a small minority of believers; namely the bigots, the intolerant, the fundamentalists, and the jihadists"? Should judges, who after all are not theologians, bear the responsibility of distinguishing between "fundamentalists," who can be insulted, from "moderates" who cannot be, on the grounds that the latter are supposedly better representatives of the Muslim community in its entirety?

If satire, irony, and caricature were given the status of fundamental freedoms, their expression, being by nature excessive, would necessarily have to be unlimited. Some object that "to blaspheme Islam is to humiliate society's weaker members"[20] and in particular the poorest immigrants from North Africa. Still others reply that it is perfectly acceptable to mock religion in a liberal democracy and that treating the religions of immigrants differently from those of the host country's residents would violate the principle of equality. As Flemming Rose, the former director of the Danish *Jyllands-Posten*, said, "If a believer demands that I, as a nonbeliever, observe his taboos in the public domain, he is not asking for my respect, but for my submission."[21] If one adheres to the remarks made by the French judges in the Muhammad-caricatures case, freedom of expression applies to all ideas, including those that "offend, shock or disturb, *as dictated by principles of pluralism and tolerance*" in a society characterized by the "coexistence of numerous beliefs . . . within the same nation."[22] Tolerance, in this view, is not just the matter of the coexistence of distinct faith communities within the same territorial space. Tolerance is an active principle founded on the shock of ideas. It is therefore not without risks, and therein lies its grandeur.

How far can one expand the limits of tolerance today? Ferocious criticism, wounding and insulting satire, and disturbing images are still allowed in many places. But unofficial censorship exists and functions as an insidious, hidden boundary. Intimidation breeds fear, and even the most sophisticated security measures cannot prevent self-censorship and abstention. Although it is difficult to admit, evidence suggests that "violence pays." We should not forget the long history of prohibitions and the criminalization of blasphemy. Voltaire, the author of *Fanaticism, or Mahomet the Prophet*, was forced into exile; Molière's *Tartuffe* was banned twice by religious zealots hostile to the court at Versailles, and today certain high-school teachers hesitate to assign the latter play to Muslim students claiming to be shocked by Molière's attacks against religion; Salman Rushdie's *Satanic Verses* provoked a death sentence against the author, who was forced to live in hiding for nine years; and twelve journalists and cartoonists at *Charlie Hebdo* were gunned down by two Islamic terrorists.

Armed fanaticism remains the basic obstacle to tolerance and freedom of expression. Today book and newspaper publishers, museum curators, and directors of art galleries all censor themselves out of fear of provoking reprisals by vigilante theologians. "Crush infamy!" ("*Écrasez l'infâme*") said Voltaire, but it is "infamy" that is trying to crush us with its Kalashnikovs and diktats. There are precious few brave souls in the publishing business today who have remained true to the example of Voltaire, Rushdie, or *Charlie Hebdo*. But the lessons learned from the millions who marched throughout France on January 11, 2015, to honor the victims of the *Charlie Hebdo* shooting shall not be forgotten. Demonstrating peacefully against violence and in defense of free speech is a way to refuse intimidation and to show that the right to mock, upset, or ridicule the most fanatical followers of any religion is entirely consistent with the fundamental liberties of a secular republic and its principle of separation between church and state.

EPILOGUE FOR THE
AMERICAN EDITION

Tolerance in the Age of Terrorism

S hould we tolerate the intolerant? Should we prohibit speech or art that is blatantly provocative or deeply offensive to some groups? Is censorship or self-censorship a valid strategy to calm the anger of true believers? I have tried to answer all of these questions in the last two chapters, but these debates rage on, fueled by a seemingly endless number of controversial incidents since the French publication of this book in 2016. I will briefly analyze two of these incidents. The first concerns the heated discussions about wearing burkinis on the beaches of southern France. The second examines the riots that took place in Charlottesville, Virginia, on August 12, 2017. These riots opposed neo-Nazis, KKK members, armed militia, and alt-right sympathizers against progressives, antifa members, and other groups opposed to white supremacists. Never had the question of the limits of tolerance been in clearer focus, yet those limits remain difficult to define.

THE LIMITS OF FREEDOM OF SPEECH IN GERMANY AND FRANCE

The violence of the Charlottesville demonstrations reveals yet again the differences that exist between the United States and Europe when it comes to freedom of speech and the right of peaceful assembly. From a European perspective, the authorization of a gathering that brought together neo-Nazis, armed militias, and members of the alt-right near the campus of Virginia's most prominent university (the University of Virginia) is incomprehensible. It is hard to imagine such a provocative demonstration being allowed by European municipal authorities—partly because the occurrence of violence was predictable but also because existing laws prohibit the public display of Nazi symbols and other public expressions of racial hatred. Free speech is more restricted and regulated in Europe than in the United States, in large part for a specific historical reason: the still fresh memories of the crimes committed by the Nazis and their enablers.

In Germany, giving the Nazi salute in the street, even in jest, is a crime punishable by up to three years in prison. In August 2017, two Chinese tourists were caught giving the Nazi salute in front of the Reichstag and were ordered to pay a fine of six hundred euros each. At first glance, German citizens seem to enjoy complete freedom of speech and assembly. Article 8 of the German Basic Law states that "All Germans shall have the right to assemble peacefully and unarmed without prior notification or permission." But this freedom of assembly is not without limits. It is directly restricted in the very next clause, which specifies that "outdoor assemblies . . . may be restricted by or pursuant to a law," particularly if these activities, as indicated in Article 9 of the Basic Law, "are directed against the constitutional order" of the nation. For example, a law adopted in 2005 concerning public assemblies forbids any gathering in a place likely to compromise the dignity of victims of the Third Reich. Thus, a march organized by members of the far-right National Democratic Party of Germany (NPD), which was to take place in Berlin on May 8, 2005, was forbidden because the planned route included passing in front of the Memorial to the Murdered Jews of Europe (the Holocaust Memorial). For similar reasons, demonstrations by the NPD or neo-Nazis at or near concentration camps have also been forbidden.[1] With its landmark Wunsiedel decision (November 4, 2009), the German Federal Constitutional Court determined that praising Nazism can no longer be tolerated because of "the extraordinary injustice and horror that National Socialist domination inflicted on Europe and much of the world."[2]

It should be kept in mind that in Germany, human dignity is a fundamental right protected by the first article of the country's Basic Law.[3] As a result, not all political opinions can be protected, particularly if they attack human dignity or, in certain cases, offend a foreign head of state. Satire, as we have seen in chapter 10, is much more restricted in Germany than in France. For example, President Erdogan of Turkey was allowed to sue the comedian Jan Böhmermann for defamation because of an "offensive" and "humiliating" poem that was read aloud on the ZDF television channel in March 2006. "Hyperbole in the name of art" is permitted, provided that it does not intentionally challenge the right to dignity.[4]

In France, freedom of speech and assembly is also regulated by a set of laws that establish clear-cut boundaries. The penal code prohibits the wearing or public display of a "uniform, sign, or emblem that recalls the uniforms, insignia, or emblems that were worn or exhibited by members of organizations classified as criminal" by the International Military Tribunal of Nuremburg.

Individuals who violate this prohibition may be fined and/or sentenced to twenty to 120 hours of public work. Any guns in the possession of such persons must be confiscated, and such persons are forbidden from owning any weapon for up to three years after the violation.⁵ Other laws, such as Article 24 of the Press Law of 1881, forbid all "provocations favoring discrimination, hatred, or violence" against persons because of their ethnic, national, or racial origins or their religious affiliation. The same law makes it a crime to question the existence of crimes against humanity, and this offense is punishable by imprisonment or fines of up to 45,000 euros.⁶ Given such a context, no French municipality would ever authorize marches openly manifesting racial hatred like those organized in Skokie and Charlottesville.

These restrictions and prohibitions in France and Germany are understandable in light of the weight accorded to history and to the suffering caused by the Nazis and their collaborators. Less comprehensible and less excusable were the rules forbidding the wearing of the burkini—a sort of beach burka—on the beaches of southern France.

BURKINIS AND THE LIMITS OF THE "BODY POLITIC"

The outlawing of the burkini—the modest swimwear revealing only the face, hands, and feet that was worn by a few Muslim women on three beaches of the French Riviera (Nice, Villeneuve-Loubet, and Cagnes-sur-Mer) in the summer of 2016—sent shockwaves across the country and abroad, especially after a photo showing four armed policemen forcing a woman to publicly remove her burkini on the Promenade des Anglais beach in Nice circulated on the internet. This incident triggered a mostly absurd and sterile debate in the media about the dignity of women and the place of religion in the public sphere. The burkini was invented in 2004 by an Australian fashion designer of Lebanese origin, Aheda Zanetti, to facilitate the athletic activities of Muslim women who were reluctant to abandon a cumbersome burka or a lighter, traditional hijab. Zanetti had designed the burkini "to make sure we blended in with the Australian lifestyle," and she tested the quality of her invention first in her own bathtub and then by swimming in a public pool for the first time in her life. The burkini, in her words, symbolized "leisure and happiness and fun and fitness." Objecting to such an outfit, in her view, could hardly be anything but regressive, since it would have the effect of saying to Muslim women, "get off the beach and back into your kitchens!"[7]

Although first conceived as an instrument of emancipation for Muslim women, the burkini was denounced by mayors on the Côte d'Azur as soon as it was introduced in France in 2016 as a tool of oppression, an attack on women's dignity and public order, and an ostentatious display of religious fanaticism. France seemed to be falling into a repressive spiral: after banning the hijab from public primary and secondary schools and the niqab from the public square, now there were ardent cries to ban the burkini from beaches; others called for an extension of the hijab ban to all French universities. There seemed to be no limit to the stigmatization of a minority religion noted for the modesty of its clothing. Thankfully, France's highest administrative court, the Conseil d'État, ruled in favor of the burkini and reaffirmed solid legal principles. The burkini, according to this court, neither threatened public order nor violated the principle of equality between men and women. The wearing of this bathing suit reflected the wearer's free choice and was not unique to Muslim women. Not all women wish to wear a bikini, and, as explained by Jean-Marc Sauvé, the vice president of the Conseil d'État, it was not the court's business to set forth official norms for the most appropriate bathing attire to be worn on public beaches: "What costume should it be? A one-piece? A two-piece? Look at the paintings by Eugène Boudin of bathers on the beaches of Normandy in the nineteenth century. They suggest that the norms in this area are subject to substantial change."[8] The burkini could not be prohibited on grounds of public order or on principles of equality and human dignity. The Conseil d'État had ruled in a much earlier case that the tossing of dwarfs in circuses or public festivals should be banned because it violated human dignity and public order. But, as Sauvé later explained, that was a limited and particularly striking case of humiliation unrelated to the burkini case. The decision in the burkini case, he further explained, is consistent with a long line of precedents based on three distinct constitutional principles: the "freedom to come and go" as one pleases in the public sphere, the "personal freedom to dress" as one wishes (except for nudity or indecency), and the "freedom to express one's religious beliefs."[9] The contested burkini bans were thus all annulled, lifted, or suspended by the court.[10]

THE EXTREME LIMITS OF TOLERANCE
FROM SKOKIE TO CHARLOTTESVILLE

The German and French examples show that, in liberal democracies, tolerance is not an absolute. Because of the weight of history and painful memories linked to particular circumstances, free speech operates within limits so as not to reopen old wounds. Solutions are rarely uniform or universal. In Great Britain, Italy, Germany, the United States, and Canada, wearing a headscarf is usually permitted, including in schools, whereas in France it is banned in all public schools from pre-K through high school, and the full-face veil is prohibited in all public places. Other countries, such as Belgium, Austria, and Denmark, have also passed laws banning the burka and the niqab.[11]

In the United States, in contrast, freedom of dress, but above all freedom of speech and freedom of assembly, are almost limitless, as was demonstrated by the ill-fated "Unite the Right" rally that took place in Charlottesville. This rally had been authorized by local authorities in accordance with a legal tradition dating back to the famous 1977 ruling permitting a neo-Nazi march in Skokie, Illinois, a suburb of Chicago (see chapter 10). In that case, neo-Nazis had been given permission to express their racial hatred while using all the signs and symbols of the Third Reich: the Hitler salute, swastikas, and torches symbolizing an Aryan brotherhood. It was clear that their march would upset the many Jews who lived in this suburb. A U.S. federal court nonetheless ruled that the march could not be prohibited because there was no evidence that it would provoke a situation of "imminent lawlessness."

Charlottesville municipal authorities believed, perhaps naively, that the planned rally would not be any riskier than the Skokie march.[12] Perhaps they were not sufficiently aware that the neo-Nazis would be accompanied by hundreds of demonstrators belonging to other white-supremacist organizations, including armed militias and members of the alt-right, and that such a provocation would inevitably be challenged by young progressives hostile to their message of hatred. What followed was a brutal confrontation that left many injured on both sides and caused the death of a young woman who was deliberately run over by a self-proclaimed alt-right demonstrator who rammed his car into a crowd of counterprotesters.

In a way, the Charlottesville riots marked the outer limits of free speech in the United States.[13] The old rule of thumb—allow anything and everything so long as there is no imminent and intentional violence—seemed no longer to work. It is obvious that with a large gathering of extremists and counterdemonstrators, violence was not just probable but almost certain—especially if the underequipped and understaffed local police force was unprepared or unwilling to separate the protesting belligerents. The very notion of "imminent lawlessness" is therefore unsatisfactory and should be reexamined by the judiciary. The key question is how to distinguish clearly between the probable and the imminent in a situation comparable to what took place in Charlottesville. How should the police defend public order? Can they truly anticipate the likely number of demonstrators when the internet's turbocharged social networks can rapidly mobilize thousands of protesters from across the country? The very notion of "imminent lawlessness" comes in many different forms, and the hateful speeches of U.S. white supremacists and neo-Nazis are basically the same as the hate-filled preaching of British, Belgian, French, or Spanish radical imams who incite their followers to commit acts of terrorism. How should we deal with such manifestations of hatred? Anthony Lewis in his book *Freedom for the Thought That We Hate* gives the best answer: "Perhaps judges, and the rest of us, will be more on guard now for the rare act of expression—not the burning of flags nor the racist slang of an undergraduate—that is genuinely dangerous. I think we should be able to punish speech that urges terrorist violence to an audience, some of whose members are ready to act on the urging. That is imminent enough."[14]

In the end, the question is: How can we suppress violent discourse without violating a person's First Amendment rights? And how can we be sure of the imminence or the existence of a causal relationship between an act of violence and a sermon, speech, video, or tweet calling for violence? As a general matter, words are not actions, and the only remedy available to prevent an act of terrorism is heightened police surveillance, better protection of likely targets, and the mobilization of equipment and personnel to prevent the rioting of angry crowds. There is, however, a red line: A speech or a sermon that advocates violence and is likely to lead to violence—based on credible evidence—should be prohibited. Free speech, when pushed to its limits, is dangerous and can have unpredictable, sometimes violent, consequences. Such a risk is inherent to a liberal political order and should be accepted in spite of its consequences, to better defend the inalienable rights of free speech and freedom of assembly, without which there can be no democracy and no genuine tolerance.

NOTES

NEW INTRODUCTION FOR THE
AMERICAN EDITION

1. The English language is richer than French in this respect because it has two distinct terms to describe the same concept: "toleration" and "tolerance." *Toleration* implies the notion of a constraint to be put up with or weight to be borne or the acceptance of an opinion or behavior that is not really approved of. *Tolerance* more often designates the absence of prejudice, open-mindedness, and the rejection of all dogmatism. See the articles "Toleration" and "Tolerance" in the *Oxford English Dictionary*, 2nd ed., vol. 18 (Oxford: Clarendon, 1989).

2. See the article "Tolérance" in the *Grand Robert de la langue française*, which refers to the promulgation of the Edict of Nantes and states that "civil tolerance" is "the freedom accorded by the reigning power to practice a religion other than the official one." Paradoxically, the Edict of Nantes, which has been called the "Edict of Tolerance," does not itself use the term "tolerance"—presumably, it has been suggested, because the term carried a negative connotation at the time.

3. Voltaire, letter 6, "On the Presbyterians," in *Letters Concerning the English Nation*, as cited in Desmond M. Clarke, introduction to Voltaire, *Treatise on Toleration* (first published as *Traité sur la tolérance à l'occasion de la mort de Jean Calas*, 1763), ed. and trans. D. M. Clarke (London: Penguin, 2016), xxii.

4. Montesquieu, lettre 85, in *Lettres Persanes* (1721), ed. Laurent Versini (Paris: Garnier Flammarion, 2016), 207.

5. Immanuel Kant, "An Answer to the Question: What Is Enlighten-ment?" (1784), in *Kant's Political Writings*, ed. Hans Reiss (Cambridge: Cambridge University Press, 1971), 58–59.

6. Immanuel Kant, "On the Common Saying: 'This May Be True in The-ory, but It Does Not Apply in Practice'" (1793), in *Kant's Political Writ-ings*, 85. For further details on Kant's complex concept of tolerance, see Rainer Forst, *Toleration in Conflict: Past and Present* (Cambridge: Cam-bridge University Press, 2016), 266–69, 324–29, 434–36 (first published as *Toleranz im Konflikt*, 2003). Kant's tolerance, according to Forst, con-stituted "an essential virtue of democracy" (435).

7. Mirabeau's declaration of August 22, 1789, to the National Assembly is quoted in the article "Tolérance," in Emile Littré, *Dictionnaire de la langue française* (Paris: Gallimard/Hachette, 1958), 7:1026.

8. As Washington argued, "It is now no more that toleration is spoken of, as if it was by the indulgence of one class of people, that another enjoyed the exercise of their inherent natural rights." See his Letter to the Hebrew Congregation in Newport, Rhode Island, August 18, 1790, https://founders.achives.gov/documents/Washington/05-06-02-0135.

9. Thomas Paine, *The Rights of Man* (1791–1792), in *The Thomas Paine Reader*, ed. Michael Foot and Isaac Kramnick (Harmondsworth: Pen-guin, 1987), 231.

10. See Peter Jones, *Essays on Toleration* (London: ECPR Press/Rowman and Littlefield, 2018); Bhikhu Parekh, *Rethinking Multiculturalism: Cultural Diversity and Political Theory* (Cambridge, MA: Harvard University Press, 2000); Michael Walzer, *On Toleration* (New Haven, CT: Yale University Press, 1997); Will Kymlicka, *Multicultural Citi-zenship* (Oxford: Clarendon, 1995); Denis Lacorne, *La crise de l'identité américaine. Du melting-pot au multiculturalisme* (Paris: Gallimard, 2003); and see chapter 7, "Multicultural Tolerance."

11. Wendy Brown, *Regulating Aversion: Toleration in the Age of Identity and Empire* (Princeton, NJ: Princeton University Press, 2006), 10, 78–79.

12. Brown, *Regulating Aversion*, 188–90.

13. Brown, *Regulating Aversion*, 6–8.

14. This is what the German philosopher Rainer Forst, in a rich dialogue with Wendy Brown, describes as the "respect conception" of tolerance. My argument here is derived from this particular conception. See Wendy Brown and Rainer Forst, *The Power of Tolerance: A Debate*, ed. Luca Di Blasi and Christoph F. E. Holzhey (New York: Columbia

University Press, 2014), 25, 78–85. For further details on different conceptions of tolerance, see Forst, *Toleration in Conflict*, 26–32.

15. On this question, see chapter 9, "New Restrictions, New Forms of Tolerance."

16. What truly matters, as argued by Cécile Laborde in a recent and important book, is the "ethical salience" of religion and culture: "Individuals act with integrity when they are faithful to relationships of community—be they cultural, linguistic, or religious—that are of central importance to their lives." *Liberalism's Religion* (Cambridge, MA: Harvard University Press, 2017), 224.

17. On the notion of "regimes of toleration," see Walzer, *On Toleration*, 14–36.

18. On the methodological advantage of a "long" historical perspective, see David Armitage and Jo Guldi, "Le retour de la longue durée: une perspective anglo-américaine," *Annales, Histoire, Sciences Sociales* 2 (2015): 289–318.

19. On the lack of a "linear path" in the history of tolerance, see Alexandra Walsham, *Charitable Hatred: Tolerance and Intolerance in England, 1500–1700* (Manchester: Manchester University Press, 2006), 287.

20. See Sudipta Kaviraj, "Modernity, State, and Toleration in Indian History," in *Boundaries of Toleration*, ed. Alfred Stepan and Charles Taylor (New York: Columbia University Press, 2014), 233–66; and Karen Barkey, "Empire and Toleration: A Comparative Sociology of Toleration within Empire," in *Boundaries of Toleration*, 203–232.

21. For further details, see chapter 4, "Tolerance in the Ottoman Empire."

22. See Stephen Holmes, "John Rawls and the Limits of Tolerance," *New Republic*, October 11, 1983, 39–47; and Perez Zagorin, *How the Idea of Religious Tolerance Came to the West* (Princeton, NJ: Princeton University Press, 2003), 11.

23. Susan Mendus, "The Changing Face of Toleration," January 26, 2014, *Reset DOC* (Dialogues on Civilizations), https://www.resetdoc.org /story/the-changing-face-of-toleration/.

24. See chapter 6, "On Blasphemy."

I. TOLERANCE ACCORDING TO JOHN LOCKE

1. Pierre Du Chastel, "Deux sermons funêbres prononcez es obsèques de François Ier de ce nom" (1543), in Malcolm C. Smith, "Early French

Advocates of Religious Freedom," *Sixteenth Century Journal* 25 (1994): 1, 32–35.

2. "Lettre du Roy à Monsieur de Lisle son Ambassadeur à Rome," in *Instructions et letter des Rois très-chrétiens, et de leurs ambassadeurs, et autres actes concernant le concile de Trente* (1561), 4th ed. (Paris, 1564), 92.

3. Michel de L'Hospital, "Déclaration aux États généraux d'Orléans," December 1560; cited in Nicolas Le Roux, *Les guerres de religion, 1559–1629* (Paris: Belin, 2009), 48.

4. Joseph Lecler, *Histoire de la tolérance au siècle de la Réforme* (1955; Paris: Albin Michel, 1994), 440.

5. Étienne Pasquier, *Exhortation aux princes et seigneurs du Conseil privé du Roy, pour obvier aux séditions qui occultement semblent nous menacer pour le faict de la Religion* (1761), cited in Le Roux, *Les guerres de religion*, 441. Despite what Lecler says, Pasquier is in fact the author of the *Exhortation*. See Smith, "Early French Advocates of Religious Freedom," 37–38.

6. Lecler, *Histoire de la tolérance au siècle de la Réforme*, 441.

7. Sebastian Castellio, *Contra libellum Calvini* (1554); cited in Lecler, *Histoire de la tolérance au siècle de la Réforme*, 338.

8. Castellio, *Contra libellum Calvini*, 334.

9. Sebastian Castellio, *Traité des hérétiques*; cited in Lecler, *Histoire de la tolérance au siècle de la Réforme*, 325. On this ideal of tolerance, see Perez Zagorin, *How the Idea of Religious Tolerance Came to the West* (Princeton, NJ: Princeton University Press, 2003), 93–144.

10. See John Marshall, *John Locke: Resistance, Religion, and Responsibility* (Cambridge: Cambridge University Press, 1994), 319.

11. Roger Woolhouse, *Locke: A Biography* (Cambridge: Cambridge University Press, 2009), 119–52, 197–263.

12. Marshall, *John Locke*, 329–35. On the subversive activities of Locke and his employer Shaftesbury, see Richard Ashcraft, *Revolutionary Politics and Locke's Two Treatises of Government* (Princeton, NJ: Princeton University Press, 1986).

13. See Marshall, *John Locke*, 358.

14. The death sentence pronounced against Michel Servet, who was burned alive for heresy on the Champel hill in Geneva in 1553, had been well documented in the writings of Sebastian Castellio, cited earlier.

15. John Locke, *A Letter Concerning Toleration and Other Writings* (1686), ed. Mark Goldie (Indianapolis, IN: Liberty Fund, 2010), 8.

16. Locke, *A Letter Concerning Toleration*, 13, 9.

17. Locke, *A Letter Concerning Toleration*, 10

18. Locke, *A Letter Concerning Toleration*, 21.

19. Locke, *A Letter Concerning Toleration*, 21.

20. Locke, *A Letter Concerning Toleration*, 15, 12.

21. Locke, *A Letter Concerning Toleration*, 12.

22. Locke, *A Letter Concerning Toleration*, 12, 14.

23. Locke, *A Letter Concerning Toleration*, 13.

24. John Locke, *An Essay Concerning Toleration* (1667), in *A Letter Concerning Toleration and Other Writings*, ed. Goldie, 108, 109.

25. For example, Pierre Bayle in his famous *Commentaire philosophique sur ces paroles de Jésus-Christ "Contrains-les d'entrer"* (1686). See Jean-Michel Gros, "Bayle: de la tolérance à la liberté de conscience," in *Les fondements philosophiques de la tolérance*, ed. Yves Charles Zarka, Franck Lessay, and John Rogers (Paris: PUF, 2002), 1:308–10.

26. Gros, "Bayle," 308.

27. See the first edition of the *Dictionnaire de l'Académie française* (1694), quoted in Élisabeth Labrousse, "Une foi, une loi, un roi?" in *La révocation de l'édit de Nantes* (Geneva: Labor et Fides, 1985), 95n1.

28. For Locke, faith is a matter of reason, not enthusiasm. It derives from a critical reading of the Scriptures, a critical appraisal of historical testimonies, and a search for convincing proof. See the chapter "The Theology of a Reasonable Man, 1667–1683," in Marshall, *John Locke*, 119–154.

29. Locke, *A Letter Concerning Toleration*, 20.

30. Locke, *A Letter Concerning Toleration*, 59.

31. In England, freedom of worship was only accorded to dissenters with the passage of the Toleration Act of 1689. That law still excluded Unitarians, who do not believe in the Trinity, as well as Catholics, Jews, and atheists. The first synagogues of the modern era were not authorized in the Dutch Republic until 1639, with the so-called Portuguese synagogue, and in Great Britain starting in 1690 under ~~George~~ III.   *William*

32. Locke, *A Letter Concerning Toleration*, 39. Locke is alluding here to Michel Servet's execution for idolatry and blasphemy in Geneva in 1553.

33. Locke, *A Letter Concerning Toleration*, 41.

34. Thomas Hobbes, *Leviathan* (1651), ed. C. B. Macpherson (Harmondsworth: Penguin, 1975), book 2, chap. 31.

35. Locke, *A Letter Concerning Toleration*, 55, 60.

36. Pierre Bayle, *Commentaire philosophique sur ces paroles de Jésus-Christ, "Contrains-les d'entrer"* (1686); reprinted in Pierre Bayle, *De la tolérance*, ed. Jean-Michel Gros (Paris: Presses-Pocket, 1992), 257. See also Hubert Bost, *Pierre Bayle* (Paris: Fayard, 2006), 295–96.

37. Bayle, *Commentaire philosophique*, 257.

38. Locke, *An Essay Concerning Toleration*, 107, 109.

39. Locke, *An Essay Concerning Toleration*, 117.

40. Locke, *An Essay Concerning Toleration*, 123.

41. Locke, *An Essay Concerning Toleration*, 123, 124.

42. Locke, *An Essay Concerning Toleration*, 123.

43. See Marshall, *John Locke*, 53.

44. Locke, *A Letter Concerning Toleration*, 50–51.

45. Locke, *A Letter Concerning Toleration*, 51.

46. Locke, *A Letter Concerning Toleration*, 44.

47. Thomas Jefferson, *Notes on the State of Virginia* (New York: Harper and Row, 1964), 152.

48. Locke, *A Letter Concerning Toleration*, 23.

49. Locke, *An Essay Concerning Toleration*, 146.

50. John Locke, "The Constitutions of Carolina," in *A Letter Concerning Toleration and Other Writings*, ed. Goldie, 146–148.

51. Locke, *A Letter Concerning Toleration*, 39.

52. Locke, *A Letter Concerning Toleration*, 40.

53. Locke, *A Letter Concerning Toleration*, 52–53.

54. Pierre Bayle, "L'athéisme ne conduit pas nécessairement à la corruption des mœurs," in *Pensées diverses sur la comète*, in Pierre Bayle, *Pensées sur l'athéisme*, ed. Julie Boch (Paris: Desjonquères, 2004), 78ff.

55. Locke, *A Letter Concerning Toleration*, 53.

56. Pierre Bayle, *Réponse aux questions d'un provincial*, quoted in Jean-Michel Gros, introduction to Pierre Bayle, *De la tolérance*, 34.

57. See Jean-Fabien Spitz's comment, in J. Locke, *Lettre sur la tolérance et autres textes* (Paris: Garnier-Flammarion, 1992), ed. Spitz, 236n86; and, more generally, J.-M. Gros, introduction to Pierre Bayle, *De la tolérance*, 32–35; as well as John Marshall, *John Locke: Toleration and Early Enlightenment Culture* (Cambridge: Cambridge University Press, 2006), 694–700.

58. See the article "Atheist, Atheism," in Voltaire, *The Philosophical Dictionary* (1764–1770; London: Wynne and Scholey, 1802), 27–28, 24, 25.

59. Voltaire, "Atheist, Atheism," 25.

60. René Pomeau, *La religion de Voltaire* (Paris: Nizet, 1956), 196.

2. VOLTAIRE AND MODERN TOLERANCE

1. Voltaire, *The Henriade: An Epic Poem, in Ten Cantos. Translated from the French of Voltaire, Into English* . . . (n.p., Burton and Co., 1797), canto 2 (verses 291–94), 45.

2. Voltaire, *The Henriade*, canto 2 (verses 306–10), 46. On the massacre, see the excellent studies by Arlette Jouanna, *La Saint-Barthélemy: les mystères d'un crime d'état* (Paris: Gallimard, 2007); Nicolas Le Roux, *Les guerres de religion, 1559–1629* (Paris: Belin, 2009), 115–73, 517–22; and Denis Crouzet, *La nuit de la Saint Barthélemy: un rêve perdu de la Renaissance* (Paris: Hachette Pluriel, 2012).

3. Voltaire, "Histoire abrégée des événements sur lesquels est fondée la fable du poème de *La Henriade*," in *Les œuvres complètes de Voltaire/The Complete Works of Voltaire* (Geneva: Institut et Musée Voltaire, 1970), 2:302.

4. Voltaire, *Essai sur les mœurs et l'esprit des nations* (1756), in *Les œuvres complètes de Voltaire*, ed. Bruno Bernard, John Renwick, Nicholas Cronk, and Janet Godden (Oxford: Voltaire Foundation, 1970–2016), vols. 22–27.

5. Voltaire, *Essai sur les mœurs*, tome VI, 26A:32. Socinianism is the religious doctrine of Lelio Sozzini (Siena, 1525–Zurich, 1562). It rejects the dogma of the Trinity and the divinity of Christ. Socin is one of the founders of Unitarianism.

6. Voltaire, "Remarques pour servir de supplément à *l'Essai sur les mœurs*," in *Textes annexes*, tome IX of *Essai sur les mœurs*, 27:57.

7. Ernest Renan, "What Is a Nation?" March 11, 1882, lecture delivered at the Sorbonne. http://web.archive.org/web/20110827065548http://www.cooper.edu/humanities/core/hss3/e_renan.html.

8. Voltaire, *Treatise on Toleration*, ed. and trans. Desmond M. Clarke (London: Penguin, 2016), 34. First published in French as *Traité sur la tolérance. À l'occasion de la mort de Jean Calas* (1763).

9. Voltaire, "Fifth Letter on the Anglican Religion," in *Philosophical Letters; or, Letters Regarding the English Nation* (1734), ed. John Leigh, trans. Prudence L. Steiner (Indianapolis, IN: Hackett, 2007), 15.

10. Voltaire, "Sixth Letter on the Presbyterians," in *Philosophical Letters*, 20.

11. Voltaire, "Seventh Letter on the Socinians, or Arians, or Antitrinitarians," in *Philosophical Letters*, 21–22. In fact, the *Act of Toleration* passed in 1689 under William and Mary did not extend to Catholics or antitrinitarians.

12. Voltaire, "Sixth Letter on the Presbyterians," 19.

13. Voltaire, "Fifth Letter on the Anglican Religion," in *Philosophical Letters*, 15. In fact Voltaire exaggerates. It wasn't so much conversion that took place but merely a formal pledge of allegiance under oath to the Anglican Church.

14. Voltaire, "An Additional Chapter," in *Treatise on Toleration*, 137. As a result of this generous action, King Louis XV was nicknamed "Louis le Bien-Aimé" (Louis the Beloved).

15. Voltaire, *Treatise on Toleration*, chap. 4, "Is Toleration Dangerous and Which Nations Permit It?" 25.

16. Voltaire, *Treatise on Toleration*, 25. The explorer Paul Ricaut, the author of *The Present State of the Ottoman Empire* (1668), had obviously been a source for Voltaire. The Gebers were followers of Zoroaster; the Banians were Hindus.

17. Voltaire, *Treatise on Toleration*, 21–22.

18. Voltaire, *Treatise on Toleration*, 22.

19. Voltaire, *Treatise on Toleration*, 24.

20. Voltaire, *Treatise on Toleration*, 24. The Pretender, Charles Edward Stuart, nicknamed "Bonnie Prince Charlie" (1720–1788), was the grandson of James II (1633–1701).

21. Protestants' access to a civil status allowed them to finally validate their marriages, register the birth of their children, and declare the death of family members. It now sufficed to appear before a royal judge or civil officer to make a declaration of marriage.

22. Montesquieu, "Of Laws in Relation to Commerce, Considered in Its Nature and Distinctions," in *The Spirit of Laws*, translated from the French, with corrections and additions communicated by the Author (London: John Nourse and P. Vaillant, 1750), vol. II, Book XX, chap. I, 1.

23. Voltaire, "Sixth Letter on the Presbyterians," 20; Voltaire, "Tolérance: Toleration," in *Philosophical Dictionary*, ed. and trans. Theodore Besterman

(London: Penguin, 2004), 388. This entry was written by Voltaire in 1765 for the second edition of the *Dictionary*.

24. Voltaire, "Sixth Letter on the Presbyterians," 20.

25. Section 1 of the entry "Tolerance," in Voltaire, *Questions sur l'Encyclopédie par des amateurs*, ed. Nicholas Cronk and Christiane Mervand, tome VIII in *Les œuvres complètes de Voltaire*, 43:374. Benjamin Franklin was highly skeptical of Voltaire's description of the tolerant regimes of North America. He thus wrote from Pennsylvania to his friend Henry Bouquet on September 30, 1764: "I will give you a passage of it, which being read here at a time when we are torn to pieces by factions religious and civil, shows us that while we sit for our picture to that able painter, tis no small advantage to us, that he views us at a favourable distance." Cited in Voltaire, "Tolerance," n4.

26. Voltaire, "Sixth Letter on the Presbyterians," 20.

27. James Madison, "Federalist, no. 51," in James Madison, Alexander Hamilton, and John Jay, *The Federalist Papers* (1788), ed. Isaac Kramnick (Harmondsworth: Penguin, 1987), 321. For further discussion of churches and factions in the *Federalist Papers*, see Denis Lacorne, *Religion in America: A Political History*, pbk. ed. (New York: Columbia University Press, 2014), 19–20.

28. Voltaire, "Prêtre: Priest," in *Philosophical Dictionary*, 346. The exact sources are, respectively, Matthew 22:21, Mark 9:33, and John 23:36.

29. Voltaire, "Remarques pour servir de supplément à *l'Essai sur les mœurs*," 22.

30. Voltaire, "Prêtre: Priest," 346–47. Voltaire observes that "the Turks are wise in this respect. It is true that they journey to Mecca; but they do not allow the sherif of Mecca to excommunicate the sultan. They do not go to Mecca to buy permission not to observe *ramadan*.... They do not pay the last year of their revenues to the sherif" (347).

31. John Locke, *A Letter Concerning Toleration* (1689), in *A Letter Concerning Toleration and Other Writings*, ed. Mark Goldie (Indianapolis, IN: Liberty Fund, 2010), 24.

32. Voltaire, "Prêtre: Priest," 346.

33. Voltaire, "Eighth Question," in "Religion" (1765), in *Philosophical Dictionary*, 359.

34. Voltaire, "Eighth Question," 359.

35. Voltaire, "Eighth Question," 359.

36. Voltaire, "Fourth Letter on the Quakers," in *Philosophical Letters*, 12.

37. Voltaire, "Fourth Letter on the Quakers," 14.

38. Voltaire, "Fourth Letter on the Quakers," 14.

3. TOLERANCE IN AMERICA

1. Abbé Raynal, *A Philosophical and Political History of the Settlements and Trade of the Europeans in the East and West Indies*, 8 vols., trans. J. O. Justamond (London: W. Strahan and T. Cadell, 1783). This is a translation of the revised *Histoire philosophique et politique des établissements et du commerce des Européens dans les deux Indes*, 10 vols., followed by an "Atlas géographique" (Geneva: Jean Léonard Pellet, 1781). I will refer to this French edition (often referred to as *L'histoire des deux Indes*) for passages that were not included in the English edition.

2. See the contribution of Hans Jürgen Lüsebrink in the general introduction to the critical edition of the *Histoire philosophique et politique des établissements et du commerce des Européens dans les deux Indes*, ed. Anthony Strugnell et al. (Ferney-Voltaire: Centre international d'étude du XVIIIe siècle, 2010), 1:xlv, xlviii–li.

3. Denis Diderot, *Lettre apologétique de l'abbé Raynal à M. Grimm*; quoted in Michel Delon, "L'appel au lecteur dans l'Histoire des deux Indes," in *Lectures de Raynal: L'histoire des deux Indes en Europe et en Amérique au XVIIIe siècle*, ed. Hans Jürgen Lüsebrink and Manfred Tietz (Oxford: The Voltaire Foundation, 1991), 53.

4. On Voltaire's method and Raynal's imitation of it, see J. G. A. Pocock, *Barbarism and Religion*, vol. 2, *Narratives of Civil Government* (Cambridge: Cambridge University Press 1999), 72–136.

5. Raynal, *Philosophical and Political History*, vol. 8, book 19, 14.

6. Raynal, *Philosophical and Political History*, 14.

7. Raynal, *Philosophical and Political History*, 23.

8. Raynal, *Philosophical and Political History*, 23.

9. Raynal, *Philosophical and Political History*, 23.

10. Raynal, *Philosophical and Political History*, vol. 7, book 17, 231.

11. Raynal, *Philosophical and Political History*, 233.

12. Raynal, *Philosophical and Political History*, 236.

13. On Lovewell's Indian hunts and his triumphant return to Boston with scalps, for which he was paid one hundred pounds per scalp by city officials, see "Lovewell's Fight," in *Maine Stories*, http://www.mainestory

.info/maine-stories/lovewells-fight.html. Lovewell died the following year in the battle of Pequawket, present-day Fryeburg, Maine, which pitted his militia against Abenakis and Penobscots.

14. Raynal, *Philosophical and Political History*, vol. 7, book 17, 244.

15. Raynal, *Histoire philosophique et politique des établissements et du commerce des Européens dans les deux Indes*, vol. 8, book 17, 337. This episode is not related in the English edition.

16. Raynal, *Histoire philosophique et politique*, 338.

17. Raynal, *Histoire philosophique et politique*, 338, 339.

18. Raynal, *Histoire philosophique et politique*, 339.

19. The *Fundamental Constitutions of Carolina* were adopted in 1669. Locke had been hired to write these texts by Anthony Ashley Cooper (one of the lord proprietors of the colony). See David Armitage, "John Locke, Carolina, and the Two Treatises on Government," *Political Theory* 32, no. 5 (2004): 602–27.

20. Raynal, *Philosophical and Political History*, vol. 7, book 18, 343.

21. Raynal, *Philosophical and Political History*, 345. On Locke's opposition to any official church in the Carolinas, see John Marshall, *John Locke: Resistance, Religion, and Responsibility* (Cambridge: Cambridge University Press, 1994), 74n1.

22. Raynal, *Philosophical and Political History*, vol. 7, book 18, 345.

23. Raynal, *Philosophical and Political History*, 357.

24. Voltaire, "Fourth Letter on the Quakers," in *Philosophical Letters*, ed. John Leigh (Indianapolis, IN: Hackett, 2007), 13.

25. Voltaire, "Fourth Letter on the Quakers," 289–90.

26. Voltaire, "Fourth Letter on the Quakers," 298.

27. See Denis Lacorne, *Religion in America*, 2nd ed. (New York: Columbia University Press, 2014), 2–12.

28. Raynal, *Philosophical and Political History*, vol. 8, book 19, 13.

29. Raynal, *Philosophical and Political History*, 12.

30. For Raynal, tolerance's progress was irreversible: "Industry and the means of information have now prevailed among the nations . . . : the human mind is undeceived with regard to its former superstitions. . . . Every thing has concurred, for these two last centuries, to extinguish that furious zeal which ravaged the globe." *Philosophical and Political History*, 12.

31. The colony's first official name was "The Providence Plantations in the Narragansett Bay." It would later be officially designated as "Rhode

Island and Providence Plantations." On the revolutionary character of Roger Williams's message in the seventeenth century, see Perez Zagorin, *How the Idea of Religious Tolerance Came to the West* (Princeton, NJ: Princeton University Press, 2003), 196–208; and, more recently, John M. Barry, *Roger Williams and the Creation of the American Soul: Church, State, and the Birth of Liberty* (New York: Viking, 2012).

32. Roger Williams, *The Bloudy Tenent of Persecution, for cause of Conscience, discussed, in a Conference between Truth and Peace* (1644); quoted in Joseph Lecler, *Histoire de la tolérance au siècle de la Réforme* (1955; Paris: Albin Michel, 1994), 801.

33. Williams, *The Bloudy Tenent*, 800. This is an allusion to Hebrews 4:12, "For the word of God is quick and powerful, sharper than any two-edged sword" (King James Bible).

34. Williams, *The Bloudy Tenent*; quoted in Barry, *Roger Williams and the Creation of the American Soul*, 336.

35. Lecler, *Histoire de la tolérance*, 800. Williams is the first to use the metaphor of a "wall of separation" between the garden of the church and the wilderness of the world. On this topic, see Lacorne, *Religion in America*, 147–52.

36. Williams, *The Bloudy Tenent*; quoted in Lecler, *Histoire de la tolérance*, 795–96.

37. Quoted in Barry, *Roger Williams and the Creation of the American Soul*, 321. Williams could have added Catholics to this list because he included them in his regime of tolerance, along with Jews and Pagans, despite his strong hostility toward all manifestations of "Papism." Lecler, *Histoire de la tolérance*, 801.

38. This according to a Dutch Reformed Church minister preaching in New England and quoted in Barry, *Roger Williams and the Creation of the American Soul*, 254.

39. See Evan Haefeli's remarkable book *New Netherland and the Dutch Origins of American Religious Liberty* (Philadelphia: University of Pennsylvania Press, 2016).

40. Haefeli, *New Netherland*, 171.

41. The Flushing Remonstrance, quoted in Haefeli, *New Netherland*, 177.

42. Haefeli, *New Netherland*, 171.

43. With the Treaty of Breda signed at the end of the Second Anglo-Dutch War (1665–1667), the Dutch renounced all claims to New Netherland,

but they obtained control of Surinam as compensation. For a brief period in 1673, the Dutch regained possession of New York, which they then returned to the British in February 1674.

44. Haefeli, *New Netherland*, 256.

45. See the article "Church," section 5, *Duke of York Laws* (1665–1775), https://www.nycourts.gov/history/legal-history-new-york/documents/charters-duke-transcript.pdf.

46. A "proprietary colony" granted by the Duke of York to two friends, Sir George Carteret and John Berkeley.

47. Haefeli, *New Netherland*, 260–61.

48. "Concessions and Agreements of the Lords Proprietors [Sir George Carteret and John Berkeley] of the Province of New Jersey," 1665; quoted in Haefeli, *New Netherland*, 263. As Haefeli correctly points out: "Colonial America was not a place where new ideas about religion freedom emerged. Rather it was a place where, occasionally, European dreams of religious toleration could find a home unavailable in Europe" (285).

49. Constitution of Massachusetts, 1780, part 1, articles 3 and 2, respectively.

50. See article XVI of the Virginia Declaration of Rights (1776).

51. 10,929 signatures were collected against the General Assessment bill submitted to the Virginia General Assembly in October 1784 and backed by supporters of the Episcopal Church.

52. James Madison, "Memorial and Remonstrance Against Religious Assessments," June 20, 1785, in National Archives, *Founders Online*, https://founders.archives.gov/documents/Madison/01-08-02-0163. On the political and religious debates at that time, see Noah Feldman, *Divided by God* (New York: Farrar, Straus and Giroux, 2005), 27–46; and Lacorne, *Religion in America*, 150–52.

53. J. Madison, "Memorial and Remonstrance."

54. Thomas Jefferson, "A Bill for Establishing Religious Freedom," June 18, 1779, in National Archives, *Founders Online*, https://founders.archives.gov/documents/jefferson/01-02-02-0123-0004-0082. This bill was adopted by the Virginia State Assembly on January 16, 1786.

55. See the article "États-Unis," in the *Encyclopédie méthodique. Économie politique et diplomatique sur la tolérance*, ed. J. N. Démeunier (Paris: Panckoucke, 1786), 2:400.

56. James Madison, cited in the *Gazette of the United States*, June 10, 1789, in *Creating the Bill of Rights*, ed. Helen E. Veit et al. (Baltimore, MD: Johns

Hopkins University Press, 1991), 66. Madison added, "those choicest flowers in the prerogatives of the people, are not guarded by the British Constitution: With respect to these, apprehensions had been entertained of their insecurity under the new Constitution; a bill of rights therefore, to quiet the minds of people upon these points, may be salutary" (67). For further details, see Jack Rakove, *James Madison and the Creation of the American Republic*, 3rd ed. (Glenview, IL: Pearson, 2006).

57. Speech of Rabaut Saint-Étienne to the Assemblée nationale regarding the discussion of the *Déclaration des droits de l'homme*, on the motion of M. le comte de Castellane: "No man should be bothered for his religious opinions, nor troubled in the exercise of his religious beliefs," August 23, 1789; quoted at length in Michel Kneubühler, ed., *De la tolérance aux droits de l'homme. Écrits sur la liberté de conscience, des guerres de religion à la Révolution française* (Paris: Paroles d'Aube, 1998), 126.

58. "Letter of August 17, 1790, to the Hebrew Congregation of Newport," quoted in Howard M. Sachar, *A History of the Jews in America* (New York: Vintage, 1992), 26. On this letter, see also Martha C. Nussbaum, *The New Religious Intolerance* (Cambridge, MA: Harvard University Press, 2012), 70–71.

59. The American "civil code," which has never existed, is Rabaut Saint-Étienne's way of alluding to the federal Constitution of 1787, to the declarations of rights of the American states most favorable to religious liberties, and, probably, to the proposal of a Bill of Rights addressed to the House of Representatives by James Madison on June 8, 1789. On this proposal, see "James Madison Introduces the Bill of Rights," National Constitution Center, June 8, 2018, https://constitutioncenter.org/blog/on-this-day-james-madison-introduces-the-bill-of-rights.

4. TOLERANCE IN THE OTTOMAN EMPIRE

1. Paul Veyne, *Quand notre monde est devenu chrétien (312–394)* (Paris: Albin Michel, 2007), 24–31, 193–94.

2. Montesquieu (Charles de Secondat, baron de Montesquieu), *The Spirit of the Laws*, ed. Anne M. Cohler, Basia C. Miller, and Harold S.

Stone (Cambridge: Cambridge University Press, 2010), part 2, book 11, chap. 6, 157.

3. Voltaire, "The Sermon of Rabbi Akib, given in Smyrna, on November 20, 1761 (translated from the Hebrew)," in *Voltaire's Revolution: Writings from His Campaign to Free Laws from Religion*, ed. and trans. G. K. Noyer (Amherst, MA: Prometheus, 2015), 112.

4. I am borrowing this expression from Karen Barkey, "Empire and Toleration: A Comparative Sociology of Toleration Within Empire," in *Boundaries of Toleration*, ed. Alfred Stepan and Charles Taylor (New York: Columbia University Press, 2014), 217.

5. Starting at the end of the fourteenth century, "Rumelia" (a term derived from the Turkish *Rumeli*: land of Romans, in other words, the Roman Empire of the Orient) designated territories known today by the names Romania, Albania, Serbia, Bosnia and Herzegovina, Bulgaria, Greece, Kosovo, and Montenegro.

6. Gilles Veinstein, "L'Europe ottomane," in *L'Europe et l'islam: quinze siècles d'histoire*, ed. Henry Laurens, John Tolan, and Gilles Veinstein (Paris: Odile Jacob, 2009), 165–66.

7. Karen Barkey, "Islam and Toleration: Studying the Ottoman Imperial Model," *International Journal of Politics, Culture, and Society* 19, nos. 1–2 (2007): 16. "Latins" refers to Roman Catholics. Armenians belonged to the Armenian Apostolic Church, one of the oldest independently organized Orthodox churches in the Orient. It does not recognize the ecumenical patriarch of Constantinople; its supreme patriarch is the Catholicos of All Armenians.

8. I am borrowing here again from Barkey, "Islam and Toleration," 16. Also on this topic, see the excellent study by Hamit Bozarslan, *Histoire de la Turquie: de l'empire à nos jours* (Paris: Texto, 2015).

9. Veinstein, "L'Europe ottomane," 165.

10. In periods when Islam became more intransigent, the dhimmis— literally the "people of the dhimma"—had to prove that they had paid the capitation by wearing a type of receipt around their necks. This receipt constituted "both a guarantee of safety and a mark of infamy." Paradoxically, "the heavy tax imposed on Jews incited some of them to convert to Islam, but the converts put the Treasury in the difficult position of having to increase the tax on those who must still pay it."

Georges Bensoussan, *Juifs en pays arabes: le grand déracinement, 1850–1975* (Paris: Tallandier, 2012), 50–51.

11. On these prohibitions, see C. E. Bosworth, "The Concept of Dhimma in Early Islam," in *Christians and Jews in the Ottoman Empire: The Functioning of a Plural Society*, ed. Benjamin Braude and Bernard Lewis (New York: Holmes & Meier, 1982), 45–49; Bensoussan, *Juifs en pays arabes*, 47–48; Michael Brenner, *A Short History of the Jews* (Princeton, NJ: Princeton University Press, 2010), 70–76.

12. Bensoussan, *Juifs en pays arabes*, 49.

13. Karen Barkey, *Empire of Difference: The Ottomans in Comparative Perspective* (Cambridge: Cambridge University Press, 2008), 121.

14. Bosworth, "The Concept of Dhimma in Early Islam," 49.

15. Bosworth, "The Concept of Dhimma in Early Islam," 46–47.

16. Benjamin Braude, "Foundation Myths of the Millet System," in *Christians and Jews in the Ottoman Empire*, 69–83. According to Braude, the instability of the term is proof of the "absence of an institutionalized policy toward non-Muslims" (74).

17. Here I am following Barkey, *Empire of Difference*, 132–33. Barkey disagrees with the restrictive interpretation of Braude and affirms instead the idea of an old and stable institutionalization of what must be called, for lack of a better term, "the millet system."

18. See the stimulating interview of Aron Rodrigue by Nancy Reynolds, "Difference and Tolerance in the Ottoman Empire," *Stanford Humanities Review* 5, no. 1 (February 27, 1996), http://www.stanford.edu/group/SHR/5-1/text/rodrigue.html.

19. Karen Barkey, "Rethinking Ottoman Management of Diversity," in *Democracy, Islam, and Secularism in Turkey*, ed. Ahmet Kuru and Alfred Stepan (New York: Columbia University Press, 2012), 22–23.

20. Barkey, "Rethinking Ottoman Management of Diversity," 24.

21. Quoted in Barkey, *Empire of Difference*, 136.

22. See the *Nomikon* (1788) of Bishop Theophilos of Kampania, quoted in Richard Clogg, "The Greek Millet in the Ottoman Empire," in *Christians and Jews in the Ottoman Empire*, 186–87.

23. Barkey, *Empire of Difference*, 135.

24. Jean-François Bayart, *L'Islam républicain: Ankara, Téhéran, Dakar* (Paris: Albin Michel, 2010), 82.

25. See Victor Roudometof, "From Rum Millet to Greek Nation: Enlightenment, Secularization, and National Identity in Ottoman Balkan Society, 1453–1821," *Journal of Modern Greek Studies* 16 (1998): 17–38.

26. Roudometof, "From Rum Millet to Greek Nation," 31.

27. Avigdor Levy, *The Sephardim in the Ottoman Empire* (Princeton, NJ: Darwin, 1992), 53–63; Mark Epstein, "The Leadership of the Ottoman Jews in the Fifteenth and Sixteenth Centuries," in *Christians and Jews in the Ottoman Empire*, 104–5.

28. Jacob Barnai, "The Development of Community Organizational Structure: The Case of Izmir," in *Jews, Turks, Ottomans*, ed. Avigdor Levy (Syracuse, NY: Syracuse University Press, 2002), 37–43.

29. In Turkish, Jews forcibly displaced to Istanbul (and by extension the Romaniotes) were named *sürgün* (those who had been displaced); the Sephardim who arrived after the fall of Constantinople were called *kendi gelen* (those who came by their own choice). In Hebrew, the former were called the Benei Romania, the latter the Benei Sepharad. Levy, *The Sephardim in the Ottoman Empire*, 59–61.

30. Levy, *The Sephardim in the Ottoman Empire*, 62, 69. It is at this time that institutions representing neighborhoods (*ma'amad*) replaced or superseded religious organizations representing different congregations.

31. Gilles Veinstein, "Un paradoxe séculaire," in *Salonique, 1850–1918*, ed. G. Veinstein (Paris: Autrement, 1992), 46.

32. Veinstein, "Un paradoxe séculaire," 47.

33. Veinstein, "Un paradoxe séculaire," 54.

34. The most severe form of punishment was the death penalty. The rabbi Juda Covo of Salonica was summoned by the tax authorities of the Sublime Porte to explain the poor quality of deliveries of wool cloth earmarked for the janissaries of the imperial army. His explanation was judged unsatisfactory, and he was condemned to death and hanged. Veinstein, "Un paradoxe séculaire," 54.

35. See Marie-Carmen Smyrnelis, ed., *Smyrne, la ville oubliée? 1830–1930* (Paris: Autrement, 2006).

36. Barkey, *Empire of Difference*, 110–14.

37. Olivier Christin, *La paix de religion: l'autonomisation de la raison politique au XVIIe siècle* (Paris: Seuil, 1997), 210.

38. Christin, *La paix de religion*, 208. The Edict of Nantes produced the same result: it "reinforced the authority of the state, conceived at once as absolute and arbitrating, as a uniter above parties and particularities" (208).

39. It should be noted that Emperor Joseph II promulgated a "Patent of Tolerance" in 1780, Frederick William II (King of Prussia) a "Patent of Tolerance" ("Woellner's Edict") in 1788, and Louis XVI an "Edict of Tolerance" (the "Edict of Versailles") in November 1787. On tolerance in Prussia and the Habsburg monarchy, see Rainer Forest, *Toleration in Conflict: Past and Present* (Cambridge: Cambridge University Press, 2016), 329–33. On the opposing "tolerant trajectories" of the Habsburg versus the Ottoman empires, see Barkey, "Empire and Toleration," 222–27.

40. Aron Rodrigue, "From Millet to Minority: Turkish Jewry," in *Paths of Emancipation: Jews, States, and Citizenship*, ed. Pierre Birnbaum and Ira Katznelson (Princeton, NJ: Princeton University Press, 1995), 242–43.

5. TOLERANCE IN VENICE

1. Benjamin Ravid, "The Religious, Economic, and Social Background and Context of the Establishment of the Ghetti of Venice," in *Gli Ebrei e Venezia secoli XIV–XVIII*, ed. Gaetano Cozzi (Venice: Edizioni Comunita, 1987), 211–14; Riccardo Calimani, *Histoire du ghetto de Venise* (1988; Paris: Tallandier, 2008), 18–40; Donatella Calabi, *Ghetto de Venise, 500 ans* (Paris: Liana Levi, 2016).

2. Ravid, "The Religious, Economic, and Social Background," 215. See also Richard Sennett, *Flesh and Stone: The Body and the City in Western Civilization* (New York: Norton, 1994), 224–26. The preachings of the Frari during Lent were particularly fierce—Jews were accused of causing public disturbances, performing ritual crimes, and having illicit sexual relations with Christians.

3. Ravid, "The Religious, Economic, and Social Background," 218–19.

4. The Venetian armies had been defeated by the united forces of the League of Cambrai in the famous Battle of Agnadello in April 1509.

5. This is the view put forward by Robert Finlay in a 1982 paper published in the *Proceedings of the American Philosophical Society*, quoted in Ravid, "The Religious, Economic, and Social Background," 219.

6. Decision of the Senate, quoted in Calimani, *Histoire du ghetto de Venise*, 55–56. The "Council" was a governmental organization that prepared the Senate's laws.

7. Sennett, *Flesh and Stone*, 231–34; Benjamin Ravid, "The Venetian Government and the Jews," in *The Jews and Early Modern Venice*, ed. Robert C. Davis and B. Ravid (Baltimore, MD: Johns Hopkins University Press, 2001), 10.

8. Ravid, "The Religious, Economic, and Social Background," 211.

9. Ravid, "The Religious, Economic, and Social Background," 226–27.

10. Ravid, "The Venetian Government and the Jews," 1819; Benjamin Ravid, "The Establishment of the Ghetto Nuovissimo," in *Studies Dedicated to the Memory of Umberto Cassuto on the Hundredth Anniversary of his Birth*, ed. H. Beinart (Jerusalem: Magnum, 1988), 35–54. There were 1,600 Jews in the Ghetto Nuovo and Ghetto Vecchio in 1589, 2,414 residents after the addition of the Ghetto Nuovissimo in 1633, and 4,870 in 1654. Calabi, *Ghetto de Venise*, 42.

11. According to Gallicciolli, as cited in Calimani, *Histoire du ghetto de Venise*, 48–49.

12. Each group, or *natione*, had its own synagogue. The Ghetto Nuovo had six places of worship, including the Scuola Grande Tedesca, the Scuola Canton, and the Scuola Italiana, which can still be visited today. Two active synagogues, still visible today, are located in the Ghetto Vecchio: the Scuola Levantina and the Scuola Ponentina or Spagnola. Calabi, *Ghetto de Venise*, 71–83.

13. David J. Malkiel, "The Ghetto Republic," in *The Jews of Early Modern Venice*, ed. R.C. Davis and B. Ravid, 132–40.

14. Sennett, *Flesh and Stone*, 230–31. The enormous building of the Fondaco dei Tedeschi still exists. Today it houses a luxury mall.

15. Ravid, "The Religious, Economic, and Social Background," 237–39. At an earlier time, during the Venetian-Ottoman War (1570–1573), Venice's Muslim residents (and Ottoman Jews) were interned and their property confiscated. They were liberated at the end of the war and recovered their possessions but still feared the vengeance of the Venetians and wished to live separately in their own protected quarters (234).

16. "Anonymous Petition of 1602," quoted in E. Natalie Rothman, *Brokering Empire: Trans-Imperial Subjects Between Venice and Istanbul* (Ithaca, NY: Cornell University Press, 2012), 200.

17. Ravid, "The Religious, Economic, and Social Background," 241–42.

18. Ravid, "The Religious, Economic, and Social Background," 244–45.

19. For an excellent analysis of the archives of the Pia Casa dei Catechumeni (the Pious House of the Catechumans), founded in Venice in 1557 on the initiative of the city's Jesuits and notables, see Rothman, *Brokering Empire*, 122–50.

20. Three-quarters of the converts were Muslims, and approximately one-quarter were Jews. The latter were mostly residents of Venice who spoke and wrote Italian and belonged to "social, family, business, and intellectual networks" that extended far beyond the confines of the ghetto. Rothman, *Brokering Empire*, 122–50.

21. In 1658, the Iberian Jewish community of Amsterdam was estimated at three thousand by the Spanish ambassador to the United Provinces, roughly 3 percent of the city's population. An additional hundred lived in Rotterdam. J. Marshall, *John Locke, Toleration, and Early Enlightenment Culture* (Cambridge: Cambridge University Press, 2006), 148.

22. According to a "statute" adopted in 1616 by Amsterdam's burgomasters, cited in Evan Haefeli, *New Netherland and the Dutch Origins of American Religious Liberty* (Philadelphia: University of Pennsylvania Press, 2012), 111–12.

23. Haefeli, *New Netherland*, 112. The Dutch Jews did not become full citizens until the time of the French Revolution. Venetian Jews were emancipated when the troops of General Bonaparte occupied the city in July 1797. The provisional municipal government decreed, "So that there no longer subsists any visible division among the citizens of this city, we order that the gates which formerly enclosed the ghetto be destroyed." Calimani, *Histoire du ghetto de Venise*, 302.

24. Quoted in Marshall, *John Locke, Toleration, and Early Enlightenment Culture*, 393–94.

25. Marshall, *John Locke, Toleration, and Early Enlightenment Culture*, 394. Some conversions were not freely accepted: janissaries were recruited by force from within the Christian population and obliged to convert to Islam.

26. Marshall, *John Locke, Toleration, and Early Enlightenment Culture*, 395. Ricaut was the secretary of the British ambassador to Constantinople.

27. See chapter 1 in this volume.

28. Pierre Jurieu, *Histoire du calvinisme et celle du papisme mises en parallèle* (1683); quoted in Marshall, *John Locke, Toleration, and Early Enlightenment Culture*, 549–50.

29. This chronicle written in Hebrew dates from 1523. It is quoted and discussed in Benjamin Lellouch, "Les juifs dans le monde musulman du XVe au XIXe siècle," in *Les Juifs dans l'histoire du monde: de la naissance du judaïsme au monde contemporain*, ed. Antoine Germa, B. Lellouch, and Évelyne Patlagean (Seyssel: Champ Vallon, 2001), 264.

30. Lellouch, "Les juifs dans le monde musulman du XVe au XIXe siècle," 265.

6. ON BLASPHEMY

1. *Grand Robert de la langue française.* In (Roman Catholic) canon law, blasphemy is included in a list of public utterances (oral or written) that "deeply injure good mores" or constitute "injuries or incite hatred or contempt for religion or the church." Article 1369 of the Code of Canon Law.

2. The sentence was handed down on February 28, 1766, by the court of Abbeville, sustained on appeal by the Parlement de Paris on June 4, 1766, and carried out in Abbeville on July 1, 1766.

3. Voltaire, *Relation de la mort du chevalier de La Barre, par M. Cass[en] avocat au Conseil du Roi, à Monsieur le Marquis de Beccaria* (1766), in *Œuvres complètes de Voltaire*, ed. Robert Granderoute (Oxford: Voltaire Foundation, 2008), 63B:549.

4. Voltaire, *Relation de la mort du chevalier de La Barre*, 551. Voltaire is alluding here to chapter 26 of Rabelais's *Tiers livre* ("Comment Panurge prend conseil de frère Jan des Entommeures") and its long and prodigious list of names for the male organ: "Escoute Couillon mignon: couillon moignon, c. paté, c. plombé, c. feutré, c. madré, c. de stuc, c. arabesque, c. troussé à la levresque, c. asceuré, c. calandré, c. diapré, c. martelé, c. juré, c. grené, c. endesvé, c. palletoqué, c. lyripipié, c. vernissé," etc. Rabelais, *Œuvres complètes* (Paris: Gallimard, 1994), 432.

5. Voltaire, *Relation de la mort du chevalier de La Barre*, 568.

6. Voltaire, *Relation de la mort du chevalier de La Barre*, 570.

7. Published in 1764, Voltaire's *Dictionnaire philosophique portatif* was burned in the public square of several Swiss and Dutch towns. It was

added to the Index of Prohibited Books by the Catholic Church and condemned by the Parlement de Paris in 1765.

8. Cesare Beccaria, *Dei delitti e delle penne* (*On Crimes and Punishments*) was first published in Livorno in 1764 and translated into French in 1765.

9. The 1972 Pleven law was incorporated into the still valid 1881 Law on the Press. Jacques de Saint Victor, *Blasphème: brève histoire d'un "crime imaginaire"* (Paris: Gallimard, 2016), 88–90.

10. Gwénaële Calvès, "Les discours de haine et les normes internationales," *Esprit* 418 (October 2015): 65.

11. Richard Webster, *A Brief History of Blasphemy: Liberalism, Censorship, and* The Satanic Verses (Southwold, Suffolk: Orwell Press, 1990), 22–23.

12. Elliott Visconsi, "The Invention of Criminal Blasphemy: *Rex v. Taylor* (1676)," *Representations* 103 (Summer 2008): 31. See also David Edwards, "Toleration and the English Blasphemy Law," in *Aspects of Toleration*, ed. John Horton and Susan Mendus (London: Methuen, 1985), 74–98.

13. Mark Hill and Russell Sandberg, "Blasphemy and Human Rights: An English Experience in a European Context," *Derecho y Religion* 4 (2009): 148.

14. Peter Mayer, quoted in Kenan Malik, *From Fatwa to Jihad: The Rushdie Affair and Its Legacy* (London: Atlantic Books, 2009), 10, 11.

15. Salman Rushdie, *Joseph Anton: A Memoir* (London: Vintage, 2013), 112.

16. Rushdie, *Joseph Anton*, 112, 121.

17. Malik, *From Fatwa to Jihad*, 30.

18. The following clarification is provided by the author: the prostitutes of a brothel in the imaginary city of Jahilia had taken "the names of the Prophet's wives to arouse their clients," whereas the wives themselves were presented as "living chastely in the harem." Rushdie, *Joseph Anton*, 115.

19. Rushdie, *Joseph Anton*, 74.

20. Rushdie, *Joseph Anton*, 116.

21. Quoted by Rushdie, *Joseph Anton*, 43, following the commentary of Tabari (839–923), a famous interpreter of the Qur'an and the founder of a school of Islamic law.

22. Rushdie, *Joseph Anton*, 43–44.

23. Rushdie, *Joseph Anton*, 41. According to Rushdie, this story is confirmed by other *hadith* compiled by Ibn Ishaq, Waqidi, and Bukhari. It is not, therefore, the invention of Tabari alone.

24. Rushdie, *Joseph Anton*, 45.

25. Salman Rushdie, *The Satanic Verses* (London: Viking/Penguin, 1988), 102–26.

26. Quoted in Webster, *A Brief History of Blasphemy*, 95.

27. Webster, *A Brief History of Blasphemy*, 88, 96, 101.

28. Rushdie, *Joseph Anton*, 152. Some years later, another archbishop of Canterbury, George Carey, denounced the novel as an "outrageous slur" against the Prophet Muhammad, adding that "We must be more tolerant of Muslim anger" (309).

29. Rushdie, *Joseph Anton*, 121.

30. Rushdie, *Joseph Anton*, 123.

31. This is Rushdie's somewhat grandiloquent description of the book burning. He then cites Heinrich Heine's famous line, "Dort, wo man Bücher verbrennt, verbrennt man am Ende auch Menschen." Rushdie, *Joseph Anton*, 128, 129.

32. Quoted in Malik, *From Fatwa to Jihad*, 8. The fatwa was written on February 13, 1989, and read the next day on Radio Teheran.

33. Rushdie, *Joseph Anton*, 130. In 2003 the Iranian foundation 15 Khordad increased the bounty money to include "expenses." Rushdie jeered: "Keep your receipts, assassins, you can reclaim that business lunch" (353).

34. Malik, *From Fatwa to Jihad*, 123–25; Victoria La' Porte, *An Attempt to Understand the Muslim Reaction to the Satanic Verses* (Lewiston: Edwin Mellen, 1999).

35. Malik, *From Fatwa to Jihad*, 125.

36. Malik, *From Fatwa to Jihad*, 124.

37. See the opinion of Lord Justice Watkins in *Regina v. Chief Metropolitan Stipendiary Magistrate, ex parte Choudhury*, 1 All ER 306, April 9, 1990; quoted in Kevin Smullin Brown, "Reforming England's Blasphemy Law," *Islam and Christian Muslim Relations* 14, no. 2 (2003): 189.

38. Hill and Sandberg, "Blasphemy and Human Rights," 150n39.

39. European Commission for Democracy Through Law/Venice Commission, Strasbourg, October 22, 2008, annex II, "Analysis of Domestic Law Concerning Blasphemy, Religious Insult and Inciting Religious

Hatred in Albania, Austria, Belgium . . . on the Basis of Replies to a Questionnaire," 86.

40. *People v. Ruggles*, 8 Johns. 290 (N.Y. Sup. Ct. 1811).

41. Quoted in Sarah Barringer Gordon, "Blasphemy and the Law of Religious Liberty in Nineteenth-Century America," *American Quarterly* 52, no. 4 (December 2000): 685.

42. Gordon, "Blasphemy and the Law of Religious Liberty," 686.

43. Robert Bray, *Reading with Lincoln* (Carbondale: Southern Illinois University, 2010), 67–69; Andrew Murphy, "Religion and the Presidency of Abraham Lincoln," in *Religion and the American Presidency*, ed. Gaston Espinosa (New York: Columbia University Press, 2009), 155; and, more generally, Stephen Mansfield, *Lincoln's Battle with God: A President's Struggle with Faith and What It Meant for America* (Nashville, TN: Thomas Nelson, 2012). We may recall that Lincoln refused to have his children baptized.

44. Murphy, "Religion and the Presidency of Abraham Lincoln," 154.

45. Gordon, "Blasphemy and the Law of Religious Liberty," 684–85.

46. According to three major Supreme Court decisions: *Gitlow v. New York*, 268 U.S. 652 (1925); *Cantwell v. Connecticut*, 310 U.S. 296 (1940); and *Everson v. Board of Education*, 330 U.S. 1 (1947), respectively.

47. Opinion of Justice Roberts, *Cantwell v. Connecticut*.

48. Opinion of Judge Baylson, *George Kalman v. Pedro Cortes*, U.S. District Court for the Eastern District of Pennsylvania, Civil Action no. 09684 (June 30, 2010), citing the Supreme Court's opinion in *Lamont v. Postmaster General of the U.S.*, 381 U.S. 321 (1995).

49. "A Brief History of 'Piss Christ,'" *Artinfo*, December 25, 2013, blogs.artinfo.com/artintheair/2013/12/25/a-brief-history-of-piss-christ.

50. "Le 'Piss Christ' de Serrano détruit par des ultra-catholiques à Avignon," *France Soir*, August 2, 2012.

51. Gary Younge, "After the Elephant Dung: Chris Ofili," *Guardian*, January 16, 2010; Michael Barbaro, "For Mayoral Hopeful Who Lost Fight to Remove Art, No Regrets," *New York Times*, March 27, 2013.

52. Philippe Dagen, "La guerre entre l'art et l'Église est-elle rouverte?" *Le Monde*, April 22, 2011; François Boespflug, *Caricaturer Dieu? Pouvoirs et dangers de l'image* (Paris: Bayard, 2006), 163–80.

53. This expression appears in the 1743 "Avis de l'éditeur" of the French edition, written by Voltaire himself, and in his Italian dedication of the work to Pope Benoît XIV published two years later. See Voltaire, *Le fanatisme ou Mahomet le Prophète* (1744), in *Œuvres*, "encadrée" ed. (Geneva: Cramer et Badin, 1775), 3:310. The play was first performed at the Comédie française in Paris in 1742. It was later banned by the Paris Parlement on grounds that it contained an apology for regicide and was targeting Catholicism as much as Islam. In other writings, notably *L'examen de Milord Bolingbroke ou le Tombeau du fanatisme* (1767), Voltaire defends "mahométisme," which he finds "more sensible than Christianity."

54. Palmira, a slave loved by Muhammad, is in fact the sister of Zaphna and the daughter of Alcanor—facts she is unaware of. Zaphna is also in love with Palmira, "Thou sov'reign of my soul and all its powers." Voltaire, *Le fanatisme ou Mahomet le Prophète*, 20.

55. Voltaire, *Mahomet: A Tragedy in Five Acts*, trans. James Miller (1744) (New York: D. Longworth, 1809), act 3, p. 40.

56. Tariq Ramadan, "Lettre ouverte à M. Hervé Loichemol," *Tribune de Genève*, October 7, 1993.

57. For a review of these incidents, see the face-off between Tariq Ramadan and Caroline Fourest: Tariq Ramadan, "Se prendre pour Voltaire?" *Spirituality*, February 23, 2006; Caroline Fourest, "Tariq Ramadan ment sur la pièce de Voltaire," February 11, 2007; and Hervé Loichemol, "Une fatwa contre Voltaire ?" *Le Monde*, February 14, 2006. For a careful and rather positive review of Voltaire, see the article "Voltaire" in "Citations d'hommes célèbres sur l'Islam" (Quotations of famous men about Islam), *Islammedia*, 2011.

58. Malik, *From Fatwa to Jihad*, 145–46.

59. Jytte Klausen, *The Cartoons That Shook the World* (New Haven, CT: Yale University Press, 2009), 14. In French on the same topic, see Jeanne Favret-Saada, *Comment produire une crise mondiale avec douze petits dessins*, 2nd expanded ed. (Paris: Fayard, 2015).

60. Klausen, *The Cartoons That Shook the World*, 15.

61. As quoted in Klausen, *The Cartoons That Shook the World*, 20.

62. Quoted in Klausen, *The Cartoons That Shook the World*, 16. For a detailed review of the whole affair and its aftermath, see Flemming Rose, *The*

Tyranny of Silence: How One Cartoon Ignited a Global Debate on the Future of Free Speech (Washington, DC: Cato Institute, 2014). See also Elizabeth Winkler, "The Man Behind the Most Infamous Cartoon of All Time," *New Republic*, December 9, 2014.

63. "A letter (October 21, 2005) from Prime Minister Rasmussen in reply to the complaint of eleven Arab and Muslim ambassadors," quoted in Klausen, *The Cartoons That Shook the World*, 66.

64. In the Pakistan incident (June 2, 2008), which al-Qaeda claimed to have carried out, a car bomb that exploded in front of the Danish embassy killed eight people, all Muslims. Three months earlier Osama bin Laden had denounced the caricatures as a "new crusade" instigated by Pope Benoît XVI. Klausen, *The Cartoons That Shook the World*, 45.

65. Klausen, *The Cartoons That Shook the World*, 38–53, 106–13. One hundred forty-three daily newspapers in fifty-six countries reprinted one or more of the caricatures. Klausen, *The Cartoons That Shook the World*, 50. See also Malik, *From Fatwa to Jihad*, 147–48.

66. Basile Ader, "Je suis Charlie," *Légipresse* 323 (January 2015). For a more detailed presentation, see the special issue of the review *Legicom* devoted to "Liberté d'expression et religion." *Legicom* 55 (July 2015).

67. This lawsuit was initiated by a moderate Muslim organization, the Société des habous et des lieux saints de l'islam, under the auspices of the Grand Mosque of Paris. This organization's effort was then backed by other groups such as the Union des organisations islamiques de France (UOIF) and the Ligue islamique mondiale.

68. TGI de Paris, 17e chambre, March 22, 2007, *Société des habous et des lieux saints de l'islam et al. c. Ph. Val*; my emphasis. It should be noted that, according to France's highest court, the Cour de Cassation, there is no right to the respect of religious beliefs. See *Cass. Civ.* 1, November 14, 2006, no. 05-15.822. The crime of insult only applies if the act in question expressly targets "a group of persons on the basis of their religious affiliation." Attacks against religious images, symbols, or pious objects cannot be banned because they do not "personally and directly target" believers protected by the law. See Gwénaële Calvès, "Sur un prétendu droit au respect des croyances religieuses," in *Les politiques du blasphème*, ed. Amandine Barb and Denis Lacorne (Paris: Karthala, 2018), 77–93.

69. See Gwénaële Calvès, *Envoyer les racistes en prison? Le procès des insulteurs de Christiane Taubira* (Paris: LGDJ, 2016), 40. See also de Saint Victor, *Blasphème*, 97–98; and his contribution to *Les politiques du blasphème*, 23–38.

70. TGI de Paris, March 22, 2007; my emphasis.

71. Malik, *From Fatwa to Jihad*, 148–49; Klausen, *The Cartoons That Shook the World*, 138–39.

72. On the iconographic evolution of representations of Muhammad, see the research of Christiane Gruber, professor of Islamic art at the University of Michigan. For summaries, see Gruber, "The Qur'an Does Not Forbid Images of the Prophet," *Newsweek*, January 9, 2015; and "How the 'Ban' on Images of Muhammad Came to Be," *Newsweek*, January 19, 2015.

73. On these legal debates, see Leonard A. Leo, Felice D. Gaer, and Elizabeth K. Cassidy, "Protecting Religions from 'Defamation': A Threat to Universal Human Rights Standards," *Harvard Journal of Law and Public Policy* 24, no. 2 (Spring 2011): 769–84; and Blandine Chelini-Pont, "La controverse actuelle sur la diffamation des religions (1999–2009)," *Cahiers de l'Institut d'anthropologie juridique*, special issue on "L'offense. Du 'torrent de boue' à l'offense au chef de l'Etat," 26 (2011): 399–430.

74. Resolution 66/167 adopted by the General Assembly of the United Nations on December 19, 2011.

75. Rushdie, *Joseph Anton*, 629. Rushdie was of course referring to the study by Klausen.

76. John Donatich, quoted in Christopher Hitchens, "Yale Surrenders," *Slate*, August 17, 2009. The publisher reportedly made his decision after consulting diplomats, Middle East specialists, and intelligence experts. See Patricia Cohen, "Yale Press Bans Images of Muhammad in New Book," *New York Times*, August 13, 2009. The Gustave Doré illustration of Muhammad, which was to be included but was ultimately excluded, has been printed many times in Great Britain, France, and the United States. See, for example, Dante Alighieri, *Dante's Inferno*, trans. Henry Francis Cary, ill. Gustave Doré, (Chicago: Belford, Clark and Cy, 1885), 149.

77. Timothy Garton Ash, "Defying the Assassin's Veto," *New York Review of Books*, February 19, 2015. See also Paul Fahri, "News Organizations

Wrestle with Whether to Publish *Charlie Hebdo* Cartoons After Attack," *Washington Post*, January 7, 2015.

78. Ash, "Defying the Assassin's Veto." See also, more recently, Timothy Garton Ash's powerful *Free Speech: Ten Principles for a Connected World* (London: Atlantic Books, 2016).

7. MULTICULTURAL TOLERANCE

1. Michael Walzer, *On Toleration* (New Haven, CT: Yale University Press, 1997), 83–92; Will Kymlicka, *Multicultural Citizenship* (New York: Oxford University Press 1995), 112–124; Charles Taylor et al., *Multiculturalism: Examining the Politics of Recognition* (Princeton, NJ: Princeton University Press, 1994), with contributions by Anthony Appiah, Amy Gutman, Jürgen Habermas, Steven Rockefeller, Michael Walzer, and Susan Wolf.

2. Jocelyn Maclure and Charles Taylor, *Secularism and Freedom of Conscience* (Cambridge, MA: Harvard University Press, 2011), 53, 57.

3. Richard Lyman Bushman, *Mormonism* (New York: Oxford University Press, 2008), 87–88.

4. *Reynolds v. United States* 98 U.S. 145 (1878), at 164.

5. Francis Lieber, a Prussian immigrant, was the author of the famous thirteen-volume *Encyclopædia Americana* and finished his career as a professor of history, political science, and law at Columbia University. He is quoted by name in the Reynolds case. For more on Lieber's influence, see Noah Feldman, *Divided by God* (New York: Farrar, Straus and Giroux, 2005), 106.

6. See Tacitus, *Germania*, in *Agricola, Germania, Dialogus*, ed. Jeffrey Henderson, 2nd rev. ed., Loeb Classical Library (Cambridge, MA: Harvard University Press, 2006), section 19, 159–60.

7. *Reynolds v. United States*, at 167.

8. John Stuart Mill, *On Liberty* (1859) (London: Penguin, 1974), 161.

9. Bushman, *Mormonism*, 98. See also "The Religion-Making Imagination of Joseph Smith," in Harold Bloom, *The American Religion: The Emergence of the Post-Christian Nation* (New York: Touchstone, 1992), 96–111.

10. *Wisconsin v. Yoder* 406 U.S. 205 (1972), at 210, 212.

11. *Wisconsin v. Yoder*, at 222.

12. *Wisconsin v. Yoder*, at 223, 224. In France, the Constitutional Council (Conseil constitutionnel) grants lawmakers a certain right to allow for difference and certain forms of exemption to the principle of equality, specifying, for example, about workplace discrimination motivated for religious reasons, that "the principle of equality does not forbid the law-maker from deciding certain things differently in different situations . . . so long as . . . the difference in treatment that results is in direct relation to the aim of the law that it establishes." Decision no. 96-375DC of April 9, 1996, Rec. CC; quoted in Xavier Delsol, Alain Garay, and Emmanuel Tawil, *Droit des cultes: personnes, activités, biens et structures* (Paris: Dalloz, 2005), 177.

13. Brian Barry, *Culture and Equality: An Egalitarian Critique of Multiculturalism* (Cambridge, MA: Harvard University Press, 2001), 178–81.

14. Bhikhu Parekh, *Rethinking Multiculturalism: Cultural Diversity and Political Theory* (Cambridge, MA: Harvard University Press, 2000), 243–45.

15. *Goldman v. Weinberger*, 475 U.S. 503 (1986), at 507, 519.

16. A quarter of British armed forces in India and surrounding regions were turban-wearing Sikhs.

17. "À la rencontre des sikhs de Seine-Saint-Denis: pourquoi les sikhs n'ont-ils pas compris la loi de 2004?", *Sikh-Saint-Denis*, February 1, 2012, sikh-saintdenis.wordpress.com/2012/01/02/quelle-est-la-signification-dut urban/.

18. http://www.jw.org/fr/temoins-de-jehovah/faq/temoins-dejehovah -pourquoi-refus-transfusions-sanguines/; http://www.jw.org/fr/la-bible -et-vous/questions-bibliques/bible-et-transfusions-sanguines.

19. See the American Academy of Pediatrics, "Religious Objections to Medical Care," *Pediatrics* 99 (1997): 279; quoted in Kent Greenawalt, *Religion and the Constitution*, vol. 1, *Free Exercise and Fairness* (Princeton, NJ: Princeton University Press), 403. Cases cited in this work relate to court rulings in many states, including Delaware, New York, Massachusetts, and California.

20. Greenawalt, *Religion and the Constitution*, 404.

21. See the opinion of Chief Justice Lamer and of concurring judges Cory, Iacobucci, and Major, *B. (R.) c. Children's Aid Society of Metropolitan*

Toronto (1995), 1 RCS 315; http://www.canlii.org/fr/ca/csc/doc/1995
/1995canliii15/1995canliii15.html.

22. Maclure and Taylor, *Secularism and Freedom of Conscience*, 101.

23. Paragraph 3 of Article L1111-4 of the Code de la santé publique (Code
of public health).

24. Conseil d'État, *Ordonnance du juge des référés*, August 16, 2002,
no. 249552, Mme Valérie Feuillatey and Mme Isabelle Feuillatey (a case
at the CHU hospital in Saint-Étienne; the patient, Mme V. Feuillatey,
was a Jehovah's Witness). In this particular case, the patient received
a blood transfusion against her will.

25. Paragraph 5 of Article L1111-4 of the Code de la santé publique, http://
www.lexinter.net/JPTXT/droit_de_donner_le_consentement_a
_un_traitement_medical.htm.

26. See the circular of February 25, 2008, from the French minister of the
interior about the criminalization of sectarian excesses in *Laïcité et liberté religieuse: recueil de textes et de jurisprudence* (Paris: Éditions des
Journaux officiels, Paris, 2011), 405–8.

27. J. Loriau, C. Manaouil, D. Montpellier, M. Graser, and O. Jarde,
"Chirurgie et transfusion chez les patients Témoins de Jéhovah. Mise
au point médico-légale," *Annales de chirurgie* 129 (2004): 267; see also
Article 223-6 of the Code penal. The maximum punishment for failure to provide assistance to a person in danger is five years in prison
and a 75,000-euro fine.

28. M. K. Viele and R. B. Weiskopf, "What Can We Learn About the
Need for Transfusion from Patients Who Refuse Blood? The Experience with Jehovah's Witnesses," *Transfusion* 34 (1994): 396–401.

29. See *R. c. Edwards Books* (1986), 2 R.C.S. 713; and José Woehrling
and Rosalie Jukier, "Religion and the Secular State in Canada," in
Religion and the Secular State: National Reports–2010, ed. Javier
Martinez-Torron and W. Cole Durham (Salt Lake City, UT: Inter-
national Center for Law and Religious Studies, Brigham Young
University, 2010), 194–95.

30. Quoted in Woehrling and Jukier, "Religion and the Secular State in Canada," 195. The Canadian decision is similar to the argument used by the
U.S. Supreme Court in a very similar case concerning Orthodox Jews who
wanted to work on Sunday. See *Braunfeld v. Brown* 366 U.S. 599 (1961).

31. Woehrling and Jukier, "Religion and the Secular State in Canada," 195.

32. *Employment Division v. Smith*, 494 U.S., at 888 (1990). Justice Scalia, the author of the majority opinion, alludes to an older argument developed in *Sherbert v. Verner* (1963).

33. *Employment Division v. Smith*, at 888. Justice Scalia is quoting here from an earlier decision: *Braunfeld v. Brown*, 366 U.S., at 606 (1961) (my emphasis).

34. *Employment Division v. Smith*, at 885, 879, citing the Reynolds case discussed at the beginning of this chapter.

35. *Employment Division v. Smith*. This is in fact what state legislatures did, including those in Oregon, Texas, Wisconsin, Colorado, Kansas, Iowa, and Idaho. In Idaho, taking mescaline was only authorized on Native American reservations. In 2004, a new federal law, the Religious Freedom Restoration Act, restored the particularly demanding test of "compelling public interest" to justify any interference of a law with the religious practices of an individual. On these debates, see Greenawalt, *Religion and the Constitution*, 74–85.

36. Stephen Macedo, *Diversity and Distrust: Civic Education in a Multicultural Democracy* (Cambridge, MA: Harvard University Press, 2000), 190–95.

37. Macedo, *Diversity and Distrust*, 196.

38. This is what Macedo defines as "prudential accommodationism." See Macedo, *Diversity and Distrust*, 195–200.

39. Barry, *Culture and Equality*, 242–43.

40. The Supreme Court has noted that in Pennsylvania between 30 and 50 percent of the Amish leave their church. *Wisconsin v. Yoder*, 406 U.S. 205 (1972), at 249n2.

41. Dissenting opinion of Justice Douglas in *Wisconsin v. Yoder*; quoted in Macedo, *Diversity and Distrust*, 236.

42. Macedo, *Diversity and Distrust*, 207.

43. See Taylor et al., *Multiculturalism*, 31.

44. Barry, *Culture and Equality*, 48–50. According to Barry, most Sikh immigrants in Great Britain belong to the Ramgarhia community, which combines several castes and specializes in military activities. In the twentieth century, the Ramgarhia became specialized in construction trades—carpentry, masonry, steel, tile, and the like.

45. See Chandran Kukathas, *The Liberal Archipelago: A Theory of Diversity and Freedom*, 2nd ed. (Oxford: Oxford University Press, 2007), 250–54. The author defends a liberal "politics of indifference" whereby the state would ignore all cultural or religious differentiation so as to avoid rivalry between groups.

8. OF VEILS AND UNVEILING

1. This is the definition proposed by Jocelyn Maclure and Charles Taylor in *Laïcité et liberté de conscience* (Paris: La Découverte, 2010), 61. In French, the concept of *vivre ensemble* refers to the social bond and is used by the courts as a legal principle. The English translation of Maclure and Taylor's book renders "bien vivre ensemble" as "peaceful coexistence." See their *Secularism and Freedom of Conscience*, trans. Marie Todd (Cambridge, MA: Harvard University Press, 2011), 47.

2. The burka is a piece of clothing that entirely covers the body and includes semitransparent cloth at eye level. The niqab is a veil that completely covers the face but with a rectangular opening at eye level. In France "burka" is often mistakenly used when the speaker is in fact referring to the niqab.

3. Maclure and Taylor, *Secularism and Freedom of Conscience*, 46–47.

4. David Kessler, "Laïcité: du combat au droit (interview)," *Le Débat* 77 (November–December 1993): 95–101.

5. Arrêt Kherouaa, Conseil d'État, 4/1 SSR, November 2, 1992, 130394.

6. Kessler, "Laïcité: du combat au droit," 99.

7. Kessler, "Laïcité: du combat au droit," 99.

8. Kessler, "Laïcité: du combat au droit," 100.

9. Arrêt Kherouaa, Conseil d'État, 4/1 SSR, November 2, 1992, 130394.

10. Henri Pena-Ruiz, *Qu'est-ce que la laïcité?* (Paris: Gallimard, 2003), 109–10.

11. Pena-Ruiz, *Qu'est-ce que la laïcité?*, 111–12.

12. Abderrahim Lamchichi, "Musulmans de France, politique de reconnaissance et éthique de responsabilité," *Confluence Méditerranée* 57 (2006): 33. See also the older but still influential text by the Moroccan Islamist Abdessalam Yassine (Cheikh Yassine), *Islamiser la modernité* (Casablanca: Al Ofok Impressions, 1998).

13. See the statements of Patrick Weil about the hearings transcribed in the Stasi Report in *Politiques de la laïcité au XXe siècle*, ed. Patrick Weil (Paris: PUF, 2007), 38.

14. See Françoise Gaspard and Farhad Khosrokhavar, *Le foulard et la république* (Paris: La Découverte, 1995); and John Bowen, *Can Islam Be French?* (Princeton, NJ: Princeton University Press, 2010).

15. Jean Baubérot, *Laïcité 1905–2005, entre passion et raison* (Paris: Seuil, 2004), 244.

16. Article L. 141-5-1 of the Education code, modified by law no. 2004228 of March 15, 2004.

17. Letter from Jacques Chirac to Bernard Stasi, mediator of the Republic, July 3, 2003, in *Rapport de la Commission de réflexion sur l'application du principe de laïcité dans la République remis au président de la République le 11 décembre 2003* (Paris: La Documentation française, 2004), 5–7.

18. *Rapport de la Commission*, 96, 127.

19. *Rapport de la Commission*, 129. This formulation was adopted by all members of the commission but one, who abstained.

20. *Rapport de la Commission*, 128. The report states: "What is at stake, beyond freedom of conscience, is public order."

21. Baubérot, *Laïcité 1905–2005*, 268–72. In his frank assessment of the decision, Baubérot deplores the "soft totalitarianism of the extreme center" and recommends "a burst of laughter" as the only proper response to the pseudoscience of the Stasi report.

22. Circular no. 2004-084 of March 18, 2004, from the minister of national education, relating to the implementation of the law of March 15, 2004.

23. Luc Ferry, quoted by Olivier Roy in *La sainte ignorance. Le temps de la religion sans culture* (Paris: Seuil, 2008), 268.

24. Kessler, "Laïcité: du combat au droit," 99.

25. Cécile Laborde, *Français, encore un effort pour être républicains!* (Paris: Seuil, 2010), 22–36.

26. Laborde, *Français, encore un effort pour être républicains!*, 54–55.

27. These manifestations of fear and contempt toward Islam are described well in John Bowen, *Why the French Don't Like Headscarves: Islam, the State, and Public Space* (Princeton, NJ: Princeton University Press, 2007), 82–96, 101–4.

28. The signers of the open letter "Profs, ne capitulons pas!" were Élisabeth Badinter, Régis Debray, Alain Finkielkraut, Élisabeth de Fontenay, and Catherine Kintzler.

29. Emmanuel Brenner [Georges Bensoussan], ed., *Les territoires perdus de la République: antisémitisme, racisme et sexisme en milieu scolaire* (Paris: Mille et une nuits, 2002).

30. See Philippe Portier, *L'État et la religion en France. Une sociologie historique de la laïcité* (Rennes: Presses Universitaires de Rennes, 2016), 199–242.

31. "Complaint for Declaratory and Injunctive Relief and Nominal Damages," *Hearn and United States of America v. Muskogee Public School District*, U.S. District Court for the Eastern District of Oklahoma, Civil Action no C3-598-W (October 23, 2003).

32. See "United States' Memorandum of Law . . . in Opposition to Defendants' Motion for Summary Judgment," and "United States' Motion to Intervene," *Hearn and United States of America v. Muskogee Public School District*, Civic Action no. CIV 03-598-S (May 6, 2004).

33. Terry Frieden, "US to Defend Muslim Girl Wearing Scarf in School," *CNN.com*, March 31, 2004, http://edition.cnn.com/2004/LAW/03/30/us.school.headscarves.

34. See "Plaintiff Wins in Oklahoma Headscarf Case," *Ummah, the Online Muslim Community*, May 19, 2004; "American Jewish Congress Praises Oklahoma Religious Accommodation Settlement," *American Jewish Congress*, May 19, 2004, http://archive.li/tVS4h.

35. For an excellent analysis of this affair and its consequences, see Amandine Barb, *Entre Dieu et César. Histoire politique des accommodements religieux aux États-Unis* (Aix-en-Provence: Presses Universitaires d'Aix-Marseille, 2018).

36. Jesse Lee, "Nashala's Story," *White House Blog*, June 4, 2009.

37. *Goldman v. Weinberger*, 475 U.S. 503 (1986). Justice Rehnquist wrote the court's opinion in this 5–4 decision.

38. See the concurring opinion of Justice Stevens in *Goldman v. Weinberger*.

39. 10 U.S.C. § 774-Religious apparel: wearing while in uniform (as modified in 1987).

40. Kent Greenawalt, *Religion and the Constitution*, vol. 1, *Free Exercise and Fairness* (Princeton, NJ: Princeton University Press, 2006), 160–61.

41. Amandine Barb and Denis Lacorne, "Incomprises ou méconnues: les laïcités française et américaine," in *La diplomatie au défi des religions: tensions, guerres, médiations*, ed. Denis Lacorne, Justin Vaïsse, and Jean-Paul Willaime (Paris: Odile Jacob, 2014), 205–19.

9. NEW RESTRICTIONS, NEW FORMS
OF TOLERANCE

1. Article 1 of the law of October 11, 2010, "forbidding dissimulation of the face in public space."

2. According to the Interior Ministry, in 2009 roughly 1,630 women were wearing the full-face veil in France and another 270 in overseas departments and territories. André Gerin and Éric Raoult, *Rapport de la mission d'information sur la pratique du port du voile intégral sur le territoire national* (Paris: Assemblée nationale, January 26, 2010), 28, 42, 60.

3. François Saint-Bonnet, "La citoyenneté, fondement démocratique pour la loi anti-burqa," *Jus Politicum* 7 (2012): 4–5, 22. That said, the law permitted "ministers of all churches to retain [their particular dress] during the exercise of their duties" while inside religious edifices.

4. Henri Leclerc, "Laïcité, respect des croyances et liberté d'expression," *Legicom* 55 (2015): 48.

5. Élisabeth Badinter, "Adresse à celles qui portent volontairement la burqa," *Le Nouvel Observateur*, July 9, 2009. She concluded, "Truly, you are using democratic freedoms to turn them against democracy."

6. Élisabeth Badinter, interview on the *RTL matin* radio show, October 10, 2008.

7. Maryam Borghée, *Voile intégral en France: sociologie d'un paradoxe* (Paris: Michalon, 2012), 57–93. For similar conclusions from an anthropological perspective, see Yasmina Foehr-Janssens, Silvia Naef, and Aline Schlaepfer, eds., *Voile, corps et pudeur: approches historiques et philosophiques* (Genève: Labor et Fides, 2015).

8. Borghée, *Voile intégral en France*, 91. On all of these debates, see the very stimulating work by Constantin Languille, *La possibilité du cosmopolitisme: burqa, droits de l'homme et vivre-ensemble* (Paris: Gallimard, 2015), 72–100.

9. Testimony of Gisèle Halimi, September 29, 2009, in Gerin and Raoult, *Rapport de la mission d'information*, 110, 121.

10. Testimony of Amandine Briffaut, in Gerin and Raoult, *Rapport de la mission d'information*, 49.

11. It is worth noting that to this day there have been no convictions for the crime of threatening, constraining, or abusing authority to force someone to cover her face. See Julia Pascual, "Les effets contraires de la loi sur le voile intégral," *Le Monde*, October 11–12, 2015.

12. Borghée, *Voile intégral en France*, 112. The phenomenon of re-Islamization as a part of "self-care" is well analyzed by Olivier Roy in *L'Islam mondialisé* (Paris: Seuil, 2002), 103–14.

13. Emmanuel Levinas, quoted by Abdelwahab Meddeb during the testimony of November 4, 2009, in Gerin and Raoult, *Rapport de la mission d'observation*, 117–18.

14. Testimony of Élisabeth Badinter, September 9, 2009, in Gerin and Raoult, *Rapport de la mission d'observation*, 119, 104.

15. Conseil d'État, *Étude relative aux possibilités juridiques d'interdiction du port du voile intégral*, adoptée en assemblée générale plénière, March 25, 2010, 17.

16. Conseil d'État, *Étude relative aux possibilités juridiques*, 19.

17. Conseil d'État, *Étude relative aux possibilités juridiques*, 20.

18. According to Article 21 of the charter: "Any discrimination based on any ground such as sex, race, colour, ethnic or social origin, genetic features, language, religion or belief, political or any other opinion, membership of a national minority, property, birth, disability, age or sexual orientation shall be prohibited."

19. Observation of the author during an Air France flight from Paris to San Francisco.

20. Circular of March 2, 2011, from the minister of the interior relating to the implementation of law number 2010-1192 of October 11, 2010, forbidding the dissimulation of the face in public space, in *Laïcité et liberté religieuse* (Paris: Éd. des Journaux officiels, 2011), 384–89.

21. Julia Pascual, "Loi sur le voile intégral: 'On a créé le monstre qu'on voulait éviter,'" *Le Monde*, October 10, 2015.

22. Patrick Weil, "La loi sur la burqa risque l'invalidation par l'Europe. Sa radicalité est inapplicable," *Le Monde*, November 23, 2010; Henri Tincq, "L'interdiction totale de la burqa, un casse-tête juridique," *Slate* (France), May 14, 2010.

23. Circular of March 31, 2011, from the minister of the interior, in *Laïcité et liberté religieuse*, 392.

24. Statements reported in "Morano: 'Faire du buzz sur la burqa? N'importe quoi,'" *Libération* (from Agence France Presse), October 14, 2014; and "Nadine Morano: 'Ce policier n'a pas fait son devoir,'" *Estrepublicain .fr*, October 15, 2014.

25. "Loi contre le port de la burqa, 5 ans après: où on est-on?" interview with Denis Jacob (secrétaire général d'Alternative-police-CFDT), *Atlantico*, October 12, 2015.

26. European Court of Human Rights, *Ahmet Arslan and Others v. Turkey*, February 23, 2010, req. no. 41135/98, § 23 and § 48.

27. European Court of Human Rights, *Ahmet Arslan and Others v. Turkey*, § 51.

28. ECHR (Grand Chamber), *S.A.S. v. France*, July 1, 2014, req. no. 43835/11, § 12, § 120.

29. *S.A.S. v. France*, § 141. Here the court quotes word for word the "presentation of motives" contained in the bill proposing the prohibition against dissimulating the face in public space.

30. *S.A.S. v. France*, § 129. On the extremely political prudence of this decision, see Ronan McCrea, "The French Ban on Public Face-Veiling: Enlarging the Margin of Appreciation," *EU Law Analysis*, July 2, 2014.

31. Dissenting opinion of the judges Angelika Nussberger and Helena Jäderblom, *S.A.S v. France*, § 7, § 14.

32. See Saïla Ouald Chaib, "*S.A.S. v. France*: Missed Opportunity to Do Full Justice to Women Wearing a Face Veil," *Strasbourg Observers*, July 3, 2014.

33. Dissenting opinion, *S.A.S. v. France*, § 7. And the dissenting judges add, "that goes too for clothing choices that express radical opinions."

34. Ernest Renan, *Qu'est-ce qu'une nation?*, ed. Joël Roman (Paris: Presses Pocket, 1992), 53–56.

35. Mark Chandler, "German Lawmakers Vote for Partial Burka Ban," *Evening Standard*, April 28, 2017. The bill adopted by the Bundestag prohibits civil servants, judges, and soldiers from wearing the Islamic face veil in public.

36. See Denis Lacorne, "Aux origines du multiculturalisme américain: le pluralisme ou la Kultur Klux Klan?" *Le Débat* 186 (September–October 2015): 20–32.

37. For a detailed analysis of these questions, see Denis Lacorne, "Breaching the Wall of Separation," in *Religion, Secularism, and Constitutional*

Democracy, ed. Jean Cohen and Cécile Laborde (New York: Columbia University Press, 2016), 204–21.

38. Circular of May 18, 2004, relating to the implementation of the law of March 15, 2004, setting limits on the wearing of signs and clothes manifesting a religious affiliation in primary and secondary schools, Ministry of the Interior, *Laïcité et liberté religieuse*, 52.

39. Xavier Delsol, Alain Garret, and Emmanuel Tawil, *Droit des cultes: personnes, activités, biens et structures* (Paris: Dalloz, 2005), 385.

40. See "La police des manifestations sur la voie publique," in Delsol, Garret, and Tawil, *Droit des cultes*, 199.

41. *Trunk v. City of San Diego*, 629 F.3d 1099 (9th Cir. 2011).

42. Especially important was the so-called Lemon test, defined in the case *Lemon v. Kurtzman*, 403 U.S. 602 (1971).

43. The cross weighs twenty-four tons and is forty-feet tall. Its presence dominates the military memorial area where it stands. It is surrounded by a circular base that includes 2,100 small granite plaques that bear the names and faces of veterans or groups of war veterans.

44. Judge McKeown, *Trunk v. City of San Diego*, is here referring to the opinion of Justice O'Connor in *Lynch v. Donnelly*, 465 U.S. 668 (1984).

45. Morgan Lee, "Mount Soledad Cross Controversy Ends After 25 Years," *Christianity Today*, July 22, 2015; Tony Perry, "Group Buys Land Under Mt. Soledad Cross," *Los Angeles Times*, July 21, 2015.

46. See Philippe Portier, "La régulation du religieux dans les pays européens," in *La diplomatie au défi des religions: tensions, guerres, médiations*, ed. D. Lacorne, Justin Vaïsse, and Jean-Paul Willaime (Paris: Odile Jacob, 2014), 185–203.

47. ECHR (Grand Chamber), *Lautsi v. Italy*, March 18, 2011, req. no. 30814/06, § 17, § 18.

48. *Lautsi v. Italy*, § 17, § 18. This law abolished the Lateran Accords signed in 1929 by Benito Mussolini and the representative of Pope Pius XI, Cardinal Gaspari.

49. *Lautsi v. Italy*, § 72.

50. Decision of the administrative tribunal, March 17, 2005, quoted in *Lautsi v. Italy*, § 15.

51. Decision of the Italian State Council, April 13, 2006, quoted in *Lautsi v. Italy*, § 16.

52. I borrow this term from Joseph H. H. Weiler, professor of law and the lawyer representing many governments involved in the Lautsi case. See Joseph H. H. Weiler, "*Lautsi*: Crucifix in the Classroom Redux," *European Journal of International Law* 21, no. 1 (June 1, 2010).

53. Louis-Léon Christians, "Le juge européen entre divergence des politiques religieuses et mobilité des personnes," in *La diplomatie au défi des religions*, 257–82.

54. *Lautsi v. Italy*, § 67, § 71.

55. *Lautsi v. Italy*, § 74.

56. "Living well together in a diverse society," as argued by the philosophers Jocelyn Maclure and Charles Taylor, "requires that one learn to consider normal a wide array of different identities." Jocelyn Maclure and Charles Taylor, *Laïcité et liberté de conscience* (Paris: La Découverte, 2010), 61.

IO. SHOULD WE TOLERATE THE ENEMIES OF TOLERANCE?

1. See Voltaire article "Tolérance: Toleration," in *Philosophical Dictionary*, ed. and trans. Theodore Besterman (London: Penguin, 2004), 387. The headline "Tout est pardonné" (All is forgiven) on the January 14, 2015, cover issue of *Charlie Hebdo*, published one week after the terrorist attack against the satirical magazine, was probably inspired by Voltaire. Under the headline was a cartoon of Muhammad holding a sign with the by-then-familiar expression of empathy, "Je suis Charlie" (I am Charlie).

2. The concept of fallibilism developed by Karl Popper allows him to better describe scientific theories. He considers that a theory is only valid if it can be submitted to and pass tests of refutation or falsification. If the theory is overturned, it should be replaced by another that will be scrutinized using the same tests. No established knowledge is exempt from refutation. In short, Popper refined the ground rules of what is generally called the scientific method.

3. Karl Popper, "Toleration and Intellectual Responsibility," in *On Toleration*, ed. Susan Mendus and David Edwards (Oxford: Clarendon, 1987), 26, 18–19.

4. Popper, "Toleration and Intellectual Responsibility," 21.

5. See *Collin v. Smith*, 578 F. 2d1197 (7th Cir.); and *Smith v. Collin*, 436 U.S. 953 (1978). In his dissenting opinion, Justice Blackmun noted that "we are presented with evidence of a potentially explosive and dangerous situation, enflamed by unforgettable recollections of traumatic experiences in the second world conflict."

6. In the end, the Skokie march did not take place; the neo-Nazi leader Frank Collin preferred to shift the demonstration to Chicago, on July 9, 1978. That small march (twenty-five neo-Nazis controlled by five hundred armed policemen) was almost entirely nonviolent, with the exception of a few thrown bottles. Philippa Strum, *When the Nazis Came to Skokie: Freedom for Speech We Hate* (Lawrence: University Press of Kansas, 1999).

7. On these questions, see Anthony Lewis, *Freedom from the Thought That We Hate: A Biography of the First Amendment* (New York: Basic Books, 2007); and Jeremy Waldron, *The Harm in Hate Speech*, 2nd ed. (Cambridge, MA: Harvard University Press, 2014).

8. These slogans are representative of the ideology of the Westboro Baptist Church, which condemns what they consider to be the overly tolerant stance of the U.S. military and the Supreme Court toward homosexuality.

9. *Snyder v. Phelps*, 562 U.S. 443 (2011).

10. The brothers Chérif and Saïd Kouachi along with Amedy Coulibaly were the three men who carried out the attacks on January 7, 2015, at the office of *Charlie Hebdo* and on January 9, 2015, at the Hyper Cacher supermarket at the Porte de Vincennes. All three stated they were acting on the authority of al-Qaeda in the Arabian Peninsula (AQAP).

11. *Schenck v. United States*, 249 U.S. (1919).

12. *Virginia v. Black*, 538 U.S. 343 (2003).

13. Waldron, *The Harm in Hate Speech*, 10, 85.

14. Ronald Krotoszynski Jr., "A Comparative Perspective on the First Amendment: Free Speech, Militant Democracy, and the Primacy of Dignity as a Preferred Constitutional Value in Germany," *Tulane Law Review* 78 (2003/2004): 1598–99. On notions of honor and respect in German and French cultures, see James Q. Whitman, "Enforcing Civility and Respect: Three Societies," *Yale Law Journal* 109 (2000): 1295ff.

15. Ronald Krotoszynski Jr., *The First Amendment in Cross-Cultural Perspective: A Comparative Legal Analysis of the Freedom of Speech* (New York:

NYU Press, 2006), 112. See also Jean-Claude Gardes, "Satire allemande et (auto)censure," *Ethnologie Française* 36, no. 1 (2006): 83–90.

16. Krotoszynski, "A Comparative Perspective on the First Amendment," 1598–99.

17. See Articles 24, 32, and 33 of the law on freedom of the press, July 29, 1881—Articles modified by the Pleven law of July 1, 1972, and the laws of August 6, 2012, and November 13, 2014, respectively.

18. On the decision of the Paris Tribunal de Grande Instance (TGI) on March 22, 2007, see chapter 6.

19. Cour d'appel de Paris, March 12, 2008, *Ph. Val et Société Éditions Rotatives c. Union des organisations islamiques de France* (my emphasis).

20. Emmanuel Todd, quoted in *Le Point.fr*, "Emmanuel Todd mal à l'aise avec la 'sanctification' de *Charlie Hebdo*," February 6, 2015.

21. Flemming Rose, "Why I Published Cartoons of Muhammad and Don't Regret It," *World Post*, February 19, 2015.

22. Cour d'appel de Paris, March 12, 2008 (my emphasis).

EPILOGUE FOR THE AMERICAN EDITION: TOLERANCE IN THE AGE OF TERRORISM

1. Thomas Hochmann, "De la bière et des nazis: la liberté de manifestation en Allemagne," *Jus Politicum* 17. See also Mehrdad Payandeh, "The Limits of Freedom of Expression in the Wunsiedel Decisions of the German Federal Constitutional Court," *German Law Journal* 11, no. 8 (2010).

2. *BverfGE 124, 300 Wunsiedel*, quoted in Hochmann, "De la bière et des nazis."

3. Article 1 of the German Basic Law states: "Human dignity shall be inviolable. To respect and protect it shall be the duty of all state authority."

4. Böhmermann accused the Turkish president of being a "sodomizer of goats" and of having "the breath of pig farts." See Volker Boehme-Nessler, "'Sodomiseur de chèvre' et Art—Jan Böhmermann entre droit pénal, politique extérieure et Loi fondamentale allemande," *Blogs of the Université Paris 10*, June 16, 2016, http://blogs.u-paris10.fr/article /sodomiseur-de-chevres-et-art-jan-bohmermann-entre-droit-penal -politique-exterieure-et-loi. In October 2016, German prosecutors in the city of Mainz dropped criminal charges against Böhmermann on

the grounds that there was insufficient evidence that a crime had been committed. The satirical poem was said to be "merely hyperbole in the name of art." But a civil court in Hamburg issued an injunction prohibiting Böhmermann from repeating parts of the controversial poem. See Alison Smale, "German Comedian Is Told Not to Repeat Lewd Lines About Erdogan," *New York Times*, February 10, 2017.

5. Article R645-1 of the Code pénal.

6. The "Article 24 bis" incorporates the Gayssot Law of July 13, 1990—the law that criminalizes "négationnisme," i.e., the denial of the Holocaust.

7. Aheda Zanetti: "I created the burkini to give women freedom, not to take it away." *Guardian*, August 24, 2016. See also Jan Dalley, "Fear and Clothing," *Financial Times*, September 17, 2016; and for a more detailed analysis, Jean-Claude Kaufmann, *Burquini: Autopsie d'un fait divers* (Paris: LLL, 2016).

8. Jean-Marc Sauvé, "Pourquoi le Conseil d'État a autorisé le burkini," an interview with Marie-Amélie Lombard-Latune, *Le Figaro*, October 4, 2016. The vice president of the Conseil d'Etat is de facto its president.

9. Sauvé, "Pourquoi le Conseil d'État a autorisé le burkini."

10. Conseil d'État, "Ordonnance of August 26, 2016, Ligue des droits de l'homme et al., association de défense des droits de l'homme collectif contre l'islamophobie en France," no. 402742, 402777 (about municipal decisions to prohibit the wearing of the burkini on French beaches). See also Denis Lacorne, "Faut-il au nom du 'vivre ensemble' interdire les signes religieux dans l'espace public?" *SaphirNews*, September 16, 2017, http://www.saphirnews.com/Faut-il-au-nom-du-vivre-ensemble -interdire-les-signes-religieux-dans-l-espace-public_a23957.html.

11. In Denmark, lawmakers banned all garments that cover the face, including the full-face veil. Critics of the Danish decision, such as Gauri van Gulik from Amnesty International, denounced this "blanket ban" and insisted that "All women should be free to dress as they please and to wear clothing that expresses their identity or beliefs," while recognizing that some restrictions could be imposed "for the purpose of public safety." See "Denmark Passes Law Banning Burqa and Niqab," *Guardian*, May 31, 2018. In Germany, the state of Bavaria bans the full-face veil in schools, universities, and government offices. On

April 28, 2017, the German Bundestag adopted a law imposing a selective burka ban, limited to government employees and, in particular, judges, civil servants, and members of the armed forces. Critics of the proposed legislation have argued that this was "purely symbolic policy pandering to the right-wing Alternative für Deutschland (AfD) ahead of the September 2017 elections." Lizzie Dearden, "German Parliament Votes in Favour of Partial Burqa Ban," *Independent*, April 28, 2017; Justin Huggler, "Limited Burka Ban Approved by German Parliament," *Telegraph*, April 28, 2017.

12. Sheryl Gay Stolberg and Brian Rosenthal, "Man Charged After White Nationalist Rally in Charlottesville Ends in Deadly Violence," *New York Times*, August 12, 2017. The march had been planned by white nationalists to protest the city's decision to remove the statue of Robert E. Lee, the Confederacy's top general. For further details on the planned Skokie march, see chapter 10.

13. In France, this outer limit was reached with the controversy over the Mohammad cartoons discussed in chapter 6. All religious beliefs may be mocked in the most outrageous ways, but believers themselves, taken as a group, cannot be gratuitously attacked by offensive symbols that stigmatize them and express feelings of racial or religious hatred. This subtle distinction between *beliefs* and *believers* does not exist in the United States.

14. Anthony Lewis, *Freedom for the Thought That We Hate: A Biography of the First Amendment* (New York: Basic Books, 2009), 167.

INDEX